Hiking Washington

Help Us Keep This Guide Up to Date

Every effort has been made by the authors and editors to make this guide as accurate and use-
ful as possible. However, many things can change after a guide is published—trails are rerouted,
regulations change, techniques evolve, facilities come under new management, etc.

We would love to hear from you concerning your experiences with this guide and how you
feel it could be improved and kept up to date. While we may not be able to respond to all
comments and suggestions, we'll take them to heart and we'll also make certain to share them
with the authors. Please send your comments and suggestions to the following address:

> The Globe Pequot Press
> Reader Response/Editorial Department
> P.O. Box 480
> Guilford, CT 06437

Or you may e-mail us at:

> editorial@GlobePequot.com

Thanks for your input, and happy travels!

Hiking Washington

A Guide to Washington State's
Greatest Hiking Adventures

Second Edition

Ron Adkison
Revised and updated by David Wortman

FALCON®

GUILFORD, CONNECTICUT
HELENA, MONTANA
AN IMPRINT OF THE GLOBE PEQUOT PRESS

A **FALCON** GUIDE ®

Photo credits: David Wortman, unless noted otherwise.
Maps created by XNR Productions, Inc. © The Globe
Pequot Press.

ISBN 0-7627-2607-5
ISSN 1542-863X

Manufactured in the United States of America
Second Edition/First Printing

Contents

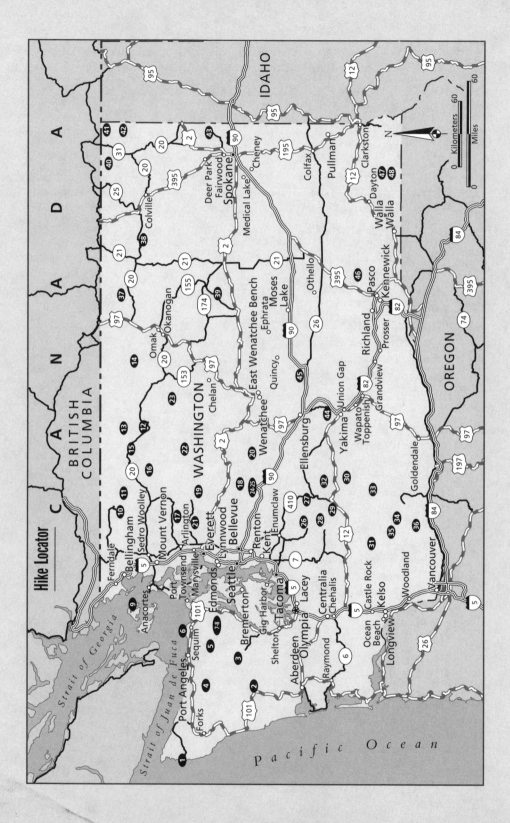

Hike Locator

North Cascades 47

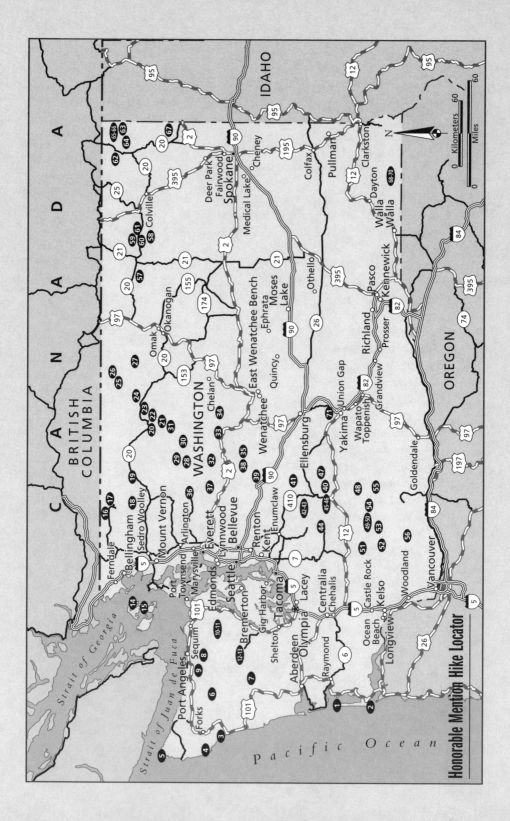

Honorable Mention Hike Locator

Preface

Washington is a land of superlatives. It is a land where mountain peaks soar above dense forests and deep river valleys . . . a land where vast wheat fields thrive in what once were parched deserts . . . a land of abundant rainfall and drought . . . a land of mountains and rugged coastlines . . . a land of deserts and forests.

Washington is so varied that it defies description. You can stand along the seacoast and stare in disbelief at the ethereal presence of giant volcanoes perpetually clad in white. You can stand on summits that see only a few weeks of spring a year and view distant deserts where summer lingers on and on.

A Land of Diversity

Diversity may best describe the landscape of Washington. Half the state is mountainous, cloaked in some of the finest coniferous forests in the nation. In their honor, Washington has been dubbed the Evergreen State. But much of the eastern half is bunchgrass steppes and parched basalt-rimmed coulees transformed almost overnight into one of the nation's breadbaskets. The mighty Columbia River supplies precious water to irrigate this region of little rain.

One-third of Washington is federally owned—that is, it's public land that belongs to each and every U.S. citizen. More than four million acres are federal wilderness, which will be left in their primitive, undeveloped state for the benefit of those who choose to explore them or those who simply need to know that wilderness exists. Large blocks of roadless land remain, and they must legally be designated wilderness if they are to be preserved.

The most familiar geographic feature in the state is the Cascade Range. The southern half, a region as coveted by loggers as hikers, is heavily forested and punctuated by volcanoes. The northern half boasts some of the most rugged, spectacular mountains in the nation.

Nearly all of the Cascade crest north of Snoqualmie Pass has been designated federal wilderness. In the south scattered parcels of pristine country, sandwiched between logging operations, have been protected. East of the Cascades much of the Selkirk Mountains and Blue Mountains lies within national forest land, but only two wilderness areas have been set aside.

To people who tend to judge value in terms of economics, wilderness may seem a wasteful folly, "locking up" resources that are "worthless" unless exploited. But the protection of wilderness affords direct economic benefits. These areas are the source of clean air and abundant oxygen, the source of clean water and subsequently generated electricity, and the last stronghold of wildlife.

For those of us who need the challenge of wild country and all the benefits of strenuous activity in a primitive setting, wilderness is everything. Indeed, we need these "wastelands" to survive. Their promise keeps us going from day to day.

The Chance to Hear a Mountain's Story

Hiking is for everybody. Look at your fellow hikers next time you are out on the trail. Representatives of every age group are enjoying wilderness and public lands to the fullest. They are also exposing themselves to a great learning opportunity.

As you hike along, keep your eyes, ears, and mind open. Be receptive to the silent story the mountains tell. Rocks reveal a mountain's history, from its advent below the ocean floor to its upheaval far above the earth's surface. Vegetation reflects the conditions under which it grows, and the trained eye can visualize the processes that created specific habitats.

By virtue of their size, mountains dramatically influence the distribution of plants, animals, and weather patterns over large areas. The Columbia Basin, for instance, owes its extreme dryness to the moisture barrier of the Cascade Range. An experienced hiker knows that vegetation is sorted by elevation, with each life zone adapted to the climatic conditions created by the mountain's great relief. While foothills bake in hundred-degree heat, temperatures on alpine peaks only a few miles away may be forty degrees cooler.

Within certain climatic and life zones, tiny "microclimates" often occur, influenced by the availability of moisture and sunlight and other factors. These microclimates may harbor plants and animals characteristic of life zones normally found great distances away.

There is much to see, do, and learn in our wildlands. As we roam the mountains, we step back in time to a simpler existence, uncomplicated by the workings of humankind. When we enter the wilderness, we become independent of the outside world. Nature's schedule is tied to the seasons and the rising and setting of the sun, not to the time clock.

John Muir's words are as appropriate today as they were when he uttered them years ago: "Climb the mountains and get their good tidings. Nature's peace will flow into you as sunshine flows into trees. The winds will blow their own freshness into you, and the storms their energy, while cares will drop off like autumn leaves."

Ron Adkison

Acknowledgments

As a hiker who's logged many miles on Washington's trails over the last ten years, being asked to update this book was a dream come true. At the same time it was nothing short of an ambitious task, and I couldn't have done it without the help of a dedicated group of friends, many of whom shared long hours on the trail and on the road. Special thanks go to Dave Cordis, Julie Furer, Greg Knutson, Norman Grant, Phillip Giarratano, Diane Hennessey, Alan Jennings, Deron Lozano, Paul Paladino, Brian Payne, Ken Pirie, Lori Seabright, Dave Shigaki, and Zack Wright for their assistance, support, and companionship. I'd also like to thank friends and coworkers at Adolfson Associates for their words of encouragement and understanding during my long hours of research and writing.

And I'd like to thank the many individuals with the various national forests, the Washington state park system, the U.S. Fish and Wildlife Service, and the Bureau of Land Management for taking the time to provide valuable review and comments on each hike description in this book.

David Wortman

Introduction

Welcome to *Hiking Washington*—the beginning of your hiking adventures in this beautiful and diverse corner of the continental United States. Despite being the third smallest state west of the Mississippi River, Washington packs a lot of punch, and inside this guidebook you'll find hikes that sample the best the state has to offer, from the wildest stretch of ocean coastline in the lower forty-eight to arid deserts. There's something for everyone—lonely wilderness beaches, temperate rain forests, alpine meadows, glaciers, lakes, rivers, and canyons, many accessible within a day's drive from the state's main population centers of Seattle and Spokane. You could spend a lifetime exploring Washington and still not see it all.

You'll find trails in this book for all abilities and in locations all across the state, from short loop trails to longer day or overnight trips, and from the remote Blue Mountains in Washington's southeast corner to the popular Alpine Lakes region. To get you started, many of the best hikes are categorized in the Hikes Index section on page 254 to let you quickly find the type of hike you're most interested in.

Washington Weather

While it's true that Washington's weather often lives up to its soggy reputation, there's much more to the story than persistent rain and cloudiness. West of the Cascade Range, moist air sweeping in off the Pacific Ocean fuels a cool, damp climate. From late fall through spring, you're most likely to encounter clouds, fog, and drizzle punctuated by larger storms across many of the state's low-elevation areas. Though there are occasional cold snaps and snow, winter temperatures in the lowlands rarely fall below freezing, typically ranging from thirty to fifty degrees Fahrenheit, while summer temperatures range from sixty-five to eighty-five.

Topography plays a large role in Washington's weather, amplifying rain and snowfall in some areas, blocking it in others. Rainfall amounts in some of the wettest coastal valleys on the Olympic Peninsula can exceed 100 inches, while areas just 25 miles east as the crow flies in the rain shadow of the Olympic Mountains may receive less than 20 inches. On slopes above 3,500 feet, most winter precipitation falls as snow, building deep snowpack, sometimes reaching more than 70 feet deep on the slopes of Mount Rainier and Mount Baker. As a consequence, snow on many higher-elevation trails in the Olympics and Cascades may not melt until well into July. Luckily for hikers, summer and early fall usually bring a distinct dry season across the region. July through mid-October are the best times for hiking, when long periods of sunny weather and mild temperatures are common.

With the Cascades acting as a moisture barrier, weather on the east side of the state is a different story, punctuated by greater temperature extremes and wider variations in precipitation. Vast portions of the state, stretching from the Cascade foothills across the Columbia Basin, are arid lands dotted by junipers and sage, or cultivated for wheat and other crops. Some areas receive as little as 7 inches of rain annually. Summers can bring on blazing heat, only occasionally broken by afternoon thunderstorms, while bitterly cold temperatures and snow are common at all elevations during winter. Higher elevations of the Selkirk Range in the far northeastern part of the state bring a return to wetter conditions, with precipitation amounts matching those in the western Cascades and heavy snows common in the winter.

Washington Flora and Fauna

Predictably, Washington's plants and wildlife are as diverse as the state's weather and landscape. Like much of the western United States, forests here are dominated by conifers. In lower elevations on the west side of the Cascades, Douglas fir and western hemlock, along with western red cedar, are among the most abundant trees you'll find along the trail. Common understory and forest floor plants include vine maple, sword fern, salal, and Oregon grape, along with several varieties of berries, mosses, and lichens. Pacific silver fir, noble fir, and mountain hemlock signal a transition to higher-elevation forests above 3,000 feet, while subalpine fir, often stunted and twisted into a dwarf form called krummholz, signals the onset of alpine conditions. Deciduous bigleaf maple, with giant leaves that live up to its name, is found on lower slopes and in low-elevation river valleys, along with red alder. Sitka spruce is abundant in coastal areas of the state but becomes more confined to wet areas farther inland. Above timberline, wildflowers such as lupine, columbine, yarrow, paintbrush, and heather carpet alpine meadows throughout the state during summer, bringing with them a profusion of color.

Capturing copious amounts of rainfall as storms sweep inland, the Hoh, Queets, Bogachiel, and Quinault Valleys on the Olympic Peninsula produce some of the world's largest trees and most ecologically productive forests. Trees reach mythological proportions here, the largest with circumferences of more than 60 feet and heights of over 200 feet. The world's largest-known hemlock and Sitka spruce trees are found in the Quinault River Valley; the largest Douglas fir is in the Queets River Valley. Ferns, mosses, and dangling epiphytes cover the ground and branches here, weaving a magical carpet of green.

Western Washington's varying vegetation and topography create habitat for a variety of wildlife. Along the coast you'll find sea lions and harbor seals, with gray whales migrating farther offshore. Tidepools here teem with a mix of anemones, starfish, mussels, and barnacles. Black-tailed deer are common in coastal forests, and large herds of Roosevelt elk inhabit river valleys. In higher elevations among boulder and talus fields, you're likely to find mammals such as the teacup-sized pika, or the larger (but lazier) marmot, often seen basking in the sun. You may also spot mountain goats in rockier alpine terrain, native to the Cascades but introduced in the Olympics and the past target of removal efforts. Black bears and cougars also inhabit Washington's forests—cougars in particular are seldom seen, while black bears can be more common visitors to highly used camping areas. Larger birds you may encounter include the great blue heron, red-tailed and Cooper's hawk, bald eagle, and osprey.

On the east side of the state, you'll find vegetation more characteristic of desert and interior west regions. The dominant vegetation here is fragrant sagebrush, typically associated with various wheatgrasses, Idaho fescue, and other bunchgrasses, along with western juniper. As you move into higher elevations, you'll find trees more common in the Rockies, including ponderosa and lodgepole pine, western and Lyall larch, western white pine, and Engelmann spruce. Cottonwoods and willows are frequent along streams.

Eastern Washington wildlife includes golden eagle, prairie falcon, and other species commonly found in high shrub-steppe deserts of the western United States. The Columbia Basin also draws thousands of ducks, geese, and migratory wading birds that nest and winter in the area's vast system of ponds and marshes. The state's Blue Mountains harbor a variety of wildlife species found in dry mountain areas, including mule deer, bighorn sheep, and Rocky Mountain elk. The eastern slopes of the Cascades, steeper and more open, are home to Rocky Mountain elk, mule deer, and many transitional species found in both mountainous and high desert ecosystems. Farther east, the Selkirk Mountains provide habitat for Rocky Mountain species found nowhere else in Washington, including moose, woodland caribou, and the state's only fully documented population of grizzly bears, listed as an endangered species.

Washington Wilderness Restrictions/Regulations

Washington's diverse landscapes and thousands of miles of trail are spread among seven national forests, three national parks, twenty-five wilderness areas, an impressive state park system, and other state and local lands. As such, use regulations vary across the state and can change from year to year, so it's a good idea to inquire about permits and use restrictions ahead of time, particularly if you're planning an overnight trip into the backcountry.

Most of Washington's trails are managed by the USDA Forest Service. To help offset shortfalls in trail and recreational road maintenance needs, parking at most Forest Service trailheads in the state now requires a Northwest Forest Pass. Hikers can purchase passes for $5.00 per vehicle for day use or obtain an annual pass for $30.00. Passes are good for any participating national forest or scenic area in Washington and Oregon. Throughout this guidebook you'll find listings of hikes requiring passes for parking. To find out more about participating national forests and locations where passes can be purchased, visit www.fs.fed.us/r6/feedemo, or call

(800) 270–7504. Permits for backcountry camping vary from forest to forest—some more popular backcountry camping areas now require advance reservations to help limit overuse. Check with the local ranger station while planning your trip.

Washington's national parks have their own fees for entering the park and for backcountry camping. Mount Rainier and Olympic National Parks collect a $10 entrance fee, and additional fees may be required for backcountry camping. Like national forests, backcountry camping may require advance reservations, so call ahead to the national park you're visiting for more information. Washington State Parks has recently implemented a day-use fee of $5.00 to offset budget shortfalls.

Getting Around Washington

Area codes: Area code 360 serves western Washington outside the central Puget Sound region. In central Puget Sound, area code 206 covers Seattle, while area code 425 serves its northern and eastern suburbs. Area code 253 serves Seattle's southern suburbs, the city of Tacoma, and surrounding communities. Area code 509 serves eastern Washington.

Roads: For winter driving and mountain pass conditions, call the Washington State Department of Transportation's Mountain Pass Report hot line at (888) 766–4636, or visit www.traffic.wsdot.wa.gov/sno-info.

By air: Seattle-Tacoma International Airport is western Washington's central airport, served by nearly all major airlines. Spokane International Airport serves eastern parts of the state, with connecting flights to farther destinations. Flights through Seattle and Spokane also connect many smaller airports in Bellingham, Lewiston, Pasco, Port Angeles, Walla Walla, Wenatchee, and Yakima. Shuttle Express and several other shuttles and taxi services provide transportation between Seattle-Tacoma International Airport and surrounding areas.

By bus: Greyhound serves most major cities in Washington and can be reached at (206) 628–5526 or at www.greyhound.com. Northwest Trailways at (800) 366–3830 operates bus service between Spokane and Seattle with stops along the way, and from Omak to Wenatchee.

By train: Amtrak offers daily north–south service from Bellingham to Portland, Oregon, with several stops along the Interstate 5 corridor. Amtrak's east–west Empire Builder route from Chicago to Portland or Seattle also makes stops along the way, providing east–west train access across the state. Call Amtrak at (800) 872–7245 or visit www.amtrak.com.

By boat: Washington has the country's largest ferry fleet, with twenty-nine boats serving twenty ports throughout Puget Sound. Regular ferries run from the west side of Puget Sound (Seattle, Edmonds, Mukilteo) and offer access to several islands and locations on the Olympic Peninsula. Contact Washington State Ferries at (888) 808–7977, or visit www.wsdot.wa.gov/ferries.

Visitor information: For more information on travel to Washington or to request a "Washington State Visitors Guide," call (360) 753–5601 or visit www.experiencewashington.com. The Outdoor Recreation Information Center, located in the REI store in downtown Seattle (222 Yale Avenue North), can provide information on hiking and other outdoor recreation opportunities in the state. Contact them at (206) 470–4060 or visit http://www.nps.gov/ccso/oric.htm.

Quick Washington Facts

The west side of the Olympic Mountains is the wettest place in the continental United States. July 26 is the day most likely to be sunny in western Washington.

- Land area: 66,582 square miles
- Largest city: Seattle (population 516,259)
- Population: 5,756,361 (1999)
- Highest point: Mount Rainier, 14,410 feet

Using This Guide

This guide contains the basic instructions and information to help you enjoy a variety of hikes located throughout the state of Washington. *Hiking Washington* features forty-eight mapped and cued hikes, seventy-one honorable mentions, and everything from advice on getting into shape to tips on getting the most out of hiking with your children or your dog.

We've divided Washington into five geographical regions: Olympic Peninsula and Coast, North Cascades, South Cascades, Northeast Washington, and Southeast Washington.

After a short summary you'll find the quick, nitty-gritty details of the hike: where the trailhead is located, the nearest town, hike length, approximate hiking time, difficulty rating, best hiking season, type of trail terrain, trail schedules and use fees, a list of maps available to the area, and what other trail users you may encounter as well as dependable directions from a nearby city right down to where you'll want to park.

The Hike section is our first-hand impression of the trail. While it's impossible to cover everything, you can rest assured that we won't miss what's important. In *Key Points,* we provide mileage cues to identify all turns and trail name changes, as well as points of interest.

In the *Hike Information* section you'll find information on where to stay, what to eat, and what else to see while you're hiking in the area.

In *Honorable Mentions,* we detail all of the hikes that didn't make the cut, for whatever reason—in many cases it's not that they aren't great hikes, but simply overcrowded or environmentally sensitive to heavy traffic. Be sure to read through these. A jewel might be lurking among them.

We don't want anyone to feel restricted to just the routes and trails that are mapped here. We hope you'll have an adventurous spirit and use this guide as a platform to dive into Washington's backcountry and discover new routes for yourself. One of the simplest ways to begin this is to just turn the map upside down and hike the course in reverse. The change in perspective is often fantastic—the hike will likely feel quite different. With this in mind, it'll be like getting two distinctly different hikes on each map.

For your own purposes, you may wish to copy the directions for the course onto a small sheet to help you while hiking, or photocopy the map and cue sheet to take with you. Otherwise, just slip the whole book in your backpack and take it all with you. Enjoy your time in the outdoors, and remember to pack out what you pack in.

Map Legend

══90══	Limited access highway
═97═	U.S. highway
─20─	State highway
─41─	Forest road
─────	Paved road
─────	Gravel road
‐ ‐ ‐ ‐ ‐	Unimproved road
---------	Trail
▬▬▬▬▬	Featured route
•───	Power line
─────	Ski lift
🚤	Boat launch
⋈	Bridge
▲	Campground
•─•	Gate
◘	Overlook/viewpoint
🅿	Parking
)(	Pass
▲	Peak
⊞	Picnic area
■	Point of interest/other trailhead
⬟	Ranger station
⌐	Spring
START 🚶	Trailhead
∥	Waterfall

Olympic Peninsula and Coast

Wedged between Puget Sound to the east and the Pacific Ocean to the west, the Olympic Peninsula and coast region of Washington stands apart as an oddity in Washington's geography. This 6,500-square-mile area takes on almost mystical qualities, from the often cloud-shrouded views of the jagged summits of the Olympic Mountains from Seattle across Puget Sound, to wilderness beaches and the deep, rain-soaked western valleys that nourish one of the planet's only temperate rain forests and some of the largest trees in the world. So special is this region that in 1976, scientists designated it a United Nations Educational, Scientific, and Cultural Organization (UNESCO) Man and the Biosphere Reserve. Today much of the area is protected by Olympic National Park and in several surrounding wilderness areas.

The Olympic Mountains are part of the Coast Ranges, stretching from southeast Alaska and Canada south into Oregon and California. About seventeen million years ago, marine sediments slid beneath the continent, crumpling and thrusting an underwater dome of basalt upward toward the surface to form the Olympics. Glaciation followed, carving rugged peaks in the range and flooding much of the surrounding lowland with meltwater carrying sand and gravel. These glacial deposits mantle much of the east and northwest sides of the Olympic Peninsula.

More than 60 miles of the peninsula's outer coast are now part of Olympic National Park, protecting the wildest stretch of coastline in the lower forty-eight states. Sculpted by pounding surf, the rocky coastline is a wonderland of arches, sea stacks, and rugged bluffs. Fog-draped forests of Sitka spruce and western red cedar hug the coast here, and wildlife species such as bears, sea otters, harbor seals, and a variety of shorebirds are common. You'll find miles of beach to explore on trails around Cape Alava and Sand Point, as well as on other trails both to the north and south of here. Tribal culture is still strong along the coast as well, home to the Makah, Ozette, Quillayute, Hoh, and Quinault reservations.

Just inland from the coast you'll find the Bogachiel, Hoh, Queets, and Quinault River Valleys, home to the region's grand temperate rain forests where trees reach mammoth proportions. Here rain is measured in feet, and the 12 to 14 feet of it that falls annually in these deep, lush valleys nourishes trees that reach up to 300 feet high and more than 20 feet in circumference. The short Lake Quinault Loop Trail and longer Enchanted Valley Trail will give you a glimpse of these grand trees and insight into the forests that once covered the western peninsula, much of it outside of the national park and wilderness areas now actively harvested for its timber.

While the Olympic Mountain peaks that rise to the east of these river valleys are not exceptionally high at just under 8,000 feet, their abrupt rise from sea level dramatically wrings moisture from the air, creating one of the largest precipitation contrasts in the country. While 14 *feet* of rain may be falling in the Quinault Valley, the town of Sequim, just 25 miles away on the dry northeast side of the Olympics, may only see 17 *inches* of rain in a year, creating the state's "banana belt," increasingly popular among retirees. Forests here take on a notably drier appearance, and many of the region's high-ridge and alpine hikes, such as Grand Valley, Royal Basin, and Mount Townsend, present spectacular open meadows filled with flowers in summer.

1 Cape Alava Loop

Wander the wild, rugged outer coast on this 8.8-mile loop trail leading through coastal forests to miles of rocky tidepools, sea stacks, and arches. With its minimal elevation gain, the loop makes for an easy day hike, but an overnight stay will reward you with golden sunsets in summer and a deep immersion in the sights, smells, and sounds of one of the country's few wilderness beaches.

Start: At the Cape Alava Trail crossing of the Ozette River, just west of the Lake Ozette ranger station.
Length: 8.8-mile loop.
Approximate hiking time: 5–6 hours.
Difficulty rating: Easy, due to minimal elevation gain and boardwalk trails to the beach.
Trail surface: Wooden boardwalk, sandy and rocky beach.
Elevation gain: 220 feet.
Land status: National park.
Nearest town: Sekiu, WA.
Other trail users: None.
Canine compatibility: Not dog friendly.
Trail contacts: Olympic National Park Wilderness Information Center, (360) 565-3100; Ozette ranger station, (360) 963-2725.

Schedule: Hikable all year, but best hiked during the drier months from July through mid-October. Overnight camping is limited by a quota system between May 1 and September 30.
Fees/permits: Wilderness permits are required for overnight stays in all backcountry areas of the park—call ahead during summer months, when these permits are in highest demand. Fees are $5.00 for a wilderness permit, plus $2.00 per person per night for backcountry camping.
Maps: USGS Ozette Lake 15-minute quad; Olympic National Park quad; Olympic National Park map.

Finding the trailhead: From U.S. Highway 101, 12 miles north of Forks and 44 miles west of Port Angeles, turn north where a sign points to Lake Ozette and Neah Bay. This county road winds through forested hills and clear-cuts for 10 miles to Washington Route 112, where you'll turn left toward the town of Clallam Bay. Drive through town, and after 11 miles turn left onto the Hoko-Ozette Road where a sign points to Lake Ozette. Follow this winding road 21 miles to the trailhead parking area at the north end of Lake Ozette. *DeLorme Washington Atlas & Gazetteer* page 90, C3.

The Hike

Lake Ozette, Washington's third largest natural freshwater lake, lies less than 2 miles from the ocean on the northern stretch of Washington's wild outer coast. Two trails depart from the north end of the lake and lead through coastal forest to the beach. These trails—one to Sand Point, the other to Cape Alava—form a scenic loop when connected by a 3-mile walk along the beach. While the loop makes for a relatively easy day hike, it's even more enjoyable as an overnighter to give yourself time to

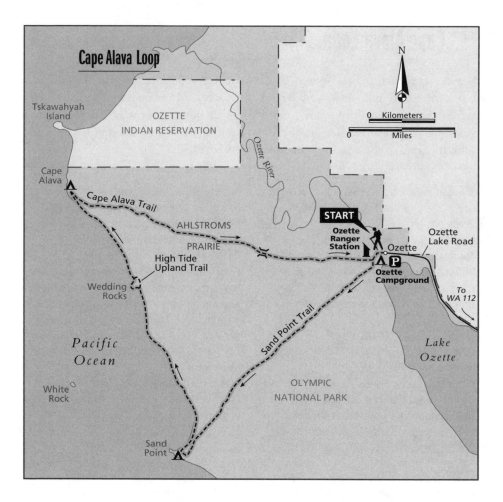

Cape Alava Loop

Tskawahyah
Island

OZETTE
INDIAN RESERVATION

Ozette River

N

0 Kilometers 1

0   Miles   1

Cape
Alava

Cape Alava Trail

AHLSTROMS

PRAIRIE

High Tide
Upland Trail

Wedding
Rocks

START

Ozette
Ranger
Station

Ozette
Lake Road

Ozette

Ozette
Campground

To
WA 112

Pacific
Ocean

White
Rock

Sand Point Trail

Lake
Ozette

OLYMPIC
NATIONAL PARK

Sand
Point

experience the sights, smells, and sounds of wilderness beach, a unique experience
along the nation's increasingly developed and crowded coastlines. Only one point
midway along the beach requires a low-tide passage, and an overland trail makes it
possible to easily pass there during higher tides.

You can take this hike in either direction, but this description will lead you first
to Sand Point, north along the beach to Cape Alava, and back to the parking area.

From the trailhead, the route bridges the sluggish, tea-colored Ozette River, col-
ored by root tannins, and heads into a western hemlock forest. Turn left at the junction after 0.2 mile, the beginning of your loop trip. From here, the trail is a cedar
boardwalk most of the way to the beach and can be quite slippery when wet. Soft-
soled shoes are recommended.

The next 2.8 miles pass through a typical coastal forest of western hemlock and
western red cedar. You'll notice that the trail is quite swampy in places and thank the

hard work of trail crews, many of them volunteers, who labored to build the boardwalk under your feet. Understory plants include salal and Oregon grape, ferns and bunchberry. And in a region of giant trees, you may wonder why many of the trees here appear so small; the area is recovering from an old burn.

As you approach the coast, you'll be drawn along by the briny scent of the beach and the increasingly loud pounding of the surf. You may also notice a change in the forests here—Sitka spruce, the dominant coastal tree (identified by its prickly needles), has replaced western red cedar in the canopy above you.

The boardwalk ends shortly before reaching Sand Point. Some hikers will continue south along the beach to Rialto Beach, a classic 20-mile coast walk. But you'll turn north and proceed along the wide sand. Cobbles and soft sand make for slow going along this stretch, particularly during high tide.

Leave yourself plenty of time for exploration here. The sheer variety of detritus washed upon the shore is amazing, and you'll hike past tidepool after tidepool teeming with mussels, ochre sea stars, anemones, blood stars, giant barnacles, nudibranchs, leaf lettuce, crabs, and limpets. As you explore, you may find yourself slowly reverting to childhood days at the beach. You'll hear the sounds of surf occasionally cut by the bark of seals hauled out on rocks offshore. Lucky hikers may, at certain times of year, also find Japanese glass fishing-net floats, a prize among beachcombers.

Midway along the hike you'll reach the rocky headland of Wedding Rocks and a high-tide passage marked with a large, round red-and-black sign. Scattered among the rocks are more than ninety Native American petroglyphs depicting various scenes. One of these petroglyphs depicts a three-masted schooner, indicating they're of fairly recent origin.

To the northwest, forested Ozette Island and other members of the Flattery Rocks group rise above the surf offshore from Cape Alava. There are several secluded campsites just landward of the beach in the spruce forest along this section of trail. Black-tailed deer are also quite common here.

Your beach walk ends at a sign pointing to the Ozette ranger station. Good campsites and fresh water from a small stream make for a good overnight stop, but you'll need reservations during summer months. This junction is located at Cape Alava, the westernmost point of land in the forty-eight contiguous states. The view to the north includes mountainous Vancouver Island.

Half a mile north of Cape Alava, on the tiny Ozette Indian Reservation, is the site of an ancient Makah Indian village. Washington State University conducted an archaeological dig here during the 1970s. Various artifacts that were recovered are currently on display at the Makah Cultural Center in Neah Bay.

From the junction, the trail quickly climbs away from the beach into a spruce forest thick with ground-covering ferns that soon becomes a hemlock-cedar forest. The cedar boardwalk resumes once again and cuts through a narrow tree-rimmed

Exploring the tidepools near Cape Alava.

meadow—a dying lake in the advanced stages of transformation. As the new meadow dries out, the forest will complete the cycle by reclaiming the site.

The route then cuts through a larger meadow, covered with ferns and grasses but steadily being invaded by forest trees. This is Ahlstroms Prairie, the site of an old homestead settled in the 1890s. From here back to the trailhead, the boardwalk leads through the coastal forest for 2 more miles, completing a diverse and rewarding Olympic coast hike.

Key Points

0.0 Start at the trailhead at the south end of parking lot, next to the Lake Ozette ranger station.

0.2 Cross the Ozette River and reach a junction and the beginning of the loop. Turn left (southwest) toward Sand Point. You'll return on the right fork from Cape Alava.

0.3 Reach the first stretch of trail boardwalk.

2.1 You'll get your first views of the beach and ocean through the trees.

2.3 Arriving at the coast, the trail splits left and right. The short right spur trail leads to nice campsites, while the left trail continues to parallel the beach in forest to more campsites. At any point along the trail, turn right, hike out to the beach, and turn right (north) along the beach to begin your hike.

4.4 Reach an upland trail, marked by a large, round red-and-black sign at the Wedding Rocks headland. There is a small campsite here. The short headland trail, your only option during high tide, climbs up and over the headland and back down to the beach. Petroglyphs can be found among the rocks here.

5.8 Arrive at Cape Alava and a junction. Turn right at the signed trail back to the trailhead. For campsites, turn left (north) at the junction just inland from the beach and cross a small stream.

6.0 Leave the forest trail and reach the boardwalk section of the trail.

7.5 Cross a small stream on a bridge with a railing.

8.1 Leave the boardwalk, returning to forest trail.

8.6 Arrive back at the loop trail junction and turn left (northeast) back toward the trailhead.

8.8 Arrive back at the parking lot and trailhead.

Hike Information

Local information

North Olympic Visitor and Convention Bureau, (800) 942-4042, www.northolympic.com.

Local events/attractions

Makah Cultural and Tribal Center, Neah Bay, WA, (360) 645-2711, www.makah.com.

Accommodations

The Lost Resort campground at Lake Ozette, (306) 963-2899, www.northolympic.com/lostresort.

Ozette campground on Lake Ozette; campsites are available on a first-come, first-served basis.

Curley's Resort, Sekiu, WA, (360) 963-2281, www.curleysresort.com.

Restaurants

The Lost Resort has a deli and small store at Lake Ozette, WA, (306) 963-2899.

2 Quinault Lake Loop Trail

This easy 4-mile loop hike will lead you through one of the peninsula's true old-growth rain forests in the Olympic National Forest's lower Quinault River Valley. Along the way you'll pass impossibly large trees blanketed in mosses and draped in delicate hanging epiphytes.

Start: From the Rain Forest Nature Trail (855) Trailhead off the Quinault Lake South Shore Road.

Length: 4-mile loop.

Approximate hiking time: 1½ hours.

Difficulty rating: Easy, due to gentle terrain and short distance.

Trail surface: Forest trail.

Elevation gain: 280 feet.

Land status: National forest.

Nearest town: Hoquiam, WA.

Other trail users: None.

Canine compatibility: Leashed dogs permitted.

Trail contacts: Olympic National Forest, Pacific Ranger District, (360) 288-2525.

Schedule: Can be hiked year-round, but you'll find the best weather from July through mid-October.

Fees/permits: A Northwest Forest Pass is required to park at the trailhead. Pick up a season pass at the Quinault ranger station near the Quinault Lodge, or pay $3.00 for a day pass at the trailhead.

Maps: USGS Quinault Lake East 7.5-minute quad; Olympic National Forest maps and Quinault Loop Trail maps are available at the Quinault ranger station near the Quinault Lodge.

Finding the trailhead: From U.S. Highway 101, 38 miles north of Hoquiam and 65 miles south of Forks, turn east onto Quinault Lake's South Shore Road. After 1.4 miles turn right into the parking lot (look for the signed trailhead for the Rain Forest Trail) on the south side of the road. *DeLorme Washington Atlas & Gazetteer* page 60, A2.

The Hike

The soggy western slopes of the Olympic Mountains boast ideal growing conditions for temperate rain forest. The two primary environmental influences creating these conditions—abundant precipitation distributed throughout the year and moderate temperatures with little annual variation—are found from southeastern Alaska to northern California. But it's here in the western river valleys of the Olympics where you'll find the most impressive temperate rain forests in the region.

As moisture-laden storm clouds sweep inland off the Pacific, they strike the western slopes of the Olympics and are forced to rise. As they rise they also cool, and since cool air is unable to hold as much moisture as warm air, their moisture is released in staggering amounts, measured in feet per year. But as the storm clouds descend the eastern side of the range toward Hood Canal and Puget Sound, the air warms again and the clouds retain much of what moisture is left, creating a dramatic rain shadow on the eastern and northern slopes of the Olympics. And while rain

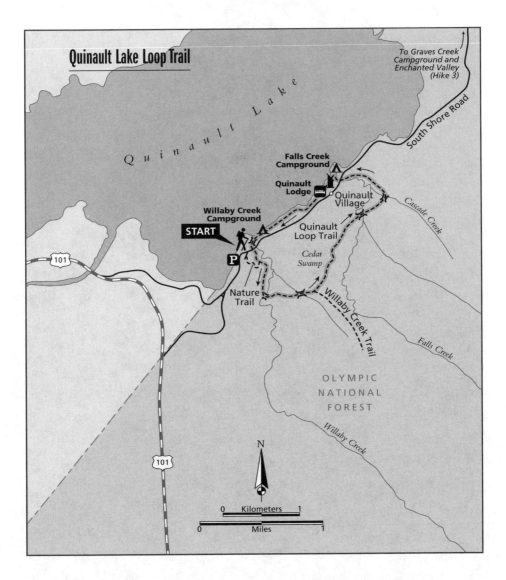

Quinault Lake Loop Trail

To Graves Creek Campground and Enchanted Valley (Hike 3)

Quinault Lake

South Shore Road

Falls Creek Campground

Quinault Lodge

Quinault Village

Willaby Creek Campground

START

Quinault Loop Trail

Cascade Creek

101

P

Cedar Swamp

Nature Trail

Willaby Creek Trail

Falls Creek

OLYMPIC NATIONAL FOREST

Willaby Creek

N

101

0   Kilometers   1

0   Miles   1

shadows are common throughout the mountains of the West, the Olympics present one of the most dramatic examples, where very wet western slopes and very dry eastern slopes vividly illustrate the phenomenon. As the lower Quinault River Valley is soaked with more than 145 inches of moisture annually, residents of the town of Sequim on the dry northeastern side of the peninsula see an average of only 17 inches. Along with the verdant Hoh, Queets, and Bogachiel River Valleys, the moderate temperatures and abundant moisture in the Quinault area create a magical forest where everything is some shade of green.

This easy and scenic loop trail through the Quinault Rain Forest is little used compared with the well-known and popular nature trails of the Hoh Rain Forest. As a result, you can enjoy and contemplate the forest here in comparative solitude. July, August, and September, the driest times of the year, are optimal months to visit, but you can come (with raincoat in hand) at any time of year.

From the trailhead, follow the trail eastward toward Willaby Creek to a fork. If you negotiate the entire 4-mile loop, you'll return on the left fork. For now, bear right at the fork, shortly meeting a junction with the Rain Forest Nature Trail. Keep left here; at subsequent junctions, follow signs for the Loop Trail.

The route proceeds through a classic rain forest, and you'll soon feel dwarfed by giant western red cedars, western hemlocks, Douglas firs, and Sitka spruces. As you drive through the logged-over region surrounding Quinault Lake, it's hard to imagine that such noble forests once blanketed the region. Vegetation here achieves mammoth proportions, including huge ferns, salmonberries, and spiny devil's-club that grows up to 10 feet tall. The shady forest floor is carpeted by mosses, ferns, the tiny white flowers and cloverlike leaves of oxalis, and beadlily, typical components of the rain-forest plant community. Much of the foliage of all trees is delicately draped with lichens and mosses.

Fallen, rotting logs form the only suitable substrate on which new plants and trees can establish themselves, and these "nurse" logs are abundant along the trail. Tree roots eventually spread around nurse logs to reach the ground, and after the nurse log decays and becomes part of the soil, a row or colonnade of trees is left, some standing above the ground on stilts of roots.

► Not only are the Olympic Peninsula's trees big—some are just plain gigantic. In fact, you'll find some of the largest-known trees of their species on record:

- Alaska cedar: 124 feet tall with a circumference of more than 37 feet, located on Olympic National Park's Big Creek Trail.
- Pacific silver fir: 218 feet tall with a circumference of over 21 feet, located in the Bogachiel River Valley.
- Western red cedar: 159 feet tall with a circumference of more than 63 feet, located near Quinault Lake.
- Sitka spruce: 191 feet tall with a circumference of 59 feet, located near Quinault Lake.

Bear left after 1.2 miles where the Willaby Creek Trail forks right, and proceed through a cedar swamp. Many picturesque half-dead red cedars and snags stand throughout this marshy area.

◄ *A giant Douglas fir, up close and personal.*

Bearing right at a junction 0.7 mile from the Willaby Creek Trail, cross Falls Creek and then Cascade Creek. At the next trail junction, bear left, cross Falls Creek, and reach the South Shore Road. The trail contours across the road along Falls Creek, opposite the campground.

This less-than-wild segment of the hike skirts the south shore of beautiful Quinault Lake before climbing through the Willaby campground and back to the trailhead.

Key Points

0.0 Start at the south end of the parking lot for trailhead for the Rain Forest Nature Trail (855).

0.3 Arrive at a junction with Quinault Loop Trail. Follow signs for Willaby Creek.

0.5 Bear left at junction with the Rain Forest Nature Trail.

1.2 Bear left where the Willaby Creek Trail forks right, proceeding through a cedar bog.

1.9 Bear right at a junction, shortly crossing Falls Creek, then Cascade Creek.

2.5 Reach a trail, signed for the Loop Trail, and turn left, crossing back over Falls Creek.

2.9 Continue across the South Shore Road and along the trail, passing the Falls Creek campground. The trail swings left along the shore of Quinault Lake.

3.8 Reach the Willaby Creek campground. Turn right and walk the campground loop road to the crossing of the South Shore Road.

4.0 The trail crosses Willaby Creek and goes under the South Shore Road. Bear right at the Rain Forest Nature Trail junction, returning to the trailhead and parking lot.

Hike Information

Local information

www.visitlakeQuinault.com, (360) 288–2900. *The Final Forest: The Battle for the Last Great Trees of the Pacific Northwest,* by William Dietrich, is a hard-hitting book about the transformation of the region's timber industry. *Champion Trees of Washington State,* by Robert Van Pelt, documents the locations of the state's largest trees.

Accommodations

Lake Quinault Lodge, (306) 288–2900. **USDA Forest Service Quinault Lake area campgrounds,** (360) 288–2525.

Restaurants

Snacks are available at the Lake Quinault Lodge and across the street from the lodge at the Quinault Mercantile.

3 Enchanted Valley

Hike this 26.2-mile round-trip backpack in the southwestern Olympics, one of the state's classic hikes into a deep rain-forest-blanketed valley. The trail follows the Quinault River from lush rain forest to a classic peak-rimmed basin in Olympic National Park. Miles of wandering lie beyond.

Start: At the Graves Creek Trailhead at the end of the South Shore Road.
Length: 26.2 miles out-and-back.
Approximate hiking time: 14–16 hours (best done as a backpack).
Difficulty rating: Difficult, due to length.
Trail surface: Forest trail.
Elevation gain: 1,493 feet.
Land status: National park.
Nearest town: Hoquiam, WA.
Other trail users: Equestrians.
Canine compatibility: Not dog friendly.

Trail contacts: Olympic National Park Wilderness Information Center, (360) 565-3100.
Schedule: Best hiked from March through mid-December due to snow at higher elevations of the trail.
Fees/permits: Fill out a permit at the trailhead register and attach it to your pack. No fee is required.
Maps: USGS Mt. Olson, Mt. Hoquiam, and Chimney Peak 7.5-minute quads; Olympic National Park quad; Olympic National Park map.

Finding the trailhead: From U.S. Highway 101, 46 miles north of Hoquiam and 65 miles south of Forks, turn east onto Quinault Lake's South Shore Road. After 1.4 miles pass the signed trailhead for the Rain Forest Trail on the south side of the road. Continue past the Quinault Lodge and Quinault ranger station after 2.1 miles. Pavement ends east of Quinault Lake after 7.7 miles. This often narrow dirt road follows the south bank of the Quinault River for another 11 miles to a parking area at the end of the road, 0.3 mile beyond the Graves Creek campground. (**Note:** As of this writing, this dirt road was washed out, so it's a good idea to check road conditions before beginning your trip.) *DeLorme Washington Atlas & Gazetteer page 76, D4.*

The Hike

Near the head of the Quinault River lies a narrow valley covered with grassy meadows and shaded by alders and bigleaf maples. White ribbons of water tumble down cliffs that rise nearly a mile above the well-named Enchanted Valley—truly one of the gems of Washington's backcountry. Come prepared with food canisters, or check on the availability of bear wires to hang your food, as bears are active along this trail.

A three-story log chalet, built in the 1930s, currently shelters the wilderness ranger at the west end of the valley. No overnight camping is allowed in the chalet, except in an emergency.

The gently rolling trail leading to the Enchanted Valley follows the course of one of the Olympic Peninsula's major drainages, the Quinault River, through a majestic lowland forest of hemlock, fir, and cedar, alternating with open groves of red alder and bigleaf maple. Numerous excellent campsites are available all along the route,

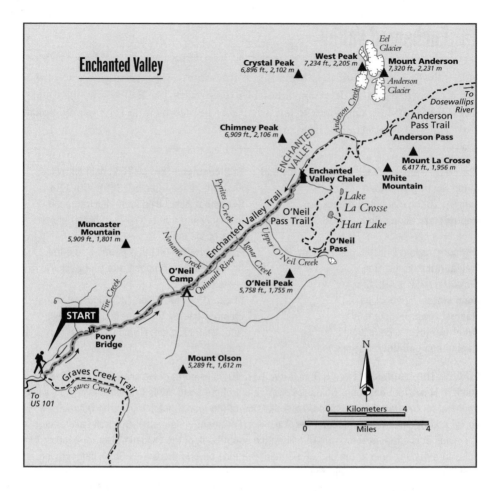

Enchanted Valley

Eel Glacier

West Peak 7,234 ft., 2,205 m

Crystal Peak 6,896 ft., 2,102 m

Mount Anderson 7,320 ft., 2,231 m

Anderson Glacier

To Dosewallips River

Anderson Pass Trail

Anderson Pass

Chimney Peak 6,909 ft., 2,106 m

Anderson Creek

Mount La Crosse 6,417 ft., 1,956 m

ENCHANTED VALLEY

Enchanted Valley Chalet

White Mountain

Pyrites Creek

Lake La Crosse

Hart Lake

O'Neil Pass Trail

O'Neil Pass

Enchanted Valley Trail

Upper O'Neil Creek

Muncaster Mountain 5,909 ft., 1,801 m

Noname Creek

Ignar Creek

O'Neil Camp

Quinault River

O'Neil Peak 5,758 ft., 1,755 m

Fire Creek

START

Pony Bridge

Mount Olson 5,289 ft., 1,612 m

Graves Creek Trail

Graves Creek

To US 101

N

Kilometers 0 — 4

Miles 0 — 4

often next to the tumultuous, milky-green glacial river. Black-tailed deer are especially common in the valley, and you may also see elk. Plan to spend at least three days to get the most out of this scenic hike, one of the classic valley-bottom hikes in the Olympics.

From the trailhead, you'll proceed steadily uphill for 2 miles through the upper limits of the rain-forest zone amid towering Douglas fir, Sitka spruce, western hemlock, and western red cedar.

The route then descends to the Pony Bridge, spanning a spectacular mini gorge on the Quinault River. There are good campsites across the bridge on the north side of the river, and this makes a good turnaround point if you're just out for a short day hike.

Silver fir begins to appear after the bridge, an indicator that you have passed above the rain-forest zone and into higher elevation forest. After 7 miles of hiking, you'll reach a spur trail leading quickly down to O'Neil camp. You may want to consider staying the night here and hiking into the valley on the second day.

Between 8 and 9.5 miles you'll catch fleeting glimpses of high peaks between Noname and Pyrites Creeks, both the locations of good campsites. At about 12.8 miles the trail descends to another bridge over the Quinault, by which you'll cross back to the south bank, quickly reaching the three-story chalet at the west end of the valley.

Rocky slopes rise on the northwest nearly 5,000 vertical feet to 6,909-foot Chimney Peak, decorated by numerous long, cascading creeks. At the head of the valley are some of the higher peaks in the Olympics: 7,234-foot West Peak and 7,320-foot Mount Anderson, separated by a small but active glacier (explaining the milky appearance of the river) at the head of Anderson Creek. Campsites are numerous throughout the valley, and drinking water is piped in from a small creek near the chalet.

From here, the trail continues beyond the valley and provides seemingly endless wandering opportunities. At a fork, you can ascend 4.9 miles to Anderson Pass—access to the Anderson Glacier—and drop to the Dosewallips River. Or you can turn right at a fork below the pass to reach the alpine Hart Lake and Lake La Crosse, high above the Enchanted Valley.

After enjoying the scenic southwestern corner of Olympic National Park, retrace the route to the trailhead—but only when you're ready.

Key Points

0.0 Start at the Graves Creek Trailhead parking area at the end of the South Shore Road.

0.2 Ignore the right-forking (southeast) Graves Creek Trail, instead continuing on the East Fork Quinault Trail.

2.5 Arrive at the Pony Bridge crossing of the river.

7.0 Arrive at a spur trail leading quickly right (southeast) down to the O'Neil camp. Camps here made a good midway stopping point.

12.8 The trail descends to a suspension bridge over the Quinault, by which you'll cross back to the south bank, quickly reaching the chalet at the west end of the valley. (**Note:** As of this writing, the bridge is out, and a ford of the river is necessary.)

13.1 Reach the chalet at the west end of the valley.

26.2 Return to the parking area and trailhead.

Hike Information

Local information
www.visitlakeQuinault.com, (360) 288-2900.
The Good Rain: Across Time and Terrain in the Pacific Northwest by Timothy Egan.

Accommodations
Lake Quinault Lodge, (306) 288-2900.

USDA Forest Service Graves Creek campground, (360) 288-2525.

Restaurants
Groceries and snacks are available at Quinault Lodge, and across the street from the lodge at the Quinault Mercantile.

4 Seven Lakes Basin

Climb just under 8 miles to the Olympic Peninsula's largest concentration of alpine lakes and tarns, perched high on the north slopes above the Sol Duc River Valley. Spend a day fishing the lakes, or explore the lake-filled basin or the inspiring views over the vast Pacific Ocean more than 5,000 feet below you from the summit of nearby Bogachiel Peak.

Start: At the Sol Duc River Trailhead.
Length: 15.6 miles out-and-back.
Approximate hiking time: 7–8 hours.
Difficulty rating: Difficult, due to length and elevation gain.
Trail surface: Forest trail.
Elevation gain: 3,050 feet.
Land status: National park.
Nearest town: Forks, WA.
Other trail users: Equestrians, except hikers-only in Seven Lakes Basin.
Canine compatibility: Not dog friendly.
Trail contacts: Olympic National Park Wilderness Information Center, Port Angeles, WA,
(360) 565–3100; Eagle (Sol Duc) ranger station, (360) 327–3534.
Schedule: Best hiked when upper portions of the trail are snow-free, from late June through October.
Fees/permits: You'll pay a park entrance fee of $10.00. Overnight backcountry camping permits are required for a fee of $5.00, plus $2.00 per person, per night.
Maps: USGS Bogachiel Peak and Mount Carrie 7.5-minute quads; Olympic National Park quad; Olympic National Park map.

Finding the trailhead: From U.S. Highway 101, 27 miles west of Port Angeles, turn left onto the Sol Duc Hot Springs Road, following this road 15 miles to its end and the trailhead. *DeLorme Washington Atlas & Gazetteer* page 76, A3.

The Hike

While the Olympic Peninsula has much to offer hikers—wild beaches, flower-filled meadows, grand forests—the region seems curiously lacking in lakes, especially considering how much rain falls here. Perhaps that's why the Seven Lakes Basin, with the largest concentration of lakes in the Olympics, has become such a coveted destination for hikers. The basin, scooped by glaciers out of the alpine country, actually contains a dozen major lakes, along with several smaller tarns cupped amid meadows on the north slopes of the Olympic Mountains. While the basin makes for a good destination for strong day hikers, it's best enjoyed as an overnighter. And while many hikers camp here and explore the trails of the surrounding high country, others take two to three days to complete an 18-mile loop trip across the High Divide and back to the trailhead following the Sol Duc River Trail. Fishing is also popular in the lakes.

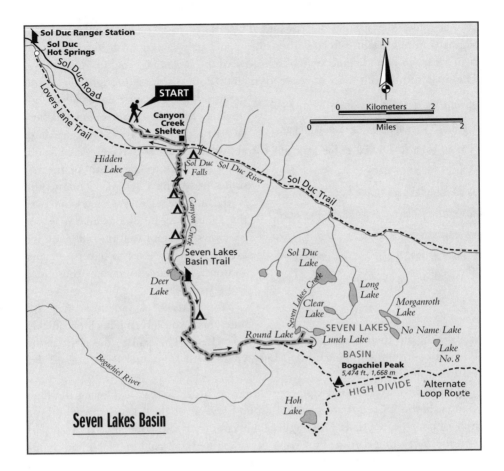

Seven Lakes Basin

The trail begins under grand forests along a well-graded trail; for the first mile of this trip, you're likely to have lots of company, sharing the trail with the throngs that come to view beautiful Sol Duc Falls, less than a mile up the trail. You'll reach the falls, cross the Sol Duc River, and soon leave many of the crowds behind you.

Over the next 3 miles, the trail climbs moderately to steeply through forest, often within sight or earshot of Canyon Creek, toward Deer Lake. In many places you'll thank the hard work of trail volunteers, who've engineered impressive sets of steps in the trail along the way. At 1.8 miles you'll cross the thundering cataract of the creek high on a bridge. Beyond this point there are several good campsites along the creek before reaching Deer Lake; while campfires are allowed here, they're prohibited in the higher elevations around Deer Lake and in the higher country beyond.

At just under 4 miles, the trail levels out and quickly drops to scenic, meadow-ringed Deer Lake. Good camps can be found along the lake, but respect the restoration that's in progress here, camping only in designated sites. For a shorter day hike, Deer Lake makes a fine turnaround point.

The trail swings around the east side of Deer Lake, past a ranger's cabin, and soon begins climbing again. After another mile you'll pass several small heather-ringed tarns with camps and climb switchbacks toward the increasingly alpine ridge above. The trail soon levels out, traverses bear-grass-dotted slopes through forest, and emerges on spectacular slopes filled with flowers earlier in summer and blueberries later in the season. Crossing high above the Bogachiel River Valley, you'll catch glimpses to the south of the icy slopes of Mount Olympus, while to the west you'll begin to get views out over the Pacific Ocean. Slopes here may not be snow-free until well into July, and ice axes may be necessary to traverse steeper sections. Be sure to check conditions before you leave.

▶ Elk are the largest mammals in Olympic National Park, weighing up to 1,000 pounds. There are an estimated 5,000 in the park, and herds can be found in many of its river valleys. Elk play an integral park in the forest's ecology, as their grazing helps to maintain the open, parklike understory in many of these valleys. During the fall rut, listen for the eerie, high-pitched squealing bugles of these majestic animals.

You'll reach a junction after 7.3 miles; here, you'll turn left, climb quickly to a notch, and then descend into Seven Lakes Basin. The trail to the right at the junction continues climbing toward lofty views from Bogachiel Peak, a good day trip from the basin.

The basin makes a good base for fishing the larger lakes or exploring the high country beyond. Camps are plentiful around several of the lakes, connected by a maze of boot-beaten trails. This fragile alpine country is also popular, so do your part to minimize further damage by staying on established trails and in established campsites. You'll also need a permit to camp here. The park limits the number of campers, so it's a good idea to reserve your permit ahead of time during summer weekends. Black bears, drawn by easy snacking on campers' food, are also common in the basin, so be prepared to hang your food well out of reach of marauding paws.

Key Points

0.0   Start at the south end of the parking lot at the Sol Duc River Trailhead.

0.1   Arrive at junction for a trail leading right (west) to the Sol Duc campground. Continue straight ahead on the main trail.

0.7   Arrive at a trail junction and shelter. Fork right (southeast) toward Deer Lake and Sol Duc Falls.

0.75 Arrive at a bridge crossing and Sol Duc Falls. Immediately after the bridge, turn right (west) onto the unsigned trail along the river toward Deer Lake and Seven Lakes Basin. To the left of the bridge are numerous campsites.

1.0   Arrive at a junction for the Lovers Lane Trail, which forks right (west) back to Sol Duc Hot Springs. Continue straight ahead.

1.8   Cross a bridge high above Canyon Creek.

2.1 Reach sign for camps along Canyon Creek off to the left (east).

2.8 Pass campsites to the east off-trail here, and again 0.5 mile farther up the trail. (**Note:** These are the last camps where fires are allowed, so you'll need a stove for higher camps.)

▶ **Native American legend says that the Sol Duc Hot Springs were created by a dragon's hot tears.**

3.9 Arrive at the shore of meadow-ringed Deer Lake. A sign directs you to campsites around the lake.

5.0 Arrive in a subalpine basin with several small tarns. An unsigned trail turns left (east) to campsites in this small basin. Continue straight ahead on the main trail.

7.3 Reach a signed junction. To the right, the trail leads to High Divide and Hoh Lake. Turn left (north) onto the Seven Lakes Basin Trail.

7.8 Arrive in the Seven Lakes Basin.

15.6 Arrive back at the trailhead and parking area.

Hike Information

Local information
North Olympic Visitor and Convention Bureau, (800) 942-4042, www.northolympic.com.

Local events/attractions
The Olympic Park Institute on Lake Crescent teaches natural and cultural history classes for adults and children, (360) 928-3720.

Accommodations
Sol Duc Hot Springs Resort, (360) 327-3583. **Olympic National Park Sol Duc,** (360) 327-3534.

Restaurants
Rain Drop Café, Forks, WA, (360) 374-6612.

5 Grand Valley

Hike from the highest trailhead in the Olympics along a spectacular open ridge, accompanied by wildflowers and whistling marmots on this 7.4-mile out-and-back hike. You'll get lofty views into the heart of the Olympic's Bailey Range and out over the Strait of Juan de Fuca. Descend to a string of emerald valley lakes, pleasant destinations for a day hike or overnight stay.

Start: On the Grand Valley Trail at the Obstruction Point Trailhead and parking area.
Length: 7.4 miles out-and-back.
Approximate hiking time: 4 hours.
Difficulty rating: Moderate, due to modest elevation gain on the return from the lake.
Trail surface: Ridgetop and forest trail.
Elevation gain: 1,650 feet on the return trip.
Land status: National park.
Nearest town: Port Angeles, WA.
Other trail users: None.
Canine compatibility: Not dog friendly.

Trail contacts: Backcountry Reservations Office, Olympic National Park, (360) 565-3100.
Schedule: Best hiked when snow-free, from July through early October.
Fees/permits: The park entrance fee is $10. Permits for backcountry camping are required and cost $5.00, plus $2.00 per person, per night.
Maps: USGS Mt. Angeles 15-minute quad; Olympic National Park quad; Olympic National Park map.

Finding the trailhead: From Port Angeles, follow the Hurricane Ridge Road south, past Olympic National Park's visitor center, paying the entry fee at the entrance station. Continue 17 miles to the large parking area on Hurricane Ridge. Just before entering the parking area, turn left at its eastern edge onto a dirt road signed for Obstruction Point. Follow the narrow, winding dirt road for 7.4 miles to the Obstruction Point Trailhead. *DeLorme Washington Atlas & Gazetteer* page 77, A5.

The Hike

A hike starting high on a ridge between heaven and earth, this rewarding trail from Obstruction Point to Grand Valley will allow you to experience the wild alpine country of the Olympics with a minimum of effort, since the trail is level or downhill most of the way and starts at the highest trailhead in the Olympics. (If you're backpacking, here's your opportunity to pack in the extra-heavy bottle of red wine.) Black-tailed deer are common here, and the piercing whistles of Olympic marmots, a species endemic to the Olympics, may accompany you on your descent into lake-filled Grand Valley.

No wood fires are allowed above 4,000 feet in this area, so be sure to bring a stove. All three lakes—Grand, Moose, and Gladys—host populations of brook trout, but fishing is generally best in Gladys Lake.

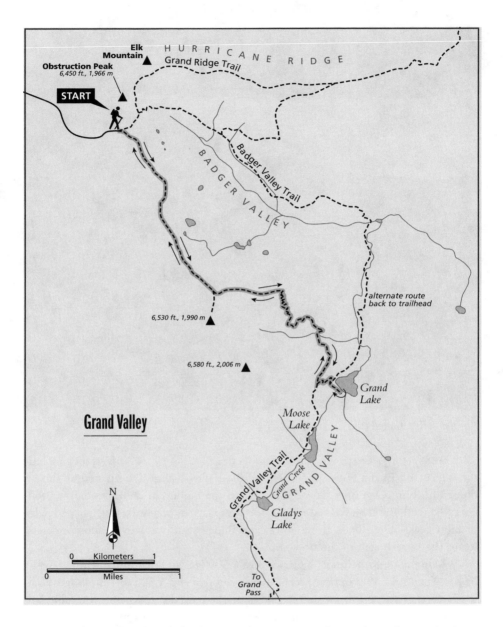

Grand Valley

From the trailhead, trails lead in two directions: northeast along the scenic alpine splendor of Grand Ridge for 8 miles to the Deer Park Trailhead, and southeast along the divide above Badger Valley. Take the right (southeast) fork—the divide route—and traverse the undulating ridge, crossing alpine fells and passing isolated clumps of stunted subalpine fir. This gentle ridge represents an ancient, gentle upland, one of the few locations in the Olympics where erosion has not worn away the broad plateau.

On the trail to Grand Valley.

The airy views are spectacular in all directions for your first 2 miles; they include the Lillian and Elwha River drainages and the Bailey Range. Dominated by the icy dome of Mount Olympus, whose West Peak is the highest in the Olympics (a modest 7,965 feet), the Bailey Range forms the western arm of a horseshoe-shaped ridge of high peaks. The divide from Hurricane Ridge southward to Mount Anderson forms the eastern arm of the horseshoe.

Where the trail reaches its high point of 6,500 feet and begins descending, you'll be presented with two options. Most hikers will descend 1,500 feet into Grand Valley, but experienced cross-country hikers might consider following the faint, up-and-down unsigned trail south along the alpine ridge for 3 miles to Grand Pass, gateway to a land of jagged peaks and alpine parks.

If you follow the steep trail down to the valley, you'll first pass scattered krummholz subalpine fir, shrublike trees stunted by the harsh environment above timberline. The route switchbacks down over 2 knee-busting miles to a bench laced with tiny creeks, passes a tarn, and descends amid increasing timber to a junction.

Emerald-green Grand Lake lies within sight 0.25 mile below and can be reached via the signed trail branching off to the left. If you're looking for another option to return to the trailhead, you can create a loop by descending toward Grand Lake and quickly turning left onto the Badger Valley Trail, first descending northward along Grand Creek and then climbing back to the trailhead via Badger Valley. This option is especially inviting during inclement weather, but it adds 900 feet to the total elevation gain.

To reach Moose and Gladys Lakes, continue forward on the main trail at the junction with the trail descending to Grand Lake and ascend the beautiful, peak-rimmed valley. Moose Lake lies 0.5 mile up the trail at an elevation of 5,050 feet, and Gladys Lake, at 5,400 feet, lies just east of the trail, 0.5 mile beyond. Be a minimum-impact camper and camp at least 200 feet from lakes and streams in subalpine areas such as Grand Valley. A day hike from any of the lakes to 6,450-foot Grand Pass makes for a rewarding excursion.

Key Points

0.0 Start at the north end of the Obstruction Point parking lot at the Grand Valley Trailhead sign.

0.55 Reach a ridge crest with views west to the Bailey Range and east to the Cascades and Puget Sound.

1.5 Reach a junction with a small trail branching right (southwest) from the main trail. This is an alternate cross-country route to Grand Pass for experienced hikers. The main trail continues straight and starts to drop toward the lake.

2.7 Cross a small stream, the first water along the trail since the trailhead.

3.4 Reach a signed trail junction; continue southwest toward Moose Lake, or turn left (north) onto a short trail to Grand Lake, visible just below you.

3.6 Arrive at a junction with the Badger Valley Trail and continue straight ahead on the trail around the lakeshore. (**Note:** The Badger Valley Trail also returns to Obstruction Point and offers a longer, steeper alternate route back to the Obstruction Point Trailhead.)

3.7 Arrive at the west shore of Grand Lake. Several campsites are located here along the forest edge.

7.4 Arrive back at the parking area and trailhead.

Hike Information

Local events/attractions
Clallam County Fair, third weekend in August.

Accommodations
Olympic National Park's Heart O' The Hills campground, (360) 452-0330.
Lake Crescent Lodge, (360) 928-3211.

Restaurants
Downriggers Restaurant, 115 East Railroad, Port Angeles, WA, (360) 452-2700.
Sirens Brewpub, 134 West Front Street, Port Angeles, WA, (360) 417-9152.

6 Dungeness Spit

On this 9.4-mile out-and-back hike, you'll walk a beach along the nation's longest sand spit to a historic lighthouse. You can spot some of the 250 species of seabirds and harbor seals that call this national wildlife refuge home along the way, and climb to the top of the lighthouse for sweeping views over the Strait of Juan de Fuca, Puget Sound, Canada's Vancouver Island, and beyond.

Start: At the north end of the parking lot for the Dungeness Spit Trailhead.
Length: 9.4 miles out-and-back.
Approximate hiking time: 5 hours.
Difficulty rating: Easy, due to the flat beach walk.
Trail surface: Sand beach.
Elevation gain: None.
Land status: National wildlife refuge.
Nearest town: Sequim, WA.
Other trail users: None.

Canine compatibility: Not dog friendly.
Trail contacts: Dungeness National Wildlife Refuge, Port Angeles, WA, (360) 457-8451.
Schedule: Open year-round from sunrise until sunset. Access road gates lock at 10:00 P.M. and open at 7:00 A.M.
Fees/permits: $3.00 entrance fee for the refuge, paid at the trailhead.
Maps: USGS Dungeness 7.5-minute quad; U.S. Fish and Wildlife Service Dungeness National Wildlife Refuge map.

Finding the trailhead: From U.S. Highway 101, turn north onto the Kitchen-Dick Road, following signs for the Dungeness Recreation Area and the Dungeness National Wildlife Refuge. At 3 miles the road bends to the east; turn left into the entrance to the refuge and recreation area. Follow signs for 0.5 mile to the trailhead parking area. *DeLorme Washington Atlas & Gazetteer* page 93, C7.

The Hike

Jutting like a delicate finger into the Strait of Juan de Fuca, the Dungeness Spit is a curious geographic oddity on the Olympic Peninsula's north coast. Erosion transported by waves and currents from cliffs to the west and from sediments flowing down the Dungeness River have interacted over time to form this 6-mile-long sandy spit, the longest spit in the United States. Now protected as part of the 360-acre Dungeness National Wildlife Refuge, the Dungeness Spit's quiet inland waters provide habitat for more than 250 species of seabirds, such as surf scoters, killdeers, Caspian terns, cormorants, and loons. Harbor seals are also common here, where mothers with pups haul out on beaches along the protected inland side of the spit.

While Dungeness Spit is a haven for wildlife, seafarers have not looked so kindly on it, nicknaming it Shipwreck Spit because of the number of voyages that have ended in tragedy in its dangerously shallow waters. Early settlers lit bonfires on the spit as beacons to ships' captains navigating the rough waters of the Strait of Juan de Fuca offshore. In 1857 a lighthouse was constructed at the end of the spit to guide

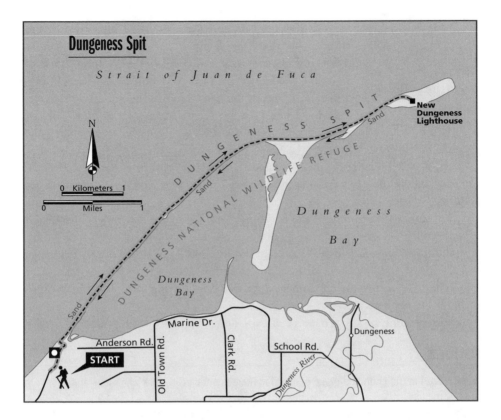

Dungeness Spit

ships safely past the hazardous waters. Still in operation today, the lighthouse, a designated National Historic Site, makes for an interesting destination on this beach walk.

Before beginning your hike, it's a good idea to check tide charts and weather. Hiking along this narrow spit—at times no more than a few hundred feet wide—is generally easier during low tide when firm, wet sand is exposed. Large storms during high tides can also send waves crashing over the spit, making hiking potentially dangerous during inclement weather.

From the parking area, the wide trail gently descends toward the beach in cool forest, quickly reaching two wooden platforms with tree-framed views east out over the spit and the Strait of Juan de Fuca. Many visitors turn back here, content with the views.

Continue descending the trail, soon reaching the base of the spit and the beginning of your walk. The calm inner harbor, marked by the line of driftwood along the top of the spit, is closed to hikers to protect shorebird habitat and haulout beaches for harbor seals.

The 5-mile hike from here out to the lighthouse can be a meditative experience, particularly in the fog that often shrouds the spit. There's no trail to follow; instead, you'll simply wander along the beach toward your destination, accompanied by the rhythmic breaking of waves on the shore. Look north across the Strait of Juan de

▶ **The Dungeness Spit is the longest natural sand spit in the United States.**

Fuca to Vancouver Island and the city of Victoria, Canada, or watch the harbor seals playfully bobbing in the surf off-shore. Look out to the east toward Whidbey and Protection Islands, or south toward Hurricane Ridge and the peaks of the Olympics. Mile markers on poles near the driftwood line help you chart your progress down the beach.

At just under 3 miles from the trailhead, the spit begins to curve to the south, bringing the lighthouse into view. Just under 2 miles later, you'll reach your destination.

The manicured grounds of the lighthouse and lighthouse keeper's residence are a sharp contrast to the wild, wind-whipped beach. Volunteers staff the lighthouse year-round, giving tours to visitors. From the top, you'll get all-encompassing views over Puget Sound, the Strait of Juan de Fuca, the Olympics, and beyond. You can also look east out over the remainder of the spit, still growing today at a rate of more than 14 feet per year.

Once content, simply retrace your steps along the beach to the trailhead.

Key Points

0.0 Start at the north end of the parking lot. There is a trailhead kiosk with maps and information.

0.36 Reach two wooden platform overlooks with views east toward the spit.

0.5 Emerge from forest trail onto the beach. Turn right (east) along the beach toward the lighthouse.

2.9 The lighthouse comes into view as the spit curves to the south.

4.7 Arrive at the lighthouse and the end of the hike.

9.4 Arrive back at the trailhead and parking area.

Hike Information

Local information
Sequim-Dungeness Valley Chamber of Commerce Visitor Information Center,
(360) 683-6690.

Local events/attractions
Celebrate Lavender Festival, Sequim, WA, early August.

Accommodations
Dungeness Recreation Area campsite,
(360) 683-5847.

Juan de Fuca Cottages, Sequim, WA,
(360) 683-4433.

Restaurants
Oyster House, Sequim, WA, (360) 385-1785.
Hiway 101 Diner, Sequim, WA,
(360) 683-3388.

7 Royal Basin

This 14.4-mile out-and-back long day hike or backpack in the northeastern Olympics in Olympic National Park features a large alpine cirque encircled by the greatest concentration of 7,000-foot peaks in the Olympics. Your destination, a trout-filled mountain lake, makes a scenic base camp for further exploration of the land of rock and ice farther up the valley.

Start: At the Upper Dungeness Trail 833.
Length: 14.4 miles out-and-back to Royal Lake.
Approximate hiking time: 8 hours.
Difficulty rating: Difficult, due to length, steep trail sections, and elevation gain.
Trail surface: Forest trail.
Elevation gain: 2,500 feet.
Land status: National forest, national park.
Nearest town: Sequim, WA.
Other trail users: None.
Canine compatibility: Not dog friendly.
Trail contacts: Olympic National Park, (360) 565-3100.

Schedule: Best hiked when snow-free, from late June through September.
Fees/permits: For an overnight stay in Royal Basin, obtain a free backcountry permit, available at the park boundary a few miles up the trail. A Northwest Forest Pass is required for parking at the trailhead. Day passes can be acquired for $3.00 at the Quilcene ranger station.
Maps: USGS Tyler Peak and Mt. Deception 15-minute quads; Olympic National Park quad; Olympic National Park map.

Finding the trailhead: Follow U.S. Highway 101 north to Sequim Bay State Park. Turn left onto the Louella Road and, after 1 mile, turn left onto the Palo Alto Road. Stay on the main road, ignoring side roads, and turn right onto Forest Service Road 2880. Pass the Dungeness Forks campground, and at 1 mile stay left on Forest Service Road 2870. After 1.5 more miles turn right onto Forest Service Road 2860. Drive another 6 miles to the Upper Dungeness Trailhead 833 parking area. *DeLorme Washington Atlas & Gazetteer* page 77, B7.

The Hike

The east side of the Olympics offers a prime example of the rain-shadow effect. Forests and underbrush here are thick but far from being overgrown and mossy, as you'll find on the very wet west side of the peninsula. Only residual snow clings to the highest peaks, not the vast fields of ice present west of the Olympics.

This "dry-side" hike will lead you through forested Royal Creek Canyon to glacier-carved Royal Basin in the shadow of the Needles, a spectacular group of jagged peaks composed of erosion-resistant basalt. Mount Deception, the second highest summit in the Olympics, rises to an elevation of 7,788 feet at the head of the basin. This peak helps illustrate the rain shadow: While Mount Olympus, only 177 feet higher, lies buried under the thickest ice cap in Washington, only a few small patches of snow and ice cling to the shadiest flanks of Mount Deception in summer.

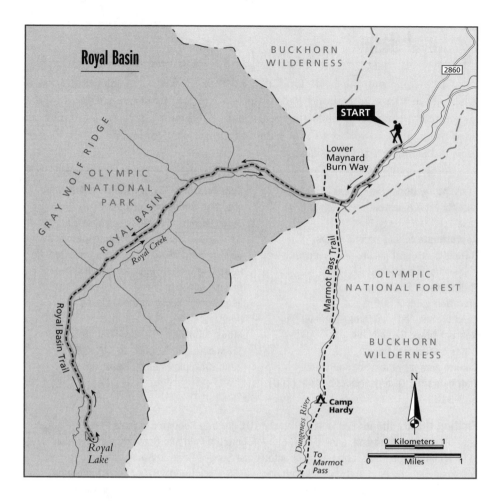

The trail begins on the west side of the road, just north of the bridge across the Dungeness River. An easy mile through a lovely forest of tall Douglas fir and western hemlock leads to a junction at a crossing of Royal Creek. Good campsites are located here.

Take the right fork, quickly entering Olympic National Park. You'll also find a register along the trail where you can self-register for a backcountry camping permit if you're planning to stay overnight.

The trail continues through lush forest, passing scattered streamside campsites, giving you only occasional views here of smooth Gray Wolf Ridge, 3,000 feet above to the west, and an unnamed ridge of 7,000-foot-plus peaks rising east of the canyon.

As you gain elevation following the drainage south, you'll pass a series of flower-filled meadows carpeting avalanche chutes in forest clearings. The grade steepens noticeably at around 4.75 miles, ending at the lower (northern) end of Royal Basin, surrounded on three sides by high, sky-piercing crags.

Head through willow-clad meadows. You'll soon pass the only campsite where wood fires are allowed.

Subalpine fir is the dominant tree here, but in the meadows you'll also see some lodgepole pine, a tree much more commonly found at higher elevations on the east side of the state. The grade soon steepens once again as you climb through forest to 5,100-foot Royal Lake, a tiny heart-shaped lake surrounded by spirelike subalpine firs. To extend your day trip or wander from your camp, explore the basin above and its meadows, rock, and ice.

After exploring what many would consider the most scenic basin in all the Olympics, simply backtrack to the trailhead.

Key Points

0.0 Start at the parking area for the Upper Dungeness Trail 833.

0.2 Ignore the unmarked trail leading uphill to the right (north). This is the Lower Maynard Burn Way Trail.

1.2 Turn right (northwest) onto the Royal Basin Trail. The left trail leads to Marmot Pass.

1.5 Reach the boundary of Olympic National Park, where you'll also find a trail register a short distance farther down the trail.

2.7 The trail drops slightly to a stream crossing.

3.2 The trail crosses another stream, and views begin to open.

6.7 Cross Royal Creek on foot logs and climb up a steep pitch.

7.2 Arrive at Royal Lake.

14.4 Arrive back at the trailhead and parking area.

Hike Information

Local information

Sequim-Dungeness Valley Chamber of Commerce Visitor Information Center,
(360) 683-6690.

Local events/attractions

Celebrate Lavender Festival, early August, Sequim, WA.

Accommodations

Sequim Bay State Park, (888) 226-7688.

Juan de Fuca Cottages, Sequim, WA, (360) 683-4433.
USDA Forest Service Dungeness Forks campground, (360) 765-2200.

Restaurants

Oyster House, Sequim, WA, (360) 385-1785.
Hiway 101 Diner, Sequim, WA, (360) 683-3388.

8 Mount Townsend

This hike climbs 3.8 miles from a rhododendron–speckled forest to a high meadow ridge that invites an afternoon of wandering. Views to Puget Sound, across the Strait of Juan de Fuca, and into the higher summits of the Olympics are spectacular, as are the sunsets from this lofty perch. In June the mountain's open, south-facing hillsides explode with colorful displays of wildflowers.

Start: At the upper trailhead for Mount Townsend Trail 839.
Length: 7.6 miles out-and-back.
Approximate hiking time: 4–5 hours.
Difficulty rating: Difficult, due to nearly 3,000 feet of elevation gain.
Trail surface: Forest trail.
Elevation gain: 2,950 feet.
Land status: National forest and federal wilderness area.
Nearest town: Quilcene, WA.
Other trail users: Equestrians.
Canine compatibility: Leashed pets are permitted.

Trail contacts: USDA Forest Service, Hood Canal Ranger District, Quilcene office, (360) 765-2200.
Schedule: Best hiked when snow-free, from June to October.
Fees/permits: A Northwest Forest Pass is required at the trailhead. Passes are $3.00 for a day pass or $30.00 for an annual pass. Both are available at the Quilcene ranger station.
Maps: USGS Mt. Townsend 7.5-minute quad; Olympic National Forest map.

Finding the trailhead: From U.S. Highway 101, 1 mile south of the town of Quilcene, turn right onto the Penny Creek Road. Stay left at the fork in the road at 1.4 miles and continue to Forest Service Road 27. Drive FR 27 for 14.2 miles to Forest Service Road 190. Turn left and follow FR 190 for 1 mile to the trailhead at the end of the road, 16.2 miles total from US 101. (Note: There are two trailheads for Mount Townsend, an upper and a lower. These directions take you to the upper trailhead. To reach the lower trailhead, bear left from FR 27 onto Forest Service Road 2760 and follow it to its end.) *DeLorme Washington Atlas & Gazetteer* page 77, B8.

The Hike

After enduring months of gloomy skies and rain, the first warm, sunny days in June send many Pacific Northwest hikers gleefully careening toward alpine trails, where they're often confronted by the grim reality that snowpack in much of the region's high country doesn't melt out until well into July. Fortunately Mount Townsend, perched on the dry eastern side of the Olympics, offers a good early-season alternative, as its south-facing meadow slopes are frequently hikable in early June. By mid-June the showy pink blooms of Pacific rhododendron brighten the lower-elevation forests here, while the mountain's expansive upper meadows become awash in the the yellows, reds, whites, and purples of wildflowers. Views from the

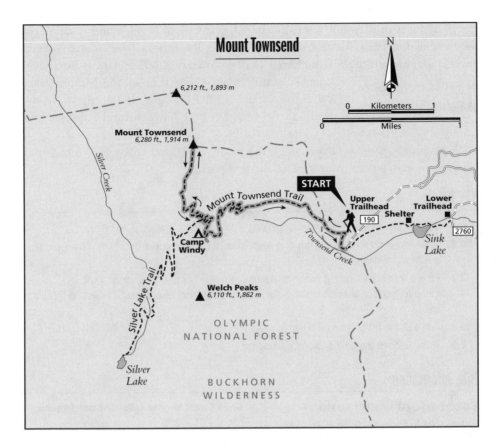

Mount Townsend

N

6,212 ft., 1,893 m

Mount Townsend
6,280 ft., 1,914 m

Silver Creek

Mount Townsend Trail

START

Upper Trailhead
190

Lower Trailhead
Shelter
2760

Sink Lake

Townsend Creek

Camp Windy

Silver Lake Trail

Welch Peaks
6,110 ft., 1,862 m

OLYMPIC NATIONAL FOREST

Silver Lake

BUCKHORN WILDERNESS

0 Kilometers 1
0 Miles 1

summit are among the most all-encompassing in the region, and the broad, open ridge invites further wandering and exploration.

Two trailheads, a lower and an upper, offer the primary access to Mount Townsend. The lower trailhead will add about a mile of walking to your trip through forest and past a shelter and small, shallow Sink Lake.

From the upper trailhead, the trail upward to the summit wastes no time, relentlessly climbing a series of switchbacks through forests of fir and hemlock, with an understory of rhododendron. After just under 1 mile of climbing, you'll pass a sign marking your entrance into the Buckhorn Wilderness.

Within the next mile forest begins to give way to meadow, with increasingly open views to the south. In early and midsummer, slopes here come alive with the reds and yellows of Indian paintbrush and columbine, purple lupine, orange tiger lily, and the whites of yarrow and valerian.

The trail continues its upward climb into the alpine country, reaching Camp Windy at just under 3 miles; a small meadow and tarn offer pleasant campsites. Here the unsigned trail to Silver Lake branches south from the trail, making for another good day hike for those camping overnight.

In about a mile, you'll reach the broad, open summit ridge and magnificent views in all directions. To the east, look down over Puget Sound; on clear days you'll be able to pick out the tiny buildings of downtown Seattle. Or stare at the snowy

▶ **The Pacific rhododendron is Washington's state flower.**

conelike summits of Mount Rainier and Mount Baker off in the distance to the southeast and northeast. To the north are the towns of Port Townsend and Sequim, along with the Dungeness Spit.

For solitude, wander farther along the lonely ridge, and when you've had your fill of the views, retrace your steps to the trailhead.

Key Points

0.0   Start at the west end of the small parking area for Mount Townsend Trail 839.

0.97 After crossing and climbing out of a small stream gully, enter the Buckhorn Wilderness at a sign along the trail.

2.7   Pass a trail branching left (west) to a small tarn and Camp Windy, where you'll find camping areas in a small meadow. An unsigned trail here also leads 5.5 miles to Silver Lake.

3.8   Arrive at the broad summit ridge.

7.6   Arrive back at the trailhead and parking lot.

Hike Information

Local events/attractions

Olympic Music Festival, Quilcene, WA, late June to early September, (206) 527-8839.

Accommodations

Old Church Inn, (360) 732-7552.

USDA Forest Service Falls View campground, (360) 765-3368.

Restaurants

Timber House, (360) 765-3339.

Honorable Mentions

Olympic Peninsula and Coast

H1 Long Beach Peninsula

The Long Beach Peninsula—the long, sandy strip of land separating sheltered Willapa Bay from the ocean—appears, like the Dungeness Spit (Hike 6), as an oddity on maps. Its northern terminus, Leadbetter Point, has several trails, ranging from 0.5 to 2 miles in length, that wind their way through shifting sand dunes and past beach grass, lupine, wild strawberry, sand verbena, sea-rocket, and beach pea to the northern tip of this long peninsula. Biologists have recorded more than a hundred species of birds here, including black brants, loons, grebes, mergansers, dunlins, American wigeons, eagles, grouse, canvasbacks, scaups, buffleheads, and scoters. Part wildlife refuge and part state park, portions of the peninsula are closed during the nesting season (April through August) to protect the nesting area of the snowy plover, a small shorebird species that reaches the northern limit of its breeding range here. Be prepared to hike in water if you plan to enjoy Leadbetter during the annual winter flood season, as the beach trails flood deeply from November through mid-May (and in some years from mid-October through the end of June).

From the town of Long Beach, follow Washington Route 103 north along the Long Beach Peninsula to its end. Follow signs for Leadbetter Point. For more information, contact Willapa National Wildlife Refuge, (360) 484–3482, pacific.fws.gov/visitor/washington.html#willapa. *DeLorme Washington Atlas & Gazetteer* page 58, D3.

H2 Fort Canby State Park

Fort Canby State Park is a gem in Washington's state park system and a great day-hiking destination year-round. It contains 7 miles of trails, 1,900 acres of saltwater and Columbia River shoreline, rocky headlands, and forest. The area is also rich with history; it's the endpoint for Lewis and Clark's expedition (there's a museum here), and it contains the Cape Disappointment Lighthouse, the oldest functioning lighthouse on the West Coast—constructed in 1856 to warn seamen of the treacherous Columbia River bar just offshore, known as the graveyard of the Pacific. In the park you'll find a 1.5-mile loop through old-growth forest, as well as several short loop trails to the Cape Disappointment and North Head Lighthouses.

To get there from the town of Ilwaco, turn south from U.S. Highway 101 onto First Street and drive 3.5 miles to the park entrance. For more information, contact Fort Canby State Park, (360) 642–3078, www.parks.wa.gov. *DeLorme Washington Atlas & Gazetteer* page 58, B1.

H3 Hoh River to Mosquito Creek

This 11-mile out-and-back hike offers another opportunity to experience Washington's wild coast. Plan your hike according to the tide table, as there are points along the beach route between the mouth of the Hoh River and Jefferson Cove that can only be negotiated at low to medium tide. From the Oil City Trailhead, the first 0.5 mile of the trail follows the north bank of the Hoh River through a forest of western hemlock, Sitka spruce, and red alder to the ocean. Numerous sea stacks, used by nesting shorebirds, lie offshore. Northwest along the beach, Hoh Head juts into the ocean, and the trail climbs a short rope ladder up the cliffs and into the hemlock-spruce forest above this point. With a reliable water supply and good campsites, Mosquito Creek, 5.5 miles from the trailhead, makes a fine destination for a weekend hike. Beyond the creek, long stretches of beach invite exploration. Tidepools, habitat for sea urchins, sea lettuce, various crabs, small fish, and much more, reward hikers who take the time to look. Harbor seals, gulls, and cormorants are all fairly common along the coast. You may also see gray whales offshore.

To get there from U.S. Highway 101, 14 miles south of Forks and 50.5 miles north of Quinault Lake, turn southwest where a sign indicates the Cottonwood Recreation Area, just north of the Oxbow campground. Ignore the left turn to the Cottonwood campground after 2.3 miles. The pavement ends after 5 miles, and a good dirt road leads to the Oil City Trailhead parking area along the Hoh River, 10 miles from the highway. For more information, contact Olympic National Park, (360) 565–3100, www.nps.gov/olym. *DeLorme Washington Atlas & Gazetteer* page 75, C5.

H4 Rialto Beach to Chilean Memorial

This 7.2-mile out-and-back day hike or backpack along the central wilderness coast of the Olympic Peninsula in Olympic National Park samples the southernmost portion of the Ozette Lake to Rialto Beach hike, a 20-mile trip lasting several days. Rialto Beach is quite popular, and you'll probably have plenty of company during the first mile or so, but the crowds will thin as you hike past Hole in the Wall—a wave-cut arch in a rocky point—and past many excellent tidepools exposed at low tide. You'll end the hike at a sheltered cove east of Cape Johnson and the Chilean Memorial, recognizing just one of many ships lost to the sea here. Wanderings along the coast from a base camp at the Chilean Memorial will add to your enjoyment of this weekend hike along a wilderness beach.

To get there, follow U.S. Highway 101 north from Forks for about 1 mile, then turn west, as indicated by a sign pointing to Mora and La Push. Turn right after 7.6 miles at the Quillayute Prairie Fire Station and follow the Mora Road for 5 miles to the large parking area at Rialto Beach. For more information, contact Olympic National Park, (360) 565–3100, www.nps.gov/olym. *DeLorme Washington Atlas & Gazetteer* page 74, A3.

H5 Cape Flattery

Not only will this short trail perched at the tip of Cape Flattery on the Makah Indian Reservation lead you 1 mile to the northwestern tip of the United States, but you'll also find 1,200-foot cliffs and jaw-dropping views of ocean and pounding surf below. Look out at storm-raked Tatoosh Island 0.5 mile offshore, and bring binoculars to help spot gray whales in spring and again in winter.

From U.S. Highway 101 east of Forks, follow Washington Route 112 north about 60 miles, through the towns of Clallam Bay and Sekiu, to the village of Neah Bay on the Makah Indian Reservation. Follow the highway through town and drive 3 miles west on the Arrowhead Road. Keep right as the road forks just before the Waatch River, passing an old air force station to the marked trailhead on the left side of the road. For more information, see www.northolympic.com/capeflatterytrail. *DeLorme Washington Atlas & Gazetteer* page 90, B3.

H6 Hoh River

Along with the Bogachiel, Queets, and Quinault, the Hoh River Valley, with its otherworldly moss-covered forests, is considered one of the true rain-forest valleys in the Olympics. A hike up the Hoh River can make a pleasant short day trip, or you can hike the full 17 miles to the valley's end and icy flanks of the Blue Glacier on Mount Olympus, the Olympics' highest peak. Along the way you'll find gigantic western cedar, Douglas fir, bigleaf maple, and Sitka spruce delicately draped with epiphytes. The largest herd of Roosevelt elk also calls this valley home. There are camps along the way at about 6 and 9 miles.

To get there from the town of Forks, follow U.S. Highway 101 south for 14 miles and turn left onto the Hoh River Road, driving 18 miles to the Hoh ranger station and the trailhead parking area. For more information, contact Olympic National Park, (360) 565–3100, www.nps.gov/olym. *DeLorme Washington Atlas & Gazetteer* page 76, B1.

H7 Pete's Creek to Colonel Bob

The entire western half of the Olympic Mountains consists of densely forested mountains dissected by a series of deep river valleys. This moderate 8.5-mile out-and-back day hike or overnighter will lead you to a rocky viewpoint in the Colonel Bob Wilderness of the southwestern Olympic Mountains. Views reach deep into the Olympics, punctuated by jagged summits. The deep trench of the Quinault River lies 4,000 feet below the peak to the north. To the southwest, the blue Pacific Ocean stretches toward the horizon.

To get there, follow U.S. Highway 101 north from Hoquiam for 24.5 miles, and turn right onto the paved Donkey Creek Road (Forest Service Road 22). After 8 miles turn left (north) onto Forest Service Road 2204, signed for the Campbell Tree

Grove campground, reaching the end of pavement in 4 miles. Following signs for Campbell Tree Grove at subsequent junctions, proceed northeastward on Forest Service Road 2204, a good gravel road, to the Pete's Creek Trailhead, 7.7 miles from pavement and 18.7 miles from the highway. For more information, contact Olympic National Forest, Pacific Ranger District, (360) 288–2525, www.fs.fed.us/r6/olympic. *DeLorme Washington Atlas & Gazetteer* page 60, A3.

H8 Hurricane Ridge to Klahane Ridge

This 9-mile out-and-back day hike in the northern mountains of Olympic National Park features wildflowers, abundant wildlife, interesting geology, and big-sky panoramas of mountains and ocean. The trail climbs through subalpine fir forest carpeted with wildflowers, including blue harebell, pearly everlasting, lousewort, red and magenta Indian paintbrush (endemic to the Olympics), phlox, red heather, avalanche lily, meadow rue, bistort, and wild pink. Views from the broken Klahane Ridge, composed of volcanic breccia and pillow basalt, are far-reaching. To the north, mountains plunge into the Strait of Juan de Fuca. Beyond rises Vancouver Island. On the mainland are the coast ranges of British Columbia, Mount Baker, and Glacier Peak. From this lofty point you can also visualize the great Cordilleran Ice Sheet that traveled south from Canada more than 10,000 years ago. This ice sheet carved out the Strait of Juan de Fuca, isolated the San Juan Islands and Vancouver Island from the mainland, and abutted the north side of the Olympics—the northern slopes of Klahane Ridge itself.

To get there from Port Angeles, follow the Hurricane Ridge Road south past the Olympic National Park's visitor center, paying the entry fee at the entrance station. Continue 17 miles to the large parking area on Hurricane Ridge. For more information, contact Olympic National Park, (360) 565–3100, www.nps.gov/olym. *DeLorme Washington Atlas & Gazetteer* Page 77, A5.

H9 Elwha River

The Elwha River on the north side of the Olympic Peninsula once supported some of the region's most productive salmon runs—that is, until two dams were built on the river for power, blocking the salmon's migration. In 1992, after years of struggle, conservationists finally succeeded in convincing Congress that the dams should be removed. In 2005 the dams will finally come down, and many hope the salmon will return. Runs are expected to reach 392,000 fish, including the huge runs of pink salmon that used to come here. This hike follows the emerald-colored Elwha River deep into the heart of its 25-mile-long valley. There are several backcountry shelters along this forested trail, giving you the option to roam as far as you'd like, from a short day hike to a several-day backcountry trip.

To get there, drive U.S. Highway 101 from Port Angeles south 8.5 miles to the Elwha River Road. Just past the Elwha ranger station, turn left onto the Whiskey Bend Road. Follow this gravel road 4.5 miles to the parking lot and trailhead. For more information, contact Olympic National Park, (360) 565–3100, www.nps.gov/olym. *DeLorme Washington Atlas & Gazetteer* page 76, A4.

H10 Tubal Cain Trail to Buckhorn Lake

A 12-mile out-and-back backpack into a glacial valley on the east side of the Olympics in the Buckhorn Wilderness, this scenic hike climbs through a "dry" east-side drainage to numerous timberline campsites above tiny but fish-filled Buckhorn Lake. Trails lead past the lake to Buckhorn and Marmot Passes, offering scenic and rewarding side trips from a Buckhorn Lake base camp. Anglers, photographers, and just plain mountain lovers will find this a rewarding introduction to the Buckhorn Wilderness and an excellent way to spend a weekend.

To get there from Port Angeles, follow U.S. Highway 101 east for 18 miles to the Louella Road across from Sequim Bay State Park. Go 1 mile and turn left onto the Palo Alto Road. This paved county road leads past farms for 5.6 miles to the end of the pavement. Bear left onto Forest Service Road 28 after 2 more miles. Follow signs at subsequent junctions that indicate the Tubal Cain Trail and Dungeness Trail. Leave FR 28, turning right onto Forest Service Road 2880 and following it past the Dungeness Forks campground. Turn left onto Forest Service Road 2870 and go 2 miles. Then turn right onto Forest Service Road 2860, pass the Upper Dungeness Trailhead, and proceed another 3 miles to the Tubal Cain Mine Trail. For more information, contact Olympic National Forest, Hood Canal Ranger District, (360) 765–2200, www.fs.fed.us/r6/olympic. *DeLorme Washington Atlas & Gazetteer* page 77, B8.

H11 Marmot Pass

The 9-mile out-and-back hike to Marmot Pass begins in old-growth forests splashed with the colorful blooms of wild rhododendron in early summer and climbs to alpine meadows and boulder fields at 6,000-foot Marmot Pass. Views from this alpine perch are spectacular, including the heart of the Olympics to the west and the Puget Sound Basin to the east.

To get there, follow U.S. Highway 101 south from Quilcene for 1 mile to the Penny Creek Road. Turn right onto Penny Creek Road. Stay left at the fork at 1.4 miles and continue to Forest Service Road 27. At the national forest boundary this road becomes paved. Drive 11 miles to Forest Service Road 2750. The trailhead is 5 miles farther down this road, located at Ten Mile Shelter. For more information, contact Olympic National Forest, Hood Canal Ranger District, (360) 765–2200, www.fs.fed.us/r6/olympic. *DeLorme Washington Atlas & Gazetteer* page 77, B7.

H12 Mildred Lakes

The strenuous 8.8-mile out-and-back trail to this lake basin in the Mount Skokomish Wilderness may conjure up any number of expletives along the way, but you'll be rewarded by the endpoint. The way to Mildred Lakes Basin follows a very strenuous, unofficial trail up and down through thick brush and over and around fallen trees, gaining 2,300 feet of elevation along the way. But at the end you'll find three sparkling lakes cupped under the jagged and imposing ridge of the Sawtooth Range. As an added attraction, the lower and upper lakes are filled with hungry cutthroat trout, some reaching 10 to 14 inches in length.

To get there from U.S. Highway 101, 13.5 miles north of Hoodsport, turn west onto the Hamma Hamma Road (Forest Service Road 25) 14 miles north of Hoodsport, where a sign points to the Hamma Hamma Recreation Area. Turn left onto FR 25 and follow it for 14 miles to the trailhead just beyond a concrete bridge over the Hamma Hamma River. For more information, contact Olympic National Forest, Hood Canal Ranger District, (360) 765–2200, www.fs.fed.us/r6/olympic. *DeLorme Washington Atlas & Gazetteer* page 77, D6.

H13 Mount Ellinor

This short, steep ascent of a mountain on the east side of the Olympics starts in cool forests before climbing 2.5 miles to the meadowy slopes of Mount Ellinor. From here, the trail follows the southern ridge to the summit, at just over 5,900 feet. From the top, soak in the views of Lake Cushman below, of Puget Sound, and of the distant Cascade Range.

To get there from just south of Hoodsport, take U.S. Highway 101 to the Lake Cushman Road and turn west. After 9 miles turn right onto the Jorsted Creek Road (Forest Service Road 24). Follow this road 1.6 miles and turn right onto Forest Service Road 2419, the Big Creek Road. You'll find the lower trailhead (the route described above) at 4.9 miles, but if you want a shorter hike, you can also drive 3 miles farther to the upper trailhead. For more information, contact Olympic National Forest, Hood Canal Ranger District, (360) 765–2200, www.fs.fed.us/r6/olympic. *DeLorme Washington Atlas & Gazetteer* page 77, D7.

North Cascades

The North Cascades region is the crowning jewel of Washington's rugged beauty, a place where climbers and mountaineers from around the world come to conquer forbidding, often cloud-shrouded summits. Range upon range of ice-mantled peaks rise above deep, forested valleys here, creating not only legendary climbing terrain, but also seemingly limitless hiking opportunities. Luckily its wilderness areas and the 684,000-acre North Cascades National Park complex also create one of the largest protected areas in the lower forty-eight states, home to salmon runs, eagles, grizzly bears, and wolves, along with more than half of all the glaciers in the continental United States.

Geologically the North Cascades are composed of faulted and folded crystalline and metamorphic rocks, along with volcanic and sedimentary rocks. The region forms the southern end of the North Cascades subcontinent, which drifted west and merged with the main North American continent some fifty million years ago. Fossils found in remote regions of the North Cascades indicate that their home was once far removed from the region, in more tropical regions of the Pacific Ocean. About the time the dinosaurs vanished, the coastal plains crumpled into folds as this Pacific microcontinent slowly merged with the main continent. Most of the rocks now exposed in the western part of the range are old oceanic crust and its overlying sedimentary layers. Over time these rocks have been scoured and shaped by glaciation into dramatic peaks, pinnacles, and deep valleys.

Mount Baker and Glacier Peak, the region's two stratovolcanoes, rise above surrounding peaks in this region. Like their cousins in the South Cascades, both are less than a million years old, relative newcomers in the surrounding landscape. Their snowy profiles provide scenic backdrops to hikes throughout the region—hikers can get an up-close view of Mount Baker by taking the Ptarmigan Ridge Trail on the northeast flanks of the mountain. Along the way to this trailhead, you'll pass Picture Lake and the dramatic backdrop of Mount Shuksan, one of the most widely photographed spots in the Pacific Northwest.

The North Cascades region stretches from Interstate 90 north to the Canadian border, and four main east–west highways—I-90, U.S. Highway 2, the Mountain Loop Highway, and the North Cascades Highway—provide access to hikes along the way. The North Cascades Highway (Washington Route 20), stretching from the city of Burlington east to the Methow Valley and beyond, is arguably one of the country's most scenic drives, passing the turquoise waters of Ross Lake and the dramatic spires above Washington Pass. The highway traverses North Cascades National Park, one of the most scenic and least developed parks in the United States. You'll find hikes along thundering streams and over open passes here, including the Panther Creek/Thunder Creek loop and a hike to Cutthroat Pass. The Alpine Lakes Wilderness, easily reached within an hour of Seattle along I–90 or US 2, is among the state's most popular hiking destinations. Lastly, the highly scenic Mountain Loop Highway, stretching from the town of Granite Falls to the town of Darrington, shouldn't be overlooked. At Barlow Pass you'll find several scenic hikes, including the climb to Gothic Basin. Leave extra time to explore the Monte Cristo townsite, once a bustling mining community, now largely a ghost town.

9 Mountain Lake–Mount Pickett Loop

This pleasant 7.3-mile loop day hike leads through dense forests and past three glacial lakes in Moran State Park on the largest of the San Juan Islands. Due to its elevation, the hike makes a great year-round destination on one of the wildest remaining
portions of the main San Juan Islands.

Start: At the Mountain Lake boat-launch area.
Length: 7.3-mile loop.
Approximate hiking time: 3½ hours.
Difficulty rating: Easy, due to minimal eleva-
tion gain.
Elevation gain: 846 feet.
Land status: State park.
Nearest town: Eastsound, WA.
Other trail users: None.

Canine compatibility: Leashed dogs are per-
mitted.
Trail contacts: Moran State Park, (360)
376-2326, www.parks.wa.gov.
Schedule: Park hours are 6:30 A.M. to 10:00
P.M. during summer, 8:00 A.M. to dusk in winter.
Fees/permits: Day parking fee $5.00.
Maps: USGS Orcas Island 15-minute quad;
"Your Guide to Moran State Park" brochure.

Finding the trailhead: For most people the only way to reach the San Juan Islands is via the
ferry from Anacortes. Drive to the end of Washington Route 20 in Anacortes, following signs indicating San Juan Ferries. Take the ferry to Orcas Island. Several daily ferries leave Anacortes
bound for Orcas Island. Ferry lines can be long on weekends, so plan ahead.

From the Orcas ferry landing, follow the main road north and then east through Eastsound
Village, turning right toward Rosario and Moran State Park after 9.2 miles. The park entrance
arch is 13 miles from the ferry landing. Continue through the arch, passing the Cascade Lake
swim area and the trailhead for Mount Constitution. Bear left onto the Mount Constitution Road,
which is 1.25 miles beyond the entrance arch and registration station. One mile up the Mount
Constitution Road, bear right at the fork. Drive past the Mountain Lake Campground to the boat-
launch area at the end of the road. *DeLorme Washington Atlas & Gazetteer* page 108, C2.

The Hike

Midway between mainland Washington and Vancouver Island, hundreds of land-
forms rise out of the Pacific, ranging from tiny rocks to large, populated islands.

Once part of the mainland, the San Juan Islands were overridden thousands of
years ago by the vast Cordilleran Ice Sheet grinding its way south from Canada.
In addition to rounding the topography of the islands, this ice sheet also formed
Puget Sound and the Hood Canal, nearly severing the Olympic Peninsula from
the mainland.

One of the more popular recreation sites in the islands, 5,600-acre Moran State
Park features four campgrounds and more than 30 miles of hiking trails. This
forested terrain is arguably the finest hiking area in the San Juans. But a trip to Orcas
Island is typically not a one-day affair. Instead, most visitors stay in one of the campgrounds and spend several days exploring the island.

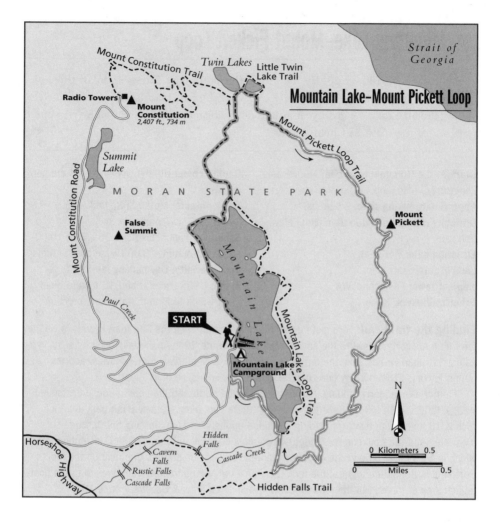

The Bonnie Sliger Memorial Trail begins north of the tiny Mountain Lake campground at the boat-launch and day-use parking area. Proceed northward along the west shore of glacier-gouged Mountain Lake, elevation 914 feet, under a canopy of western hemlock, western red cedar, and Douglas fir. Understory plants in this shady environment include Oregon grape, wild rose, whortleberry, gooseberry, bracken fern, ocean spray, and a variety of grasses.

The trail jogs east in a grassy flat shaded by large red alders, and after 1.4 miles it reaches a junction. The right fork follows the east shore of the lake and loops back to the trailhead, a pleasant hike for those with limited time. But for a longer and more interesting hike, take the left fork, which ascends the course of a small stream and climbs easily over a low saddle. Sitka spruce make a brief appearance at this 1,100-foot-high saddle, far in elevation above the wet coastal regions they typically inhabit. Numerous large, charred snags are among the remnants of the huge forests that once blanketed this island.

On the other side of the saddle, an imperceptible descent leads to a three-way junction. The left fork leads upward for 1.3 steep miles to the popular summit of Mount Constitution, also accessible by road. Take the right fork, skirting the southeast end of trout-filled Big Twin Lake (fishing in Mountain Lake is also productive), and quickly reach another junction.

You can either turn left here and loop around Little Twin Lake for a good view of the glacier-smoothed east face of Mount Constitution, or turn right and follow the south shore of the lake. The two trails rejoin at the little-used Mount Pickett Trail, ascending a gentle, southeast-trending ridge, viewless due to the dense Douglas fir forest. The way passes several former ponds, now grass-filled depressions. Keep an eye out for the abundant black-tailed deer that inhabit the area.

You'll reach a destination-and-mileage sign at the north end of an old road. Continue your trek via this road, topping out on a saddle just east of Mount Pickett after another mile. The 1,765-foot summit lies a few feet to the west, but search as you may, any hint of a vista is obscured by the dense forest. The topographic map will inform you that Mountain Lake lies less than 1 mile west, and the Pacific, rumbling with the motors of numerous watercraft, lies but a mile to the northeast.

Follow the road south as it descends from the saddle, immediately switchbacking. A faint trail branches northeastward from this bend, and experienced hikers—with the help of the topo map—can follow this route as it descends first north, then south along the eastern boundary of the park, and finally west along the southern boundary, rejoining the road partway between Mountain and Cascade Lakes.

Most hikers will continue following the course of the old road as it descends, alternating between old-growth forest and younger stands of Douglas fir and lodgepole pine. The route dips into a 1,000-foot-high saddle just before reaching a junction with a westbound track 2.2 miles from Mount Pickett.

Turn right (north) at this point, quickly descending to the south end of Mountain Lake. Then turn left and walk to the lower end of the lake, bear right at another junction, and cross the lake's outlet just below a small dam. You can enjoy a fine view of Mount Constitution and the summit observation tower from here.

The trail follows the irregular southwest shore, ending on the road opposite a park ranger's cabin, 0.5 mile from the dam. Complete the loop by walking northward on the road for 0.25 mile to the trailhead.

Key Points

0.0 Start on the Bonnie Sliger Memorial Trail at the boat launch just north of the Mountain Lake campground.

1.4 Arrive at a junction and turn left (north). The right fork loops back around the lake to the trailhead.

2.2 Arrive at a three-way junction. The left (west) fork leads upward for 1.3 steep miles to the summit of Mount Constitution. Take the right (east) fork, skirting the southeast end of trout-filled Big Twin Lake.

2.4 Reach another junction and turn right (southeast) along the south shore of Little Twin Lake. (**Note:** You can also turn left and traverse around the north shore of the lake. The two trails rejoin at the opposite end of the lake.)

3.0 Reach a destination-and-mileage sign for Mount Pickett at the north end of an old road. Continue forward as the trail reverts to road.

4.0 Reach the saddle below the summit of Mount Pickett. A faint trail branches right (northeast) from a switchback just below the saddle. Ignore this trail and continue forward on the road.

6.2 Reach a junction and turn right (north), descending to the south end of Mountain Lake.

6.5 Turn left (north) at the south end of the lake.

6.6 Reach another junction and bear right, crossing the lake outlet just below a dam.

7.1 Arrive at a road opposite the park ranger cabin.

7.3 Arrive back at the boat-launch area and trailhead.

Hike Information

Local information
Orcas Island Chamber of Commerce, (888) 376-8888.

Local events/attractions
Shearwater Adventures kayak rentals, (360) 376-4699, www.shearwaterkayaks.com. **Gnat's Nature Walks,** guided nature hikes, (360) 376-6629.

Accommodations
Doe Bay Resort, (360) 376-2291, www.doebay.com.

Moran State Park campgrounds, (360) 376-2326.

Restaurants
Café Olga, Olga, WA, (360) 376-4408. **Bilbo's Festivo,** Eastsound, WA, (360) 376-4728.

10 Ptarmigan Ridge

This 3- to 10-mile out-and-back day hike or overnighter winds its way along a spectacular alpine ridge in the Mount Baker Wilderness. The open terrain allows you to walk as far as you like. With dramatic views from the first step, you'll hike under the shadow of the northernmost Cascade volcano in Washington and the equally scenic Mount Shuksan across the valley.

Start: At the Artist Point and the Heather Meadows Recreation parking area.
Length: 3 miles out-and-back to the first viewpoint, 10 miles out-and-back to the trail's end.
Approximate hiking time: 1½ hours to the first viewpoint, 6 hours to the trail's end.
Difficulty rating: Easy to the first viewpoint; difficult to the trail's end, due to mountainous and snowy terrain.
Trail surface: Dirt trail and snow.
Elevation gain: 1,300 feet to the trail's end.
Land status: Special-use area (trailhead); federal wilderness area (trail).
Nearest town: Glacier, WA.
Other trail users: None.

Canine compatibility: Leashed dogs are permitted at the trailhead; the trail is dog friendly.
Trail contacts: Mount Baker-Snoqualmie National Forest, Mount Baker Ranger District, (360) 856-5700, www.fs.fed.us/r6/mbs/.
Schedule: Late July through September.
Fees/permits: Parking at the trailhead requires a $5.00 day pass or $30.00 annual Northwest Forest Pass. You can purchase a pass at www.fs.fed.us/r6/feedemo/ or by calling (800) 270-7504.
Maps: USGS Mt. Shuksan and Mt. Baker 15-minute quads; USDA Forest Service Mount Baker-Snoqualmie National Forest map.

Finding the trailhead: Follow the paved Mount Baker Highway (Washington Route 542) east from Kendall for 33.5 miles to its end at the large parking area at Artist's Point on Kulshan Ridge. Views from the trailhead are magnificent, including Mount Shuksan, Mount Baker, and a host of surrounding peaks. *DeLorme Washington Atlas & Gazetteer* page 110, B3.

The Hike

The trail along Ptarmigan Ridge is arguably the most scenic ridge walk in the Mount Baker area. Constant, glorious views of either Mount Baker's vast fields of ice or the glacier-carved mass of 9,127-foot Mount Shuksan will accompany you right from the beginning and all along the route.

Elevations en route are high, and the trail is generally not passable due to snow until late July or August. Even then, several permanent snowfields remain. Many hikers go only a mile or two to the first snowfields, which may be small in late summer but still quite steep. Sturdy boots are highly recommended, as is an ice ax for crossing steeper sections. If you're traveling beyond the first snowfields, use caution in changeable weather; fair weather can quickly lead to whiteout conditions as

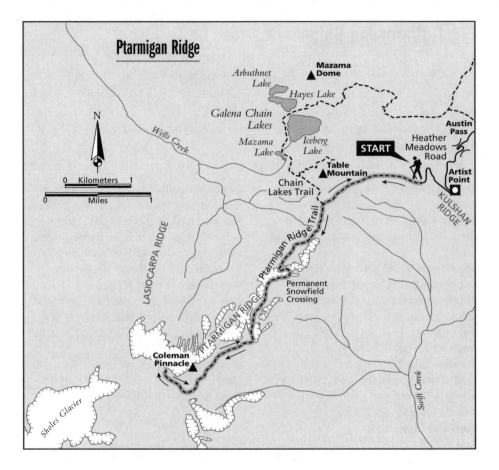

Ptarmigan Ridge

Arbuthnet Lake

Mazama Dome

Hayes Lake

Galena Chain Lakes

Mazama Lake

Iceberg Lake

Wells Creek

N

0   Kilometers   1

0   Miles   1

START

Heather Meadows Road

Austin Pass

Artist Point

KULSHAN RIDGE

Table Mountain

Chain Lakes Trail

Ptarmigan Ridge Trail

LASIOCARPA RIDGE

PTARMIGAN RIDGE

Permanent Snowfield Crossing

Coleman Pinnacle

Sholes Glacier

Swift Creek

clouds descend on the exposed ridge. Wood is scarce and no campfires are permitted anywhere on Ptarmigan Ridge, so carry a backpack stove if you're planning an overnight stay.

Beginning at the parking area, the trail descends slightly into forest to the kiosk for the Chain Lakes Trail—ignore the right-forking ridgeline route to Table Mountain from the parking area.

The trail traverses the glorious open, south-facing slopes of Table Mountain, a large alpine plateau isolated from its surroundings by the erosive forces of glaciation. Views are ever-impressive, featuring inescapable Mount Baker and its companion summit, Sherman Peak. Mount Baker's main summit, 10,778-foot Grant Peak, a nearly flat, ice-covered plateau, is separated from 10,000-foot Sherman Peak by the Sherman Crater. This crater is the most active volcanic feature in the Cascades (with the exception of Mount Saint Helens). Increasing thermal activity in the crater beginning in 1975 caused geologists to worry about an impending eruption. While

Ptarmigan Ridge Trail and snowy Mount Baker.

that didn't happen, all eyes are still on the mountain, possibly the next of Washington's volcanoes to erupt.

Other views from this south-slope traverse are superb. Southward, beyond a nearby stream-dissected bench, Swift Creek's canyon opens up to reveal a portion of Baker Lake. Beyond rise Glacier Peak and a host of other icy North Cascade crags. West of Glacier Peak is a cluster of three especially prominent peaks—Sloan Peak, Mount Pugh, and White Chuck Mountain.

You'll enter the Mount Baker Wilderness at an isolated stand of mountain hemlock. After a mile of easy walking, you'll see the Chain Lakes Trail fork right. That trail forms a popular semi-loop, passing the Galena Chain Lakes and then crossing a 5,300-foot saddle before descending past two more alpine lakes and ending at Austin Pass—a total of about 7 miles.

▶ Mount Baker Ski Area set a world record in 1999 for having the most snowfall in one year—that year a whopping 1,140 inches, or 95 feet, of snow fell on the mountain. So much snow fell that the ski area was forced to temporarily shut down when its chairlifts were buried.

Stay left at that junction and descend into the headwaters basin of Wells Creek to avoid permanent snow. From this point, grassy Skyline Divide and icy Chowder Ridge form the western horizon.

Much of this sheltered bowl was recently scoured by Little Ice Age glaciers, as evidenced by a fresh moraine you must cross before climbing back to the ridge crest.

▶ Next to Mount Rainier, Mount Baker is the most heavily glaciated volcano in the Cascades, and quite possibly the most likely to follow in the footsteps of Mount Saint Helens. While Washington's volcanoes erupt much less frequently than Hawaiian volcanoes, eruptions can be vastly more destructive. Several explosions rocked the mountain during the mid-nineteenth century, and there has been increased fumarolic activity in the mountain's crater since 1975. Scientists continue to keep a close eye on the volcano's activity. (See Hike 31, Norway Pass.)

A superb view of the cliffs, buttresses, pinnacles, and ice fields of Mount Shuksan, one of the classic peaks of the Cascade Range, unfolds from the top of the ridge.

Soon the trail jogs southward, traversing east-facing slopes with constant inspiring views of alpine wilderness. The first major permanent snowfield blocks the trail at about 1.7 miles from the Chain Lakes Trail junction, and nearly 3 miles from the trailhead. Thus far, the hike is a rewarding stroll, and average hikers should be content to stop here.

More experienced hikers can cross the snowfield (an ice ax is recommended) and then round a ridge emanating from Peak 5841, featuring more fine views. A southwestward traverse leads to another, larger snowfield on the flank of Coleman Pinnacle, its smooth, tree-covered south slopes a stark contrast to its ice-chiseled north face. About 1 mile to the southeast lies a milky-green, 5,500-foot-high alpine lake, reached via gentle, snowy slopes.

Ahead, the trail crosses more snow while traversing a headwaters bowl of Rainbow Creek. The route plunges you into an isolated stand of stunted subalpine fir and crosses a few tiny creeks, more snowfields, and wildflower-decorated fells before climbing briefly to a boulder-littered volcanic bench where the trail ends.

Just below the bench to the west lies the Sholes Glacier, riddled with crevasses created as the glacier flowed over uneven terrain, the resulting stress causing the ice to split and crack.

Ahead, to the southwest, are The Portals, passageways between a group of volcanic crags leading to the Rainbow and Mazama Glaciers and Mount Baker itself. Only experienced mountaineers should continue beyond trail's end on this bench.

Although fully exposed to the often merciless, changeable weather of the North Cascades, this bench and the aforementioned alpine lake are the best choices on this hike for an overnight stay.

Key Points

0.0 Start on the Ptarmigan Ridge Trail 682.1 signed for Chain Lakes and Table Mountain Trails on the northwest side of the Artist Point parking area.

1.1 Reach a signed junction for the trail to Chain Lakes leading off to the right (north). Continue straight ahead.

2.9 Reach the first permanent snowfield, a good turnaround point for day hikers without ice axes. (**Note:** More experienced mountaineers can continue from here another 1.1 miles beyond Coleman Pinnacle to the trail's end.)

5.8 Arrive back at the trailhead and parking area.

Hike Information

Local information

Mount Baker Experience, a local free newspaper with event listings and information. **Mount Baker Blues festival,** early August, www.bakerblues.com.

Accommodations

The Inn at Mt. Baker Bed and Breakfast, Glacier, WA, (360) 599-1776.

USDA Forest Service Silver Fir campground, (800) 280-2267.

Restaurants

Milano's, Glacier, WA, (360) 599-2863.

11 Baker River

Take this easy 5-mile out-and-back day hike or overnighter through rain forest to the southern foot of Mount Shuksan in North Cascades National Park. Along the way you'll pass through lovely old-growth forest and along the tumbling Baker River. This low-elevation hike also offers virtually year-round access for restless hikers when higher trails are snowbound.

Start: On the Baker River Trail.
Length: 5 miles out-and-back.
Approximate hiking time: 2½ hours.
Difficulty rating: Easy, due to gentle terrain and short length.
Trail surface: Dirt trail.
Elevation gain: 100 feet.
Land status: National Forest and National Park.
Nearest town: Concrete, WA.
Other trail users: None.
Canine compatibility: Not dog friendly.
Trail contacts: Mount Baker-Snoqualmie National Forest, Mount Baker Ranger District, (360) 856-5700, www.fs.fed.us/r6/mbs.

Schedule: March through mid-December.
Fees/permits: Parking at the trailhead requires a $5.00 day pass or $30.00 annual Northwest Forest Pass. You can purchase a pass at www.fs.fed.us/r6/feedemo or by calling (800) 270-7504. Backcountry permits are required for overnight camping in North Cascades National Park. Permits are available at ranger stations in Marblemount and Sedro Woolley.
Maps: USGS Mt. Shuksan 15-minute quad; North Cascades National Park quad; North Cascades National Park map.

Finding the trailhead: Drive Washington Route 20 east 14.5 miles from Sedro Woolley and turn north onto the Baker Lake Road. Follow this paved road, Forest Service Road 11, generally northeastward, avoiding numerous signed turnoffs. Pavement ends 0.3 mile beyond a junction with the right-forking road to Baker Lake resort and the left-forking Park Creek Road, 20 miles from the highway. Continue straight ahead on the main road, signed for Baker River. Drive around the north shore of Baker Lake and turn left onto Forest Service Road 1168, signed for the Baker River Trail, after another 5 miles. This rough dirt road leads northeastward through shady red alders, forks right after 0.3 mile, and ends at the large gravel parking area after another 0.2 mile. *DeLorme Washington Atlas & Gazetteer* page 110, B4.

The Hike

From the Picket Range to the Skagit River, the Baker River cuts a deep swath through the western North Cascades, draining the south slopes of the two preeminent peaks of the region, Mount Baker and Mount Shuksan. Its upper reaches are wild and trailless, while its lower section is followed by roads and impounded in two large reservoirs.

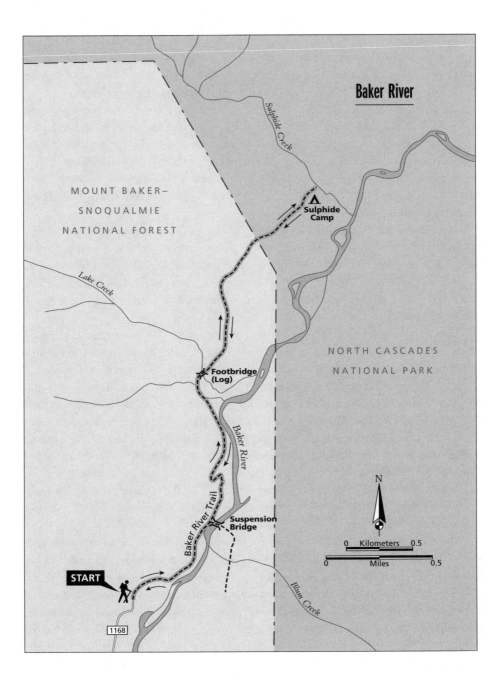

Baker River

MOUNT BAKER–
SNOQUALMIE
NATIONAL FOREST

Lake Creek

Sulphide Creek

Sulphide
Camp

Footbridge
(Log)

Baker River

NORTH CASCADES
NATIONAL PARK

N

Baker River Trail

Suspension
Bridge

Blum Creek

START

1168

0   Kilometers   0.5
0   Miles   0.5

This short trail follows the wild upper section of the river from above Baker Lake to a backcountry campsite on Sulphide Creek, below the enormous emptiness of the Sulphide Creek cirque. Above the camp Seahpo Peak and aptly named Jagged Ridge soar more than 6,000 feet from the canyon bottom to alpine heights.

This easy and scenic hike, 2.5 miles each way, is suitable for families with young children, since the trail gains little elevation. The lush forests along the Baker River are probably the best example of this type of environment in the Mount Baker area, and the contrast between nearby icy crags and the moist forests is dramatic.

Sulphide Creek offers a year-round water source, but glacial rock particles suspended in the creek may be rough on water filters. The nearby Baker River also carries a silty load from glaciers above.

The hikers-only trail begins at the west side of the parking area and heads north through a stand of young Douglas firs to the west bank of the boulder-strewn riverbed. It then enters a moss-draped forest of red alder, bigleaf maple, western red cedar (some of which are very large), vine maple, and western hemlock. At times you'll enjoy distant views up the river to the northeast, as well as to Mount Blum and other crags towering to the east.

After 1 mile silver fir joins the forest, indicating that you've reached the upper limits of the lowland-forest zone. Silver fir is a very common tree on the west side of the Cascades up to an elevation of about 6,000 feet. Its bark is silver to gray with white blotches and resin blisters on more mature trees. You can also recognize this tree by its blunt needles, notched at the tip, pointing forward along the branches. Two white lines on the underside of each needle give the tree a silvery appearance. Even with these cues, botanists sometimes have difficulty distinguishing among species of true fir, and the silver fir may be confused with both noble fir and subalpine fir where their ranges overlap.

At this point in the hike, you'll head into the heavily forested part of the trail, away from the Baker River. In fact, the Baker River is not visible again until you reach the Sulphide camp.

The trail proceeds through the lush forest with a few minor ups and downs and enters North Cascades National Park after passing a flooded area with many cedar snags—possibly an old beaver pond—finally ending at the edge of wide, swift Sulphide Creek. If you're adventurous, you may choose to attempt the swift ford of the stream and proceed up the wild Baker River. But the Sulphide camp is hard to resist, pleasantly shaded by large trees such as bigleaf maple, silver fir, and western hemlock. A fine view from the camp reaches up into the deep bowl at the head of Sulphide Creek—the largest cirque on Mount Shuksan. Jagged Ridge, crowned by toothed summits, and nearby Seahpo Peak rise northward above a thick hanging glacier.

Key Points

0.0 Start on the north side of the parking area for the Baker River/Baker Lake Trail.

0.3 Arrive at a trail register and the junction with the Baker Lake Trail. Continue straight ahead (do not cross the new suspension bridge, which leads to the Baker Lake Trail).

1.4 Pass a good vantage point of the Baker River and snowcapped peaks beyond.

1.5 Pass a flooded area of dams and snags—a side channel of the Baker River.

1.7 Cross a rocky area on a log.

2.5 Arrive at the Sulphide camp. Rock-hop across the river for views of Mount Shuksan.

5.0 Arrive back at the trailhead and parking area.

Hike Information

Local events/attractions

Float the Skagit River to view wintering bald eagles in the Skagit River Bald Eagle Natural Area. Call (206) 343-4344 or visit www.skagiteagle.org for information on float trips.

Accommodations

There are four USDA Forest Service campgrounds on Baker Lake (Shannon Creek, Panorama Point, Park Creek, and Horseshoe Cove). Contact (360) 856-5700. **Baker Lake Lodge,** (888) 711-3033, www.bakerlakelodge.com/lodge.shtml.

Restaurants

Baker Street Bar & Grill, Concrete, WA, (360) 853-7002.

12 Cutthroat Pass

This moderate 10-mile hike traverses a spectacular section of the Pacific Crest Trail from Rainy Pass to Cutthroat Pass. Along the way forests give way to the open, windswept pass surrounded by rugged peaks. Come here in fall for impressive displays of golden larch trees, which blanket the upper slopes of the basin. You can either retrace your steps from the pass, or leave a car at the Cutthroat Creek Trailhead for a scenic point-to-point hike past Cutthroat Lake.

Start: On Pacific Crest Trail (PCT) 2000.
Length: 9.6 miles out-and-back to Cutthroat Pass, 10 miles one-way to the Cutthroat Creek Trailhead with car shuttle.
Approximate hiking time: 5 hours out-and-back to Cutthroat Pass, 6 hours to the Cutthroat Creek Trailhead.
Difficulty rating: Difficult, due to length and elevation gain.
Elevation gain: 1,950 feet.
Land status: National forest.
Nearest town: Mazama, WA.
Other trail users: Equestrians, mountain bikes.
Canine compatibility: Dog friendly.

Trail contacts: Okanogan National Forest, Methow Valley Ranger Station, (509) 996-4003, www.fs.fed.us/r6/oka.
Schedule: July through September
Fees/permits: Parking at both the Rainy Pass and Cutthroat Creek Trailheads requires a $5.00 day pass or $30.00 annual Northwest Forest Pass. You can purchase a pass at www.fs.fed.us/r6/feedemo or by calling (800) 270-7504.
Maps: USGS Mt. Arriva and Washington Pass 7.5-minute quads; USDA Forest Service Okanogan National Forest map.

Finding the trailhead: Follow the North Cascades Highway (Washington Route 20) to Rainy Pass, 50.2 miles east of Marblemount or 43 miles west of Winthrop. Opposite the Rainy Pass picnic area, turn north onto a spur road that leads 0.3 mile to the parking area for the northbound Pacific Crest Trail.

To reach the Cutthroat Creek Trailhead, follow the North Cascades Highway east from Washington Pass for 4.5 miles to the Cutthroat Creek Road, and turn left (west). Follow this one-lane paved road for 1 mile to the trailhead. Or drive 30 miles west from Winthrop to the Cutthroat Creek Road. *DeLorme Washington Atlas & Gazetteer* page 112, D3.

The Hike

The Pacific Crest Trail crosses the Cascade crest at Rainy Pass, heading southward toward Lake Chelan and northward into the Pasayten Wilderness. The section north of the 4,840-foot pass travels through a spectacular swath of the Cascade crest, dominated by the saw-toothed ridges and summits of the Golden Horn Batholith, the youngest granitic rocks exposed in Washington. The dominant erosive force responsible for shaping these jagged rocks (in addition to past glaciation) is a process known

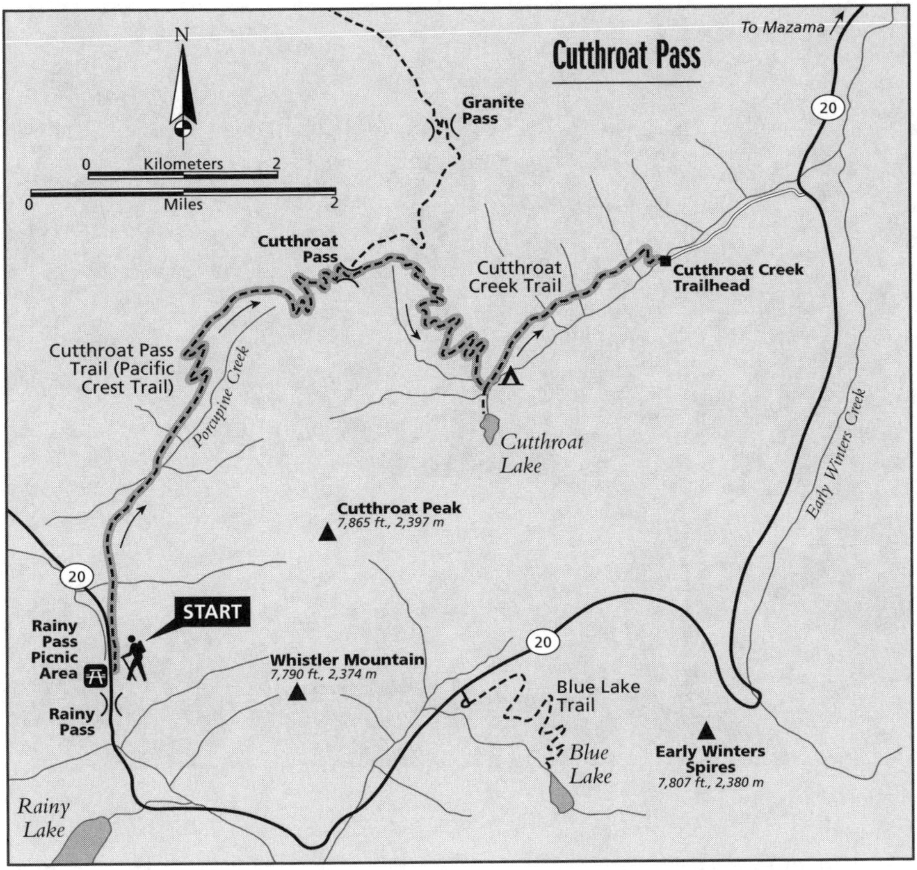

as frost wedging: Moisture seeps into cracks in the rock, wedging them apart as the water freezes and expands.

This out-and-back or point-to-point trip surveys the scenic high country above Rainy Pass. It's generally less crowded than the more popular (and easier) trail to Maple Pass on the south side of the highway. For the most scenic trip, arrange to leave a car at the Cutthroat Creek Trailhead. It's slightly longer than just retracing your steps to Rainy Pass, but the outstanding scenery on the descent to Cutthroat Lake makes the extra distance well worth hiking.

From the Rainy Pass Trailhead, you'll quickly duck into fir forest and cross a small stream below a delightful, two-tiered mini waterfall. Looking west from here you'll be able to see Black Peak—which, at 8,970 feet, is one of the highest summits in the Skagit River drainage. The divide on which this impressive peak rests is a granitic intrusion predating the Golden Horn Batholith you're traversing. Look southward before the trail bends into the Porcupine Creek drainage and you'll catch

Cutthroat Pass.

a glimpse of Lyall Glacier and the basin of Rainy Lake. You'll pass a variety of forest trees on this slope: mountain hemlock and silver fir from the west slope of the Cascades, and Engelmann spruce and subalpine fir from the drier, colder east slopes.

Just before the trail bridges Porcupine Creek, it crosses a smaller creek below a campsite, 1.5 miles from the trailhead. Granitic Dome 7520 looms boldly to the northwest. Then you'll negotiate three switchbacks to reach more open slopes and cross two small but year-round streams as you look up the canyon toward broad Cutthroat Pass, standing at timberline on the eastern skyline.

The basin above is dominated by the tough Lyall larch, which grows in exposed sites above all other trees in this region, seemingly thriving in the harshest mountain conditions. This interesting deciduous conifer, cousin to the western larch more common at lower elevations east of the Cascades, puts on a showy golden display of fall color in September and October.

The trail continues traversing south-facing slopes, crosses one more reliable creek, and crosses the headwaters of Porcupine Creek and a camping area. It then negotiates a series of switchbacks, rising toward the pass. The view grows ever more sweeping as you leave behind a few persistent larches and reach the pass.

Views are magnificent and far-ranging. To the southwest lies ice-encrusted Dome Peak, visible through the notch of Maple Pass, while Corteo Peak rises just northwest of that pass. Although Dome and Corteo Peaks reach similar elevations, Corteo supports only a few persistent snow patches in late summer—a good example of the rain-shadow effect. To the southeast you'll see a jumble of impressive, toothed summits. Due east is 8,876-foot Silver Star Mountain. South of it is jagged Kangaroo Ridge and the smooth dome of Liberty Bell, all composed of Golden Horn granodiorite.

Many backpackers out for a longer trip proceed north from here on the PCT, traversing below broken cliffs and above larch-covered benches toward the distant alpine ridges of the Pasayten country, a land that more closely resembles the Rockies than the Cascades. The beautiful alpine tarns of the Snowy Lakes lie about 5 miles farther along the PCT and make for a scenic turnaround point for a longer trip.

Just east of the pass, the Cutthroat Creek Trail forks right and descends toward the greenish blue gem of Cutthroat Lake, visible in the basin below you. If you've left a second car at the Cutthroat Creek Trailhead, this is the route you'll take. You'll descend easy switchbacks, first across open slopes and then through a timberline forest of Lyall larch, Engelmann spruce, and subalpine fir.

The route levels off on a waterless bench shaded by huge larches. Then it resumes its steady descent through a forest, where picturesque snags are as numerous as live trees. Huckleberry and manzanita carpet the slopes down to the canyon bottom. Below lies Cutthroat Lake; above the lake rise a number of jagged granitic summits.

You'll reach a junction with the short spur to Cutthroat Lake, where no overnight camping is permitted. To continue on the main trail, bear left, pass a spur trail to creekside campsites, and then descend the glacier-shaped valley of Cutthroat Creek amid mixed conifers. You'll cross the creek just before the trailhead.

Key Points

0.0 Start on Pacific Crest Trail 2000 at the north end of the parking area.

0.6 Cross a small stream.

1.6 Cross Porcupine Creek.

2.0 Pass a campsite off to the right (north) of the trail at a switchback.

2.3 Cross two streams as views open up toward Cutthroat Pass ahead of you.

3.2 Pass a campsite off to the right (east) of the trail.

4.8 Reach Cutthroat Pass and a trail junction. The trail to the left (northwest) leads to Granite Pass, continuing along the PCT. Fork right (east) toward Cutthroat Lake, visible below the pass.

8.2 Cross a stream soon after reaching an unsigned junction leading 0.1 mile to Cutthroat Lake to the right (south). Camping is not allowed at the lake.

8.4 Cross a stream on a bridge and pass another unsigned junction to the right (south)—a short spur trail leading to streamside camps.

9.8 Cross Cutthroat Creek on a bridge.

10.0 Arrive at the trailhead for Cutthroat Lake Trail 43.

Hike Information

Local information

Methow Valley Visitor Information, (509) 996-2125, www.methow.com.
Methow Valley Sports Trail Association, (509) 996-3287, www.mvsta.com.

Local events/attractions

Winthrop Rhythm and Blues Festival (summer), **Winthrop Octoberfest** (fall), (509) 996-2125, www.methow.com.

Accommodations

Mazama Country Inn, Mazama, WA, (509) 996-2681, www.mazamacountryinn.com.
USDA Forest Service Klipchuck, Lone Fir, and Early Winters campgrounds, (509) 996-4000.

Restaurants

Mazama Country Inn, Mazama, WA, (509) 996-2681.

13 Windy Pass/Tamarack Peak

Starting high and staying high, this easy 8.2-mile out-and-back hike through alpine meadows and larch-covered slopes to Windy Pass and beyond to the shoulder of nearby Tamarack Peak surveys some of the most scenic landscape along the Pacific Crest Trail (PCT). From Tamarack Peak, you can continue along to Foggy Pass and beyond into the remote Pasayten Wilderness, with the option of completing a multiday loop by returning via the Pasayten River Valley.

Start: At the Windy Pass Trailhead for the PCT.
Length: 8.2 miles out-and-back to the shoulder of Tamarack Peak.
Approximate hiking time: 4 hours out-and-back.
Difficulty rating: Easy, due to minimal elevation gain.
Elevation gain: 100 feet, on return to the trailhead.
Land status: National forest, federal wilderness area.
Nearest town: Mazama, WA.
Other trail users: Equestrians.

Canine compatibility: Dog friendly.
Trail contacts: Okanogan/Wenatchee National Forest, Methow Valley ranger station, (509) 996–4003, www.fs.fed.us/r6/oka.
Schedule: July through September.
Fees/permits: Parking at the trailhead requires a $5.00 day pass or $30.00 annual Northwest Forest Pass. You can purchase a pass at www.fs.fed.us/r6/feedemo or by calling (800) 270-7504.
Maps: USGS Slate Peak and Pasayten Peak 7.5-minute quads; USDA Forest Service Okanogan National Forest map.

Finding the trailhead: From Washington Route 20, 17 miles east of Washington Pass or 17.5 miles west of Winthrop, turn north to the crossroads of Mazama. After 0.4 mile turn left and pass the Mazama General Store. Follow this road westward up the course of the Methow River. Pavement ends after 6.6 miles, but the way becomes a good dirt road. At numerous junctions follow signs to Harts Pass. The road climbs steadily and becomes quite narrow in places; drive with care, reaching a junction for the Meadows campground after 18.3 miles. Bear right at this junction, pass a Forest Service guard station, and then turn right onto the Slate Peak Road. Continue past a parking area on your left; the signed trailhead is at the first switchback in the road, 1.3 miles from Harts Pass. Parking is limited to only about four vehicles. *DeLorme Washington Atlas & Gazetteer* page 112, C3.

The Hike

North of the Methow River, the crest of the Cascade Range assumes an entirely different character. Here imposing rocky summits give way to a series of gentle timberline peaks separated by many lower grassy and forested saddles. Slopes here are carpeted in summer by one of the most diverse assemblages of wildflowers in the state, while in fall larch-covered hillsides turn a fiery gold. Views are boundless along

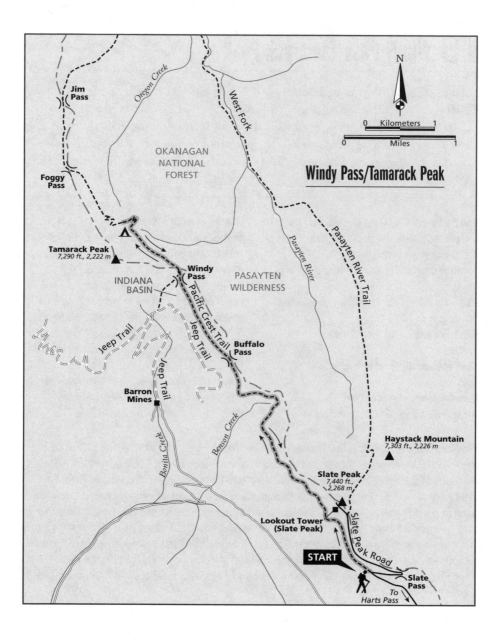

Windy Pass/Tamarack Peak

this stretch of the Pacific Crest Trail traversing between sky and earth. Much of this hike is along very exposed slopes, which should be avoided if inclement weather is imminent.

From the trailhead, begin by following the trail through scattered Lyall larches, soon reaching the PCT and bearing right. The views are immediately exceptional, including domineering Silver Star Mountain and its small glacier to the south, along with other prominent peaks such as The Needles, Tatie Peak, Mount Hardy, Fisher

Peak, Azurite Peak, and Mount Ballard. Beyond are peaks of North Cascades National Park: Snowfield Peak, Paul Bunyan's Stump, Bacon Peak, and the isolated crag of Mount Triumph. Closer at hand to the west are the dark masses of Crater Peak and Jack Mountain. Beyond them are distant North Cascades summits west of Ross Lake, and finally the snowy cone of Mount Baker.

The trail traverses the west slopes of Slate Peak's lookout-crowned summit, passing subalpine fir in krummholz form and flowers such as yarrow, lupine, false dandelion, meadow rue, blue harebell, buckwheat, stonecrop, purple aster, red Indian paintbrush, phlox, figwort, wild pink, and anemone. Beyond the slopes of Slate Peak, trailside vegetation becomes less diverse, where forest (stunted and widely scattered) includes subalpine fir, white-bark pine, Engelmann spruce, and Lyall larch.

▶ **Are there grizzly bears in Washington's Cascades? The answer is yes, but you're unlikely to see them. Wildlife biologists roughly estimate that there are only ten to twenty grizzly bears in the region stretching from southern British Columbia south to Snoqualmie Pass. Grizzlies have been declared an endangered species in Montana, Wyoming, Idaho, and Washington—the North Cascades have been designated as one of the targeted recovery areas for the species.**

After 2 miles you'll pass above an inviting larch-covered bench at the head of Benson Creek, a mere trickle late in the season. Ahead the trail traverses around the south and west slopes of Peak 6928. Here you may notice the abrupt change in the forest: The south-slope forest of subalpine fir and spruce gives way abruptly on the north slopes to cold-tolerant larch.

You'll soon reach forested Buffalo Pass and continue climbing gradually toward the west. As you hike, you won't be able to help noticing the scars of past mining activity and the townsite of Barron, below you to the west. This area is part of the productive Slate Creek mining district, where ores of gold, silver, zinc, lead, and copper were extracted around the turn of the twentieth century. The road over Harts Pass (formerly Slate Pass) was built in the 1890s to serve this area.

You'll descend to broad, 6,280-foot Windy Pass, ignoring an unsigned, left-forking jeep trail and a right-forking, northwest-bound path. While the hike to this point has been scenic, for more views continue a short distance on the PCT into the Pasayten Wilderness, one of Washington's largest and most isolated wild areas. You'll cross an impressive talus field and a stream 3.8 miles from the trailhead and 0.4 mile from Windy Pass. Trailside campsites can be found here amid a ground cover of huckleberry, red heather, and anemone.

Soon four switchbacks will bring you onto the northeast-trending ridge emanating from rocky Tamarack Peak. Subalpine firs atop the narrow ridge hug the ground, while nearby Lyall larches and white-bark pines stand erect, defying the elements. From here, for even more views, scramble farther up the peak's shoulder, or just be content with the views back toward Slate Peak and farther into the heart of the Pasayten before retracing your steps to the trailhead.

For an extended backpack loop, you can continue from here, descending past forested Foggy Pass and rocky Devil's Backbone to the West Fork of the Pasayten River, returning via the Slate Peak Trailhead.

Key Points

0.0 Start at the Windy Pass Trailhead (PCT) on the left (west) side of road.

0.1 Join the PCT leading to Harts Pass to the left (southeast). Bear right toward Windy Pass.

0.6 Pass below the lookout tower for Slate Peak, to the right and above you.

1.7 Traverse a meadow-filled basin with a small campsite just off the trail to the left (south).

1.9 Reach an unsigned trail leading off to the right (north). Continue straight ahead.

2.5 Arrive at Buffalo Pass.

3.4 Arrive at Windy Pass and an unsigned trail junction. The trail to the left (south) leads to a road and old mine area. Continue forward, soon entering the Pasayten Wilderness.

3.8 Cross a stream with a few camps in a meadow just below Tamarack Peak.

4.1 Arrive on the shoulder of Tamarack Peak.

8.2 Arrive back at the trailhead and parking area.

Hike Information

Local information
Methow Valley Visitor Information, (509) 996-2125, www.methow.com.
Methow Valley Sports Trail Association, (509) 996-3287, www.mvsta.com.

Local events/attractions
Winthrop Rhythm and Blues Festival (summer), **Winthrop Octoberfest** (fall), (509) 996-2125, www.methow.com.

Other resources
Geology of the North Cascades: A Mountain Mosaic by Ralph Haugerud, et al.

Accommodations
Mazama Country Inn, Mazama, WA, (509) 996-2681, www.mazamacountryinn.com.
USDA Forest Service Harts Pass and Meadows campgrounds, (509) 996-4000.

Restaurants
Mazama Country Inn, Mazama, WA, (509) 996-2681.

14 Tiffany Mountain

This moderate 4.8-mile out-and-back day hike takes you across grassy meadows to the gentle rocky dome of Tiffany Mountain in the Okanogan Cascades. From the summit, the mountain's steep western side drops dramatically away from you, and you'll have 360-degree views into the Pasayten Wilderness, south across the Methow Valley, and west to the distant snowy crest of the North Cascades. It's also a great spot to watch the sun set.

Start: At Freezeout Pass and the trailhead for Freezeout Trail 345.
Length: 4.8 miles out-and-back.
Approximate hiking time: 2½ hours.
Difficulty rating: Moderate, due to modest length and elevation gain.
Elevation gain: 1,742 feet.
Land status: National forest.
Nearest town: Winthrop, WA.
Other trail users: Equestrians.
Canine compatibility: Dog friendly.
Trail contacts: Okanogan/Wenatchee National Forest, Methow Valley ranger station, (509) 996–4000, www.fs.fed.us/r6/oka.

Schedule: July through early October.
Fees/permits: Parking at the trailhead requires a $5.00 day pass or $30.00 annual Northwest Forest Pass. You can purchase a pass at www.fs.fed.us/r6/feedemo or by calling (800) 270–7504.
Maps: USGS Tiffany Mountain 15-minute quad; USDA Forest Service Okanogan National Forest map.

Finding the trailhead: From Washington Route 20 at the west end of Winthrop, turn north onto the West Chewuch Road, following it for 6.9 miles along the Chewuch River. Then turn right, bridge the small river, and immediately turn left (north) onto paved Forest Service Road 37. Follow FR 37 along the east bank of the Chewuch River for 7.6 miles, bearing right at the end of the pavement. After another 5.8 miles, turn left off FR 37 and onto Forest Service Road 39. This gravel road, rough in spots, leads to Freezeout Pass and the trailhead, 3.4 miles from FR 37. *DeLorme Washington Atlas & Gazetteer* page 114, C1.

The Hike

Tiffany Mountain is part of a large roadless area along the divide between the Chewuch and Okanogan Rivers. A road up the Chewuch severs its link with the Pasayten Wilderness. The entire region from the Okanogan River westward to the Cascade crest is known as the Okanogan Cascades, a unique and rewarding place to hike.

To reach the high, open ridges and summits of the Okanogan Cascades, you must usually walk many miles. But this short hike to the crest of Tiffany offers great

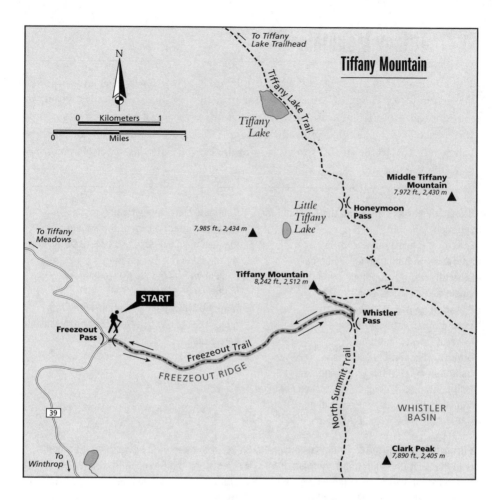

rewards for minimal effort. Three nearby lakes, several cirque basins, and peaks and more peaks visible from the summit invite daydreaming about days of wandering.

From Freezeout Pass, the trail proceeds eastward along boulder-littered Freezeout Ridge through an open forest of lodgepole and white-bark pine, subalpine fir, and Engelmann spruce. A variety of flowers color the otherwise open slopes: lupine, arnica, yarrow, stonecrop, whortleberry, senecio, purple aster, pearly everlasting, whorled penstemon, buckwheat, and red Indian paintbrush.

After a mile of steady climbing, the trail breaks out into open meadows and passes scattered, increasingly stunted trees. At times the trail splits but quickly rejoins itself heading northeastward up the broad slopes of Tiffany Mountain.

Upon reaching the foot of the mountain, the route passes a junction for Whistler Pass and climbs steep, grassy slopes, littered with granite boulders and a few persistent, ground-hugging white-bark pines and Engelmann spruces. You'll finally reach the flat, rocky summit area after just 2.4 miles of pleasant high-country walking.

Meadows on the shoulder of Tiffany Mountain.

Views from the mountain are far-reaching, including the vast rolling landscape of the Okanogan Cascades to the west, north, and south. Far to the east is the Okanogan Valley, the only major interruption in a chain of mountains stretching 500 miles from the Pacific Ocean in northwest Washington to the high plains east of Glacier National Park, Montana.

Nearby are other grassy, alpine summits, beckoning you in summer with the promise of solitude, broad vistas, and fields of grass and flowers. If you're a skier, you'll be lured back to this country in winter, when open slopes and the usually excellent dry snow conditions combine to make the high country of the Okanogan Cascades a wilderness skier's paradise.

Below the summit to the northeast is an inviting timberline lake in a deep cirque at 7,300 feet. To the north, Tiffany Lake sits amid the marshlands of upper Tiffany Creek.

Invisible from the summit is Little Tiffany Lake, elevation 7,400 feet. To get to this isolated tarn, you must walk north from the summit via the gentle alpine ridge for 0.5 mile to a broad saddle. The lake lies in a tiny cirque just north of the saddle.

Key Points

0.0 Start on the east side of the road at Freezeout Pass on Trail 345.

1.5 The main trail splits but quickly comes back together.

1.7 Arrive at a signed junction with a faint trail leading to the right (south) to Whistler Pass. Continue forward on the main trail toward the summit.

2.4 Arrive at the summit of Tiffany Mountain.

4.8 Arrive back at Freezeout Pass and the trailhead.

Hike Information

Local information

Twisp Visitor Information Center,
(509) 997–2926, www.twispinfo.com.
Methow Valley Sports Trail Association,
(509) 996–3287, www.mvsta.com.

Local events/attractions

Winthrop Rhythm and Blues Festival (summer), **Winthrop Octoberfest** (fall), (509) 996–2125, www.methow.com.

Accommodations

Virginian Resort, Winthrop, WA,
(509) 996–2535.
USDA Forest Service Falls Creek campground,
(509) 996–4000.

Restaurants

Duck Brand Hotel and Cantina, Winthrop, WA,
(509) 996–2192.
Winthrop Brewing Company, Winthrop, WA,
(509) 996–3183.

15 Panther Creek/Thunder Creek

This 11.4-mile point-to-point day hike or backpack south of Ross Lake in Ross Lake National Recreation Area surveys some of the finest forests and most striking peaks south of the Skagit River. Along the way you'll pass along two streams, one plunging through a deep canyon, the other a broad, gentle valley. Several camps along the way provide opportunities to extend your trip.

Start: At the Panther Creek Trailhead off the North Cascades Highway (Washington Route 20).
Length: 11.4 miles point-to-point.
Approximate hiking time: 6–7 hours.
Difficulty rating: Difficult, due to length and elevation gain.
Trail surface: Dirt trail.
Elevation gain: 2,300 feet.
Land status: National recreation area.
Nearest town: Marblemount, WA.
Other trail users: Equestrians on Thunder Creek Trail.
Canine compatibility: Leashed dogs permitted.

Trail contacts: North Cascades National Park Wilderness Information Center, (360) 873–4500, www.nps.gov/noca.
Schedule: Late June through October.
Fees/permits: Parking at the trailhead requires a $5.00 day pass or $30.00 annual Northwest Forest Pass. You can purchase a pass at www.fs.fed.us/r6/feedemo or by calling (800) 270–7504. A free permit is required for all overnight stays in the backcountry
Maps: USGS Ross Dam and Crater Mtn. 7.5-minute quads; North Cascades National Park quad; North Cascades National Park map.

Finding the trailhead: Since this is a point-to-point hike, there are two trailheads to locate, both just off the North Cascades Highway (WA 20). The hike begins at the Panther Creek Trailhead. To get there, follow the North Cascades Highway to the East Bank Trailhead parking area east of Ross Lake and park there. The trail begins east of the Panther Creek Bridge on the south side of the highway, 0.2 mile east of the parking area.

The hike ends at the Colonial Creek campground (south segment) on the Thunder Arm of Diablo Lake. Park in the large parking area just beyond the campground registration booth. This trailhead (8 miles west of Panther Creek) is about 4 miles east of Diablo Dam and 25 miles east of Marblemount. The trail ends at the west end of this parking area. *DeLorme Washington Atlas & Gazetteer* page 111, C8.

The Hike

The North Cascades area is a land not only of high, rugged peaks and perpetual snow but also of deep canyons, big rivers, and dense forests. This interesting long day hike or backpack trip of two or more days offers a glimpse of both sides of the North Cascades' character.

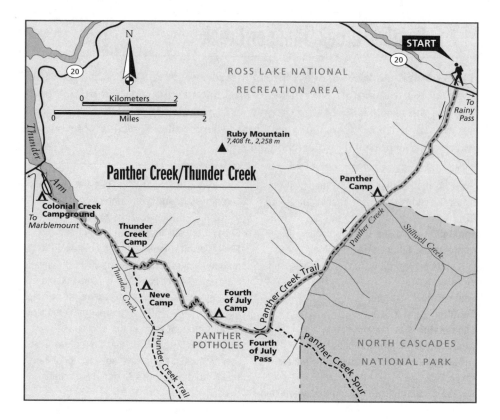

This hike surveys two very different drainages—one a deep, narrow canyon in a west-side rain shadow created by towering mountains; the other a broad, flat, densely forested valley draining a host of immense ice fields. The trail crosses a low divide between the two, and a nearby campsite boasts views to the tremendous, ice-mantled mountain peaks so common in the other half of the North Cascades.

The hike is rigorous, but three widely spaced trail camps, each in its own unique setting, allow you to plan your hike according to your ability and the type of experience you seek. Finding water is no problem along much of the route. You can expect to see many more hikers along the second half of the hike, but Panther Creek is seldom crowded.

From the trailhead, the route switchbacks upward through a moss-carpeted forest of Douglas firs and western hemlocks (the state tree of Washington). Along the way the moist forest alternates with more open stands of lodgepole pine, recognizable by its scaly bark and needles in bundles of two, which typically pioneers burned areas and is fairly common east of the Cascades.

The trail gains 700 feet during the first mile to avoid the rugged reaches of lower Panther Creek. Then it descends 600 feet into the canyon, where the noise of highway traffic is thankfully no longer audible.

Towering more than a mile above the narrow canyon bottom is 7,408-foot Ruby Mountain. The undulating trail follows along the rushing creek through mossy forest, bridges the creek, and reaches the isolated Panther camp on the west side of the creek, shaded by a canopy of western hemlocks and western red cedar.

You'll leave the streambank on a southwestward traverse and cross numerous springs and small creeks before climbing dry, hemlock-covered slopes toward Fourth of July Pass. The trail levels out and crosses a small creek before entering the broad, hemlock-and-silver-fir-carpeted saddle of Fourth of July Pass, elevation 3,500 feet.

The trail then heads west through the pass, crosses above the emerald-green Panther Potholes (two tiny lakes below the pass), and proceeds briefly downhill to the spur trail to the Fourth of July camp.

This scenic campsite lies on a sunny western slope dotted with scattered lodgepole pines, Douglas firs, and hemlocks. Campfires are allowed at this and the other two trail camps en route, and water is available nearby in this otherwise dry area. The outstanding features of this campsite are the views across Thunder Creek to Snowfield Peak, the eastern lobe of the ridge-straddling Neve Glacier, and the pyramids of Primus and Tricouni Peaks in the southwest.

Experienced and determined peak-baggers will want to scale the forested ridge northward to Ruby Mountain, its lofty summit viewpoint 3.5 miles above you.

Beyond the camp the trail descends 2,100 feet, alternately crossing dense and open forest, to the Thunder Creek Trail, an old miners' route. During a final series of switchbacks near the canyon bottom, you can enjoy a superb view across Diablo Lake to the glaciated peaks beyond.

As you turn onto the Thunder Creek Trail, you'll pass through a moist forest of red cedars and silver firs, soon reaching the spur trail to the Thunder Creek camp. This is a very pleasant site surrounded by huge trees and situated next to the large, silty creek. It's a choice location for families with young children.

The final 2 miles to the trailhead proceed through the forest, crossing the milky-green, riverlike creek via an impressive suspension bridge after 0.5 mile. The route then contours above the silty Thunder Arm of Diablo Lake.

Upon reaching a junction with a nature trail, take the middle fork to reach the parking area below at the Colonial Creek campground, passing through a walk-in camp area en route.

Key Points

0.0 Start at the Panther Creek Trailhead on the south side of the North Cascades Highway.

3.0 Cross Panther Creek on a bridge; just beyond, on the west side of the creek are camps.

6.2   Arrive at Fourth of July Pass.

7.0   Arrive at a spur trail to the Fourth of July camp (northwest of the main trail) on the ledges of Ruby Mountain.

9.2   Pass a view of Thunder Creek, Diablo Lake, and glaciated peaks beyond.

9.6   Arrive at the intersection with the Thunder Creek Trail, turning right (northwest) onto this trail.

10.0   Reach a junction with a spur trail to the Thunder Creek camp. The main trail continues straight ahead.

10.5   Cross over Thunder Creek on an impressive and sturdy iron-and-wood suspension bridge.

11.2   Reach a junction with a spur to the Thunder Creek Nature Trail. Continue straight ahead to reach the trailhead.

11.4   Reach the parking lot at the Colonial Creek campground.

Hike Information

Local information

North Cascades Institute, Marblemount, WA, offers natural and cultural history classes throughout the Cascades. Contact (360) 856-5700, or www.ncascades.org.

Accommodations

Clark's Skagit River Cabins, Marblemount, WA, (360) 873-2250.

Colonial Creek campground, (360) 873-4500.

Restaurants

Buffalo Run Restaurant, Marblemount, WA, (360) 873-2461.

16 Cascade Pass

This strenuous but short 7.4-mile out-and-back trip offers some of the best rewards for the effort in the Cascades. Climbing steeply through forest, the trail emerges into a wonderland of hanging glaciers, waterfalls, and soaring peaks. From the pass, you can continue higher into the alpine country toward Sahale Arm, or drop toward the scenic outpost of Stehekin at the north end of Lake Chelan, accessible only by boat.

Start: At the Cascade Pass Trailhead.
Length: 7.4 miles out-and-back.
Approximate hiking time: 4 hours.
Difficulty rating: Moderate, due to modest length.
Trail surface: Dirt trail.
Elevation gain: 1,800 feet.
Land status: National Park.
Nearest town: Marblemount, WA.
Other trail users: None.
Canine compatibility: Leashed pets are permitted.
Trail contacts: North Cascades National Park, (360) 873-4500, www.nps.gov/noca.

Schedule: Late July through September.
Fees/permits: Parking at the trailhead requires a $5.00 day pass or $30.00 annual Northwest Forest Pass. You can purchase a pass at www.fs.fed.us/r6/feedemo or by calling (800) 270-7504. Free permits are required for overnight camping; contact (360) 873-4500.
Maps: USGS Cascade Pass 7.5-minute quad; North Cascades National Park quad; North Cascades National Park map.

Finding the trailhead: Drive to Marblemount via the North Cascades Highway (Washington Route 20). Where the highway bends left (north), bear east onto the Cascade Pass Road and cross the Skagit River. Pavement ends after 4.6 miles. After 16.4 miles this wide gravel road (rough due to heavy use) leads to a junction with the right-forking road to the Middle and South Forks of the Cascade River. Just past this junction the road turns sharply left onto a narrow road, reaching the large parking area and trailhead after another 6.1 miles. The final 2 miles are steep and narrow—use caution. *DeLorme Washington Atlas & Gazetteer* page 97, A8.

The Hike

The North Cascades are a rugged region of soaring ice-covered peaks rising thousands of feet above deep, densely forested canyons. This range forms the westernmost extension of the longest unbroken band of east–west mountains in the contiguous United States, stretching 500 miles from the Pacific Ocean to the plains east of Glacier National Park, Montana.

It's here that the Cascade Range broadens, reaching 125 miles at its widest point, creating seemingly limitless opportunities for exploration. But impenetrable thickets of underbrush, jumbles of fallen trees, icy torrents, vast glaciers, smooth rock walls, and knife-edged ridges limit travel for most to the few established trails in the

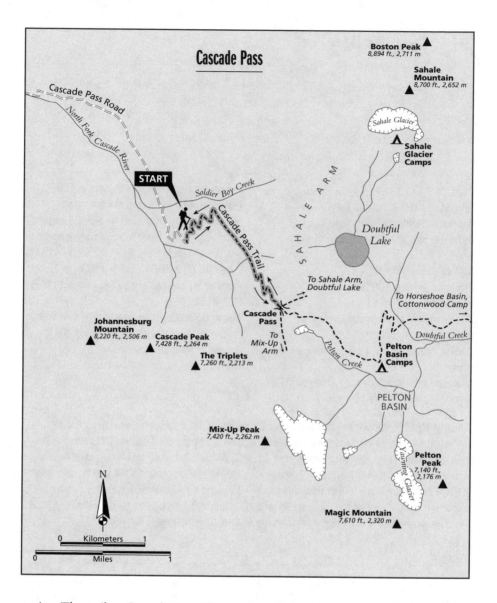

Cascade Pass

Boston Peak
8,894 ft., 2,711 m

Sahale
Mountain
8,700 ft., 2,652 m

Cascade Pass Road

North Fork Cascade River

Sahale Glacier

Sahale
Glacier
Camps

START

Soldier Boy Creek

Cascade Pass Trail

S A H A L E   A R M

Doubtful
Lake

To Sahale Arm,
Doubtful Lake

To Horseshoe Basin,
Cottonwood Camp

Doubtful Creek

Johannesburg
Mountain
8,220 ft., 2,506 m

Cascade Peak
7,428 ft., 2,264 m

Cascade
Pass

To
Mix-Up
Arm

Pelton Creek

Pelton
Basin
Camps

The Triplets
7,260 ft., 2,213 m

PELTON
BASIN

Mix-Up Peak
7,420 ft., 2,262 m

Yawning Glacier

Pelton
Peak
7,140 ft.,
2,176 m

N

Magic Mountain
7,610 m, 2,320 m

0   Kilometers   1

0   Miles   1

region. The trail to Cascade Pass offers perhaps the easiest route into the heart of the North Cascades, a chance for anyone willing to negotiate the short path to experience the grandeur of some of the world's most beautiful mountains.

The pass, a historical Indian route, was crossed by Lieutenant Henry C. Pierce in 1882 in an epic monthlong cross-Cascade journey. Later it was used by miners, whose diggings can be observed in Horseshoe Basin and at Doubtful Lake. The state of Washington had plans in the late nineteenth century to construct a wagon road across the range at Cascade Pass, getting as far as conducting railroad surveys along

Alpine wonderland near Cascade Pass. Photo by Diane Hennessey

the Stehekin River. Eventually a road was built in to Horseshoe Basin to serve the mines there, but fortunately for hikers, plans to extend it over the rugged pass were scrapped, and the road from the Cottonwood camp to Horseshoe Basin was abandoned.

The trailhead itself, surrounded by rock walls and massive glaciers, is perhaps the most beautiful spot accessible by automobile in all the North Cascades. Views from the start inspire the mountaineer in each of us. Johannesburg Mountain and its hanging glaciers loom menacingly to the southwest, while ice-capped Eldorado Peak dominates the northwestern horizon. Cascade Pass itself seems but a stone's throw away.

Views soon temporarily fade from view as the wide, easy-to-ascend trail ducks into a stand of silver fir while switchbacks climb approximately 1,400 feet for 2.5 miles. En route you'll hear the spray and thunder of a host of waterfalls draining the ice fields of Cascade Peak. Occasionally you may be startled by the roar of ice crashing down from the hanging glaciers of Johannesburg Mountain.

Beyond the switchbacks the trail passes above timberline and traverses to the pass amid the stunted forms of silver fir and mountain hemlock, trees common at higher elevations west of the Cascade crest.

Most hikers go no farther than Cascade Pass, enjoying eastward views into Pelton Basin, the headwaters of the Stehekin River, encircled by a jumble of impressive peaks seemingly in the grip of an ice age.

Distant peaks rise farther to the east, as high as those surrounding the pass. Due to the rain shadow created by the North Cascades, those mountains bear little ice on their flanks.

A choice of routes from the pass await the adventurous. A trail leads southeast along scenic Mix-Up Arm and then plunges into steep ice fields—realm of the experienced mountaineer and gateway to the famous Ptarmigan Traverse, a four- to five-day technical traverse of glorious glacier country. No camping is allowed in the fragile alpine environment of Cascade Pass and nearby Sahale Arm.

▶ Glaciers are made of fallen snow that compresses over time into large, thickened ice masses. Due to their mass, glaciers flow like slow rivers, carving and shaping the landscape as they grow and recede. Glaciers occupy 10 percent of the world's total land area; Washington State contains approximately 1,200 of them, more than all other states outside Alaska combined. Many glaciers you see today are mere remnants of past ice ages, of which there have been eight in the last 750,000 years. Scientists say we're due for another ice age in a few thousand years, but how will global warming affect it? The answer remains to be seen.

The main trail descends east for 1 mile into Pelton Basin (and campsites), passes the spur trail to the mines of Horseshoe Basin, and ends at the Cottonwood camp, 9 miles from Cascade Pass. A shuttle bus serves Cottonwood from the village of Stehekin on Lake Chelan. This is the shortest and easiest trans-Cascade hike in the North Cascades, but highly scenic and rewarding nonetheless.

Another trail leads steeply northeast from Cascade Pass, climbing grassy slopes before leveling off above a few persistent subalpine firs and mountain hemlocks struggling to survive on Sahale Arm.

Numerous trails which signs indicate are closed for restoration crisscross the slopes of the arm above the deep emerald oval of Doubtful Lake. One of these trails is open, though, and descends steeply for 800 feet to the lake in 1 mile. A ribbon of whitewater drops nearly 2,000 feet into the 5,385-foot lake, draining the Sahale Glacier.

To get to the glacier, continue to follow the trail along gentle Sahale Arm, ending where grass and alpine cushion plants give way to rock—the arctic-alpine life zone. Experienced hikers can continue (although inexperienced hikers, sometimes outfitted only in tennis shoes and shorts, unwisely proceed beyond the arm) to the Sahale Glacier, 4,000 feet above the trailhead. Several very exposed campsites are situated below the glacier, which provides an ample water supply.

Practiced climbers may contemplate an ascent of Sahale Mountain. The Class 3 summit lies above small but crevasse-riddled Sahale Glacier. The North Cascades National Park map features a photograph taken from the summit, offering further enticement to hikers who thrive on panoramic views.

Key Points

0.0 Start at the Cascade Pass Trailhead and parking area.

1.8 Arrive at the site of a large, recent avalanche, which cleared a view to the west of craggy peaks, including The Triad and Eldorado Peak.

3.7 Cross a talus slope and arrive at Cascade Pass.

7.4 Arrive back at the trailhead and parking area.

Hike Information

Local information

North Cascades Institute offers natural and cultural history classes at locations throughout the North Cascades. Contact (360) 856-5700 or www.ncascades.org.

Accommodations

USDA Forest Service Mineral Park campground, (360) 436-1155.

Clark's Skagit River Cabins, Marblemount, WA, (360) 873-2250.

Restaurants

Buffalo Run Restaurant, Marblemount, WA, (360) 873-2461.

17 Boulder River

This easy 8.6-mile out-and-back day hike or backpack in the Boulder River Wilderness will take you through beautiful old-growth forest and past cascading waterfalls. Because of its low elevation, the hike can be done virtually any time of year, even in winter when the higher elevations of the Cascades are buried under snow.

Start: At the trailhead for Boulder River Trail 734.
Length: 8.6 miles out-and-back.
Approximate hiking time: 4 hours.
Difficulty rating: Easy, due to minimal elevation gain and loss.
Trail surface: Dirt trail.
Elevation gain: 750 feet.
Land status: Federal wilderness area.
Nearest town: Darrington, WA.
Other trail users: None.
Canine compatibility: Dog friendly.
Trail contacts: Mount Baker–Snoqualmie National Forest, Darrington ranger station, (360) 436–1155, www.fs.fed.us/r6/mbs.

Schedule: Open year-round.
Fees/permits: Parking at the trailhead requires a $5.00 day pass or $30.00 annual Northwest Forest Pass. You can purchase a pass at www.fs.fed.us/r6/feedemo or by calling (800) 270-7504.
Maps: USGS Granite Falls 7.5-minute quad (the trailhead is just off the map on the Oso 15-minute quad); USDA Forest Service Mount Baker–Snoqualmie National Forest map.

Finding the trailhead: Follow Washington Route 530 to milepost 41, 8.2 miles west of the Darrington ranger station and 19.75 miles east of Arlington. Turn south at a hard-to-spot junction onto Forest Service Road 2010. This dirt road leads past the French Creek campground for 3.8 miles to the trailhead and parking area. *DeLorme Washington Atlas & Gazetteer* page 96, C2.

The Hike

The canyon of the Boulder River cuts a deep trench through the northwestern corner of the Boulder River Wilderness. Because of its low elevation, the trail along the river remains accessible to hikers year-round. In winter it's wet, but that's a special time to take this hike, when the high country of the rest of the wilderness, including Saddle Lake and Goat Flat near Three Fingers, is buried in white and the river is roaring with runoff.

The initial 0.75 mile of the trail follows an old road cut into a steep cliff, shaded by red alder, western hemlock, and western red cedar. You can see but not hear roaring Boulder Falls as the route, narrowing to a trail, passes above the remains of an old shelter. A boot-beaten path descends past the shelter site to the river.

After a mile the trail passes above Boulder Falls, accessible by another short boot-beaten path to the river, where you can sit among the boulders near the base of the

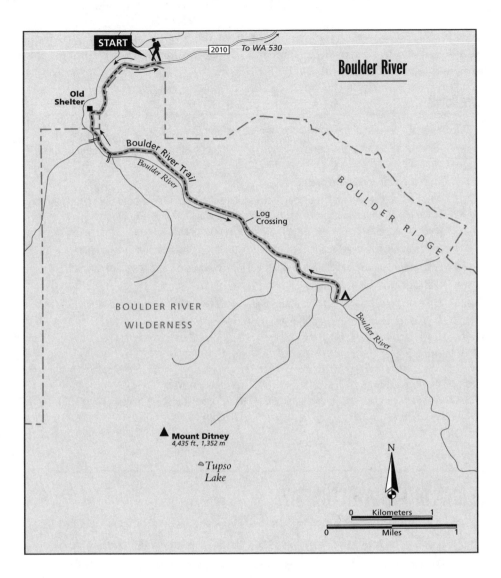

falls. This ribbon of whitewater cascades nearly 80 vertical feet and is a worthy destination alone, making for an easy day hike, particularly for families with children.

The trail continues above the east bank of the river, quickly passing a second set of falls and winding through a lush, low-elevation forest of western hemlocks, silver firs, and some very large western red cedars and Douglas firs. Then, shaded by western hemlocks and red alders, it descends to Boulder Ford camp after just over 4 miles.

At the ford you can see up the canyon to a jagged alpine ridge, especially enjoyable since views are infrequent along the trail and limited to forested slopes and ridges. And while it may be tempting to continue on, you'll have to ford the river, and the trail shown on the map—leading from the ford to Tupso Pass—has been abandoned and is overgrown and difficult to follow. Your best bet is to enjoy the river and retrace your steps to the trailhead.

Key Points

0.0 Start at west end of the parking lot for Boulder River Trail 734.

0.7 Reach a spur trail at the top of a hill off to the right (south), which leads to the remains of an old shelter.

0.8 Enter the Boulder River Wilderness.

1.1 Arrive at the first waterfall (Boulder Falls) within sight across the river to the right (south) of the trail. A small trail here leads to the first waterfall. Just 0.1 mile beyond, you'll reach a second waterfall and small viewing area just past it.

1.4 Pass several very large cedar trees off to left (north) of the trail near a switchback.

2.2 Pass yet another waterfall on the south bank of the river, off to the right of the trail.

3.0 Cross a stream on a large log.

4.3 Arrive at the riverbank and end of the trail. A few campsites can be found along the river.

8.6 Arrive back at the trailhead and parking lot.

Hike Information

Accommodations
USDA Forest Service Clear Creek campground, (518) 885–3639.

Restaurants
Back Woods Café, Darrington, WA, (360) 436–1845.

WHAT IS AN OLD-GROWTH FOREST?

There's little doubt that the Pacific Northwest's dwindling old-growth forests have sparked fierce confrontations dating back to as early as the 1950s. In the early 1990s the controversy over the northern spotted owl, which resides in old-growth forests, brought the issue to a head and resulted in dramatic reductions in timber harvest levels on national forests in Washington.

But just what is an old-growth forest? While there is no hard-and-fast answer, scientists agree that it takes more than a large tree or two to make a true old-growth forest. Many scientists define *old-growth* as forests more than 250 years old that contain large trees, fallen logs, standing snags (dead trees), and a diverse, multilayered vegetation canopy. There's not much old growth left in Washington, and the little that does remain can be found mainly in the state's national forests, wilderness areas, and parks.

18 Lake Dorothy

Hike this moderate 3- to 7-mile out-and-back day hike or backpack to Lake Dorothy, one of Washington's largest backcountry lakes, in the Alpine Lakes Wilderness. You follow a rushing stream to the lake, which offers good camping. Beyond the lake you can hike to more lakes, and even descend into the scenic Middle Fork of the Snoqualmie River.

Start: At Lake Dorothy Trail 1072.
Length: 7 miles out-and-back to the far end of the lake.
Approximate hiking time: 3 hours.
Difficulty rating: Moderate, due to modest elevation gain.
Trail surface: Dirt trail.
Elevation gain: 1,000 feet.
Land status: Federal wilderness area.
Nearest town: Skykomish, WA.
Other trail users: None.
Canine compatibility: Leashed dogs are permitted.

Trail contacts: Mount Baker–Snoqualmie National Forest, Skykomish Ranger District, (360) 677-2414, www.fs.fed.us/r6/mbs.
Schedule: Late June through October.
Fees/permits: Parking at the trailhead requires a $5.00 day pass or $30.00 annual Northwest Forest Pass. You can purchase a pass at www.fs.fed.us/r6/feedemo or by calling (800) 270-7504.
Maps: USGS Snoqualmie Lake and Big Snow Mountain 7.5-minute quads; USDA Forest Service Mount Baker–Snoqualmie National Forest map.

Finding the trailhead: From U.S. Highway 2, about 4 miles west of the Skykomish ranger station and 18.3 miles west of Stevens Pass, or 49.3 miles east of Interstate 5 in Everett, turn south onto the Old Cascade Highway (just west of a tunnel on US 2) signed for the Money Creek campground. The road immediately crosses the South Fork Skykomish River, passing the campground and then the Burlington Northern railroad tracks at 0.4 mile. Bear left at the tracks, go another 0.6 mile, and turn right (south) onto the Miller River Road Northeast (Forest Service Road 6410). Avoid a right fork (Forest Service Road 6420) and follow FR 6410, a good gravel road, for 9 miles to its end at the trailhead. Portions of the final 2 miles are subject to washouts, so it's a good idea to call ahead for the latest conditions. *DeLorme Washington Atlas & Gazetteer* page 81, D6.

The Hike

One of the largest of all Washington's backcountry lakes, 290-acre Lake Dorothy lies near the head of the East Fork Miller River. At an elevation of 3,058 feet and accessible by foot only 1.5 miles from the trailhead, Dorothy is also one of the most popular backcountry lakes in the state. Dozens of campsites lie near the trail along the east side of the deep, 1.5-mile-long lake. Fishing from the shore is best after the fall turnover, an annual event that occurs when the water temperature cools. The colder water near the bottom and the warmer water near the surface circulate until the lake

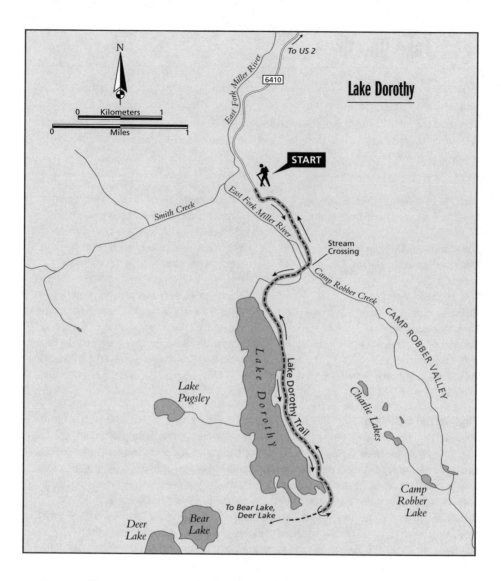

attains a uniform temperature. At that point fish begin feeding in earnest. Fishing here is also productive after the ice breaks up in early summer. During the warm summer months, some hikers pack in a rubber raft to fish the deeper waters.

Lake Dorothy is a great spot to introduce children to the backcountry, as numerous families on any summer weekend will attest. The trail is rocky, muddy, and obstructed by tree roots in many places, but it's easy to follow, and the Forest Service plans to reconstruct it in the near future.

Beginning in a montane forest of silver fir, mountain hemlock, and western red cedar, the trail climbs past several springs to the boundary of the Alpine Lakes

The inviting waters of Lake Dorothy. Photo by Dave Shigaki

Wilderness. The way stays above the east bank of the East Fork Miller River—simply a large creek at this point but full of slickrock cascades and waterfalls.

After less than a mile, you'll cross Camp Robber Creek via a steel bridge, just above its confluence with the East Fork Miller River in a beautiful area of slickrock cascades. A deep, inviting pool lies downstream below the bridge. On a hot summer day you may find it hard to resist a swim.

Beyond the bridge, the trail, rocky and full of tree roots, crosses rotting plank bridges and winds upward through a typical moist-forest plant community. Plants common along this shady stretch include huckleberry, whortleberry, bunchberry (Canada dogwood), black raspberry, queen's cup, devil's-club, vine maple, and ferns. The ground is carpeted with soft, green moss.

Rocky switchbacks soon lead to the lake's outlet stream, and a spur trail leads to the lower end of the lake. The Forest Service is revegetating various locations around Lake Dorothy to mitigate the impact of too many hikers' boots. Keep clear of these closed areas so that native vegetation can become reestablished.

The main trail continues south above the east shore, passing many fine camp-sites. The massive granite bulk of 6,680-foot Big Snow Mountain looms 4 miles to the south.

The shores of the lake are cloaked in mountain hemlock, silver fir, Alaska yellow cedar, and the five-needled white pine, many of which are dying from blister rust, a disease accidentally introduced into this country around the turn of the twentieth century by a shipment of white pine seedlings from Europe.

The trail continues from the upper end of the lake over the low, forested ridge to the west, leading to Bear and Deer Lakes after 2 more miles, and to the road along the Middle Fork of the Snoqualmie River 11.6 miles from the trailhead.

Key Points

0.0 Start at the road's end on Lake Dorothy Trail 1072.

0.4 Enter the Alpine Lakes Wilderness.

0.6 Cross Camp Robber Creek on a bridge.

1.5 Reach the north shore of Lake Dorothy.

3.5 Reach the south shore of Lake Dorothy.

7.0 Arrive back at the trailhead and parking area.

Hike Information

Accommodations

Sky River Inn, Skykomish, WA,
(360) 677-2261, www.skyriverinn.com.

19 Gothic Basin

This steep but scenic trail to rocky Gothic Basin is perched high above the Sauk River Valley and historic Monte Cristo townsite. Good camps can be found in the basin, and glacier-carved country invites further wandering from Foggy Lake under the shadows of Del Campo Peak into the heather-and-rock country beyond. For an interesting side excursion, explore Monte Cristo, an easy 3-mile walk or mountain bike ride up the road from the trailhead (4 miles from Barlow Pass).

Start: At Barlow Pass on the Monte Cristo Road.
Length: 8.6 miles out-and-back from Barlow Pass.
Approximate hiking time: 4½ hours.
Difficulty rating: Difficult, due to steep terrain.
Trail surface: Dirt trail, steep rocky stretches.
Elevation gain: 2,600 feet.
Land status: National forest, state conservation area (Washington Department of Natural Resources).
Nearest town: Granite Falls, WA.
Other trail users: None.

Canine compatibility: Dog friendly.
Trail contacts: Mount Baker-Snoqualmie National Forest, Verlot Public Service Center, (360) 691-7791, www.fs.fed.us/r6/mbs.
Schedule: July to mid-October.
Fees/permits: Parking at the trailhead requires a $5.00 day pass or $30.00 annual Northwest Forest Pass. You can purchase a pass at www.fs.fed.us/r6/feedemo or by calling (800) 270-7504.
Maps: USGS Monte Cristo 7.5-minute quad; USDA Forest Service Mount Baker-Snoqualmie National Forest map.

Finding the trailhead: From Granite Falls, take the Mountain Loop Highway 30.1 miles to Barlow Pass. Parking is provided in a parking area on the left (north) side of the road, as well as on the right. *DeLorme Washington Atlas & Gazetteer* page 97, D5; page 81, A5.

The Hike

Barlow Pass is the gateway to the exceptionally scenic headwaters of the Sauk River and the historically intriguing ghost town of Monte Cristo. Visiting the area today, it may be hard to believe that in the late 1890s the bustling town's population swelled to 2,000 as people came to the remote region to work the area's gold mines. Even as late as the early 1930s after the decline of mining, the town—accessible by direct rail service from the city of Everett north of Seattle—attracted hunters, campers, and sightseers. Today rail service is long gone, and little is left of the town but a few cabins, but the dramatic scenery remains and you'll find interesting mining remnants throughout the valley.

The trail to Gothic Basin surveys some of the best terrain above the Sauk River Valley and Monte Cristo. For the first mile or so, you'll walk along the Monte Cristo

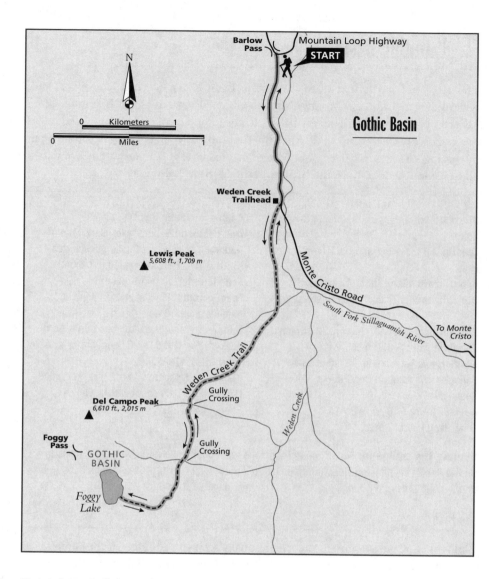

Road through forest and past occasional views down to the river below. Beyond this point the trail becomes steep, crossing several gullies that may contain snow year-round, creating dangerous crossing conditions where an ice ax may be needed for safe crossing.

The trail leaves the Monte Cristo Road at a trailhead just before a crossing of the Sauk River and begins gently ascending and descending wet areas through stately stands of hemlock and silver fir and past spiky devil's-club. You'll stay close to the river during this stretch.

After less than a mile from the Monte Cristo Road, the real climb starts and, except for some brief stretches, doesn't relent until you reach the basin. Views across the valley to the east become increasingly expansive as you climb steeply along switchbacks.

The grade briefly moderates as the trail traverses across seeps and brushy areas high above the valley through increasingly open terrain. You'll be accompanied by the sound of several ribbonlike waterfalls cascading down from the slopes of Del Campo Peak above you. Lower-elevation forests give way to mountain hemlock here, a sure sign that you're gaining altitude.

Soon after, you'll cross the first of two avalanche gullies under a tumbling waterfall. Snow may persist well into the summer season—cross with extreme care here. Snow bridges can easily collapse at any time, and a false step may send you careening down the gully below.

The way continues to open as you climb the valley, increasingly dominated by glorious rock gardens of pink heather and the sounds of cascading water. Stop at 3.4 miles to take a break and enjoy a scenic waterfall at a stream crossing.

The trail resumes climbing steeply, scrambling at times up rocks to another gully and stream where snow may linger late into the season, and then, after 0.1 mile, to yet another gully. The trail can be hard to find here—proceed up this second gully for a short distance and find the trail veering left, crossing and climbing the opposite bank.

At just over 4 miles from Barlow Pass, the climb finally relents as the trail turns west and heads through a notch and into the basin. Views of the dramatic glacier-carved landscape open before you amid tarns and hummocks of glacier-polished rock. There is no particular destination here; you can find Foggy Lake, often ice-bound late into the year cupped amid the rock, or explore up the valley toward Del Campo Peak. Campsites are found throughout the basin, but be sure to camp on rock or on already bare spots to minimize future damage in this fragile environment.

Or just find a spot to sit and soak in the magnificent views. And when you're done, simply retrace your steps to Barlow Pass.

Key Points

0.0 Start at the gated, dirt Monte Cristo Road on the south side of Barlow Pass.

0.95 Reach Weden Creek Trailhead 724. Turn right (west) at a trailhead kiosk just before the road crosses the Sauk River.

1.1 Cross a short stretch of boardwalk over a wet area.

1.6 Cross a stream on a boulder bridge cemented into the streambed.

2.8 Cross the first avalanche gully, with snow into late season.

3.4 Cross a stream and pass a scenic waterfall.

3.5 Reach a small pond and flat area. A small camping area can be found off to the east side of the trail just beyond.

3.8 Cross another gully that may contain snow late into the season.

3.9 The trail climbs through a hard-to-find section in another stream gully.

4.3 Arrive at Gothic Basin.

8.6 Arrive back at the trailhead at Barlow Pass.

Hike Information

Local events/attractions

Big Four Ice Caves, located 15 miles east of the Verlot Public Service Center on the Mountain Loop Highway, (360) 691-7791.

Accommodations

USDA Forest Service Perry Creek and Boardman Creek campgrounds, (360) 691-7791.

Restaurants

Omega Pizza and Pasta, Granite Falls, WA, (360) 691-4394.

20 Ingalls Lake

This difficult 8.6-mile out-and-back day trip or backpack to an alpine lake in the Stuart Range of the Alpine Lakes Wilderness traverses spectacular open terrain on the east slopes of the Cascades. Starting in forest, the hike quickly climbs to rocky meadows, cresting with a dramatic up-close view of imposing Mount Stuart. The lake itself is an alpine gem tucked in a rocky basin beneath the flanks of North Ingalls Peak, a popular climbing destination.

Start: At Esmerelda Basin Trail 1394.
Length: 8.6 miles out-and-back.
Approximate hiking time: 5 hours.
Difficulty rating: Difficult, due to elevation gain and rocky terrain near the lake basin.
Trail surface: Dirt trail, rock scramble.
Elevation gain: 2,400 feet.
Land status: Federal wilderness.
Nearest town: Cle Elum, WA.
Other trail users: None.
Canine compatibility: Leashed dogs permitted.
Trail contacts: Okanogan/Wenatchee National Forest, Cle Elum Ranger District, (509) 674-4411, www.fs.fed.us/r6/wenatchee.

Schedule: Mid-July through mid-October.
Fees/permits: Parking at the trailhead requires a $5.00 day pass or $30.00 annual Northwest Forest Pass. You can purchase a pass at www.fs.fed.us/r6/feedemo or by calling (800) 270-7504.
Maps: USGS Mt. Stuart 15-minute quad; USDA Forest Service Wenatchee National Forest map; Alpine Lakes Wilderness map.

Finding the trailhead: Follow Washington Route 970 about 9 miles east from Cle Elum or 3.3 miles west from U.S. Highway 97 (15 miles north of Ellensburg) to northbound Teanaway Road, and turn north (watch for a Teanaway River sign). Pavement on this county road ends after 13.2 miles. Bear right onto Forest Service Road 9737, signed for the Beverly campground and Trail 1394. Follow this often rough dirt road, avoiding numerous signed spur roads, to its end at the trailhead and picnic area 23.1 miles from WA 970. *DeLorme Washington Atlas & Gazetteer* page 66, A1.

The Hike

Sometimes termed the High Sierra of Washington, the glacier-carved, lake-dotted terrain of the Stuart Range is a mecca for hikers and climbers. Part of the Wenatchee Mountains, a major spur ridge trending southeast from the Cascade crest in the center of the range, the Stuart Range is a large batholith of quartz diorite (loosely referred to as granite) sculpted and scoured by ancient glaciers into a land of jagged summits, U-shaped drainages, and lake basins by the dozen. Rising far above surrounding peaks and ridges is the crown of the range, 9,415-foot Mount Stuart,

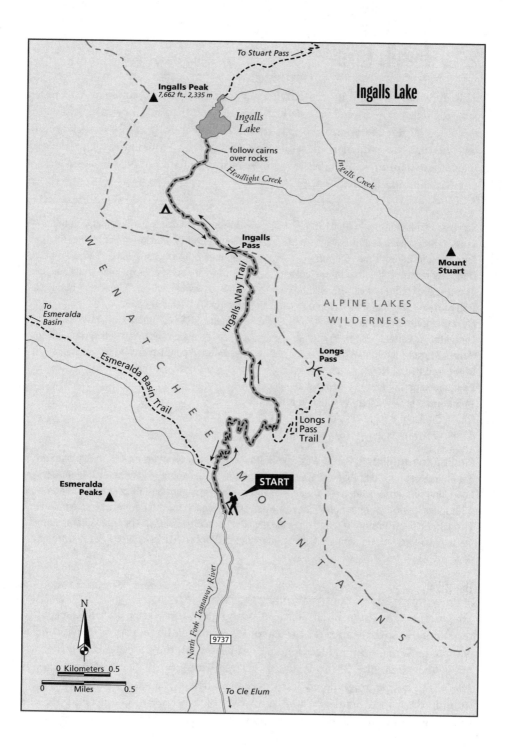

Ingalls Peak
7,662 ft., 2,335 m

Ingalls Lake

Ingalls
Lake

follow cairns
over rocks

Headlight Creek

Ingalls Creek

Ingalls
Pass

Mount
Stuart

To Stuart Pass

W E N A T C H E E

Ingalls Way Trail

ALPINE LAKES
WILDERNESS

To
Esmeralda
Basin

Esmeralda Basin Trail

Longs
Pass

Longs
Pass
Trail

Esmeralda
Peaks

START

M O U N T A I N S

N

North Fork Teanaway River

9737

To Cle Elum

0 Kilometers 0.5

0 Miles 0.5

drawing mountaineers because of its hard, stable rock, many challenging climbing routes, and rewarding views.

The hike to the Ingalls Lake Basin traverses the edge of the Stuart Range Batholith for 4.3 spectacular miles through an alpine world of impressive peaks, flower-covered hillsides, and rocky basins. While there's no camping at the lake itself, camps in the basin below the lake make a good base for alpine wanderings including Longs Pass, the Ingalls Creek Basin, and the popular technical rock climb up North Ingalls Peak or less technical scramble up South Ingalls Peak.

Beneath giant crags, the trail begins by proceeding into a Douglas fir forest, following the course of the North Fork Teanaway River, simply an inviting cascading mountain stream here in its headwaters.

You'll soon turn right onto Trail 1390, closed to all but hikers, and begin gently climbing slopes dotted with pine and fir and brightened by a variety of wildflowers. Views are almost immediately superb through the open forest up and down the Teanaway.

You'll soon reach a junction for the Longs Pass Trail, which departs for a notch visible on the skyline above. Stay on the main trail through rocky terrain dotted by increasingly stunted timber to the boundary of the Alpine Lakes Wilderness on a ridge at 6,500 feet. A ribbon of stunted trees, including subalpine fir, Lyall larch, and white-bark pine, lines this exposed ridge. Views are excellent, from the impressive fluted walls of Mount Stuart to the snowy cone of Mount Rainier in the distance off to the south.

Ingalls Lake lies less than 1 mile (as the crow flies) north across the bowl below the ridge. The route contours around the basin through stands of Lyall larch, passing a broad bench with campsites—since there is no camping at the lake, camp here if you're planning an overnight stay. Wildflowers are numerous, including pink and white heather, shooting star, buttercup, valerian, phlox, and Indian paintbrush.

At the north end of the basin, you'll climb steeply over rocks through a notch in a low, rocky, glacier-smoothed ridge to reach the lake. Rocky bluffs along the south shore of the lake make a scenic spot for lunch and a nap before the trip home.

Key Points

0.0 Start at the northeast end of the parking lot for Esmerelda Basin Trail 1394.

0.3 Cross a dry stream and turn right (east) onto Ingalls Way Trail 1390.

1.4 Arrive at a junction with the Longs Pass Trail, which leads right (east). Continue straight ahead toward Ingalls Lake.

2.2 Pass a small stream along the left (west) side of the trail with a small campsite.

2.8 Arrive at a saddle (Ingalls Pass) and enter the Alpine Lakes Wilderness.

3.0 Cross a small stream in a meadow-filled basin. Campsites can be found here and 0.1 mile farther along the trail.

3.5 Boulder-hop across a stream, following rock cairns marking the trail.

3.8 Cross two more streams, ignoring a spur trail leading right (south) down into the basin below you.

4.0 Begin scrambling up over rocky ledges, following cairns.

4.3 Reach the top of the scramble, pass through a small notch, and enter the lake basin, arriving at the south shore of Ingalls Lake.

8.6 Arrive back at the trailhead and parking lot.

Hike Information

Local information

Three Queens Outfitters/Guide Service (guided trips), (509) 674-5647.
High Country Outfitters also offers guided trips, (509) 674-4903.

Accommodations

Iron Horse Inn Bed and Breakfast, Cle Elum, WA, (509) 674-5939, www.ironhorseinnbb.com.

USDA Forest Service Beverly campground, (509) 674-4411.

Restaurants

El Caporal, Cle Elum, WA, (509) 674-4284.

21 Mount Pilchuck

This moderate 5.4-mile round-trip day hike climbs to the top of 5,324-foot Mount Pilchuck, an impressive peak perched on the western edge of the Cascades. The trail climbs through a scenic north-facing basin, often filled with the sound of rushing snowmelt. From the restored Forest Service fire lookout at the summit, you'll get some of the best views around of Puget Sound, the Olympics, and beyond.

Start: At the trailhead for Mount Pilchuck Trail 700.
Length: 5.4 miles out-and-back.
Approximate hiking time: 3 hours.
Difficulty rating: Moderate, due to elevation gain and a short summit boulder scramble.
Trail surface: Dirt and gravel trail.
Elevation gain: 2,200 feet.
Land status: National forest, Washington state parks.
Nearest town: Granite Falls, WA.
Other trail users: None.
Canine compatibility: Dog friendly.

Trail contacts: USDA Forest Service Verlot Public Service Center, (360) 691-7791, www.fs.fed.us/r6/mbs.
Schedule: Late June through November.
Fees/permits: Parking at the trailhead requires a $5.00 day pass or $30.00 annual Northwest Forest Pass. You can purchase a pass at www.fs.fed.us/r6/feedemo or by calling (800) 270-7504.
Maps: USGS Granite Falls 7.5-minute quad; USDA Forest Service Mount Baker-Snoqualmie National Forest map.

Finding the trailhead: From Interstate 5 north of Lake Stevens, take a right onto Washington Route 92 through Granite Falls to the Verlot Pubic Service Center. Go 1 mile east on WA 92, which becomes the Mountain Loop Highway, and turn right onto Mount Pilchuck State Park Road 42, a partially paved, partially gravel road. Follow this road, passing a trailhead for Heather Lake at 1.5 miles, to the signed trailhead 7 miles from WA 92. *DeLorme Washington Atlas & Gazetteer* page 96, D2.

The Hike

Mount Pilchuck is the perfect hike for first-time visitors to the area who want a taste of the Cascades, and perhaps want to reach a summit and fire lookout as well. Standing atop Pilchuck's broad rocky summit gives you the feeling of having climbed a "real mountain." The 360-degree view from the old Forest Service fire lookout cabin (restored by the Everett Mountaineers in 1989) is breathtaking. On a clear day you can make out ferries crossing Puget Sound and take in the jagged crest of the Cascades from Mount Rainier to the Canadian border. Not bad for a hike just shy of 2.7 miles. This, combined with the mountain's relatively easy access from Puget Sound, makes Mount Pilchuck a popular weekend hike.

The hike begins on the edges of the old Mount Pilchuck Ski Area. The once scarred ski slopes are slowly being reclaimed by fern, fir, and vine maple. The lower

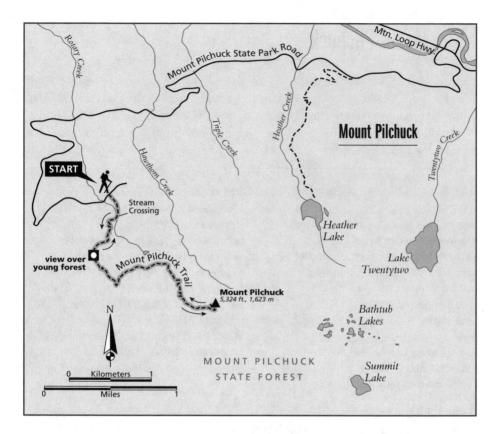

portion of trail, through old-growth forest, is wide and well engineered, with a gravel surface and steps.

Shortly before swinging to the east in less than a mile, the trail touches the eastern edge of a huge 1977 clear-cut on state land. You'll get views out to the west over the logged area toward Puget Sound.

The trail continues up and up, crossing an impressive talus slope before swinging around the north side of the mountain, where the summit comes into view above a wonderfully scenic basin of meadow, rock, snow, and cascading water. Near the top of the old ski slopes, marked by a concrete foundation alongside the trail, you'll continue to climb up through heather and over polished rock slabs. Snow may persist here on north-facing slopes well into the season.

Just east of the peak of Little Pilchuck, the trail crosses a saddle onto the south side of the mountain. Above the saddle is an old "high route" to the summit. This high trail, while quickly gaining the summit ridge crest, is a difficult boulder-hop to the summit and should only be attempted by experienced hikers. Most hikers will be happy to follow the main trail around the south side of the mountain before climbing the final set of switchbacks to the summit.

The summit of Mount Pilchuck.

Plan to spend some time here. The restored lookout cabin has an informative historic display, including old Forest Service photos and panoramic photos that identify the surrounding peaks. And of course there's the real view, from the Olympics across Puget Sound to Mount Rainier, and north toward Glacier Peak and beyond.

Key Points

0.0   Start at the south side of the parking lot on Trail 700.

0.2   Pass an unsigned fork in the trail to the left. Stay to the right and rock-hop across a stream—a good spot for a quick soak on a hot summer day.

0.5   Crest a ridge in young forest with views west toward Puget Sound.

1.0   Cross a stream on a puncheon bridge.

1.5   Arrive at a boggy plateau, soon getting your first views of the rocky summit above you.

1.7   Climb past the concrete base of a ski lift.

2.3 Break out into summit talus as you near the summit. Mount Rainier comes into view to the right (south) off the trail. (**Note:** The alternate "high route" boulder-hop begins off to the left of the trail here.)

2.7 Arrive at the summit ridge and scramble up the summit boulders to the fire lookout.

5.4 Arrive back at the trailhead and parking lot.

Hike Information

Local information

Information on Granite Falls can be found at www.granitefallswa.com.

Lookouts: Firewatchers of the Cascades and Olympics, second edition, by Ira Spring and Byron Fish (contributor).

Local events/attractions

Granite Falls and Fish Ladder, just east of town near the crossing of the South Fork Stillaguamish River.

Accommodations

USDA Forest Service Verlot and Turlo campgrounds, (360) 691-7791.

Restaurants

Omega Pizza and Pasta, Granite Falls, WA, (360) 691-4394.

22 Lyman Lakes

This 16.2-mile out-and-back backpack trip starts at a remote mining-town-turned-retreat deep in the Railroad Creek Valley and leads to the spectacular turquoise Lower Lyman Lake in the Glacier Peak Wilderness. From here, explore meadows above and glacier-fed Upper Lyman Lake, or climb to Cloudy Pass for even more rewarding views.

Start: At the Railroad Creek Trailhead at the west end of Holden Village.
Length: 16.8 miles out-and-back to Lower Lyman Lake.
Approximate hiking time: 8½ hours.
Difficulty rating: Difficult, due to length and elevation gain.
Trail surface: Dirt trail.
Elevation gain: 2,458 feet.
Land status: Federal wilderness area.
Nearest town: Chelan, WA (by boat).
Other trail users: Equestrians.

Canine compatibility: Leashed dogs are permitted.
Trail contacts: Wenatchee National Forest, Chelan Ranger District, (509) 682-2576, www.fs.fed.us/r6/wenatchee.
Schedule: Mid-July through September.
Fees/permits: None required.
Maps: USGS Holden 15-minute quad (the Glacier Peak 15-minute quad is necessary for side trips); USDA Forest Service Glacier Peak Wilderness map and Wenatchee National Forest map.

Finding the trailhead: To reach Holden Village, catch the *Lady of the Lake* from Chelan to Lucerne—a three-and-a-half-hour boat ride (call 509-682-4584, or visit www.ladyofthelake. com). Boats leave Chelan daily at 8:30 A.M. from May 1 through October 31; a fee is charged for a round trip. The Chelan Boat Company dock is located 1 mile west (toward Wenatchee) of downtown Chelan on U.S. Highway 97. The company charges a parking fee. To cut an hour off your cruise, drive 25 miles north along the west shore of Lake Chelan to Fields Point Landing, where the boat departs at 9:45 A.M. The round-trip fare is the same, and there's also a parking fee.

Upon arrival at Lucerne (Port of Holden), you'll need to catch a ride on the shuttle bus (an old school bus) up the steep Railroad Creek Valley to Holden Village and the trailhead. The ride and luggage transport takes about an hour, and no reservations are needed. A fee is charged for the round trip. *DeLorme Washington Atlas & Gazetteer* page 98, C1.

The Hike

This outing begins with a scenic 40-mile boat ride to the trailhead up the narrow, inland fjord of Lake Chelan, a monumental work of glaciation. Its deepest point is 1,486 feet, making it the second deepest lake in North America. Its bottom is 490 feet below sea level—the lowest point on the North American continent.

This memorable backpack penetrates deeper into the backcountry away from major roads than just about any other hike in the state. Glacier Peak, Washington's

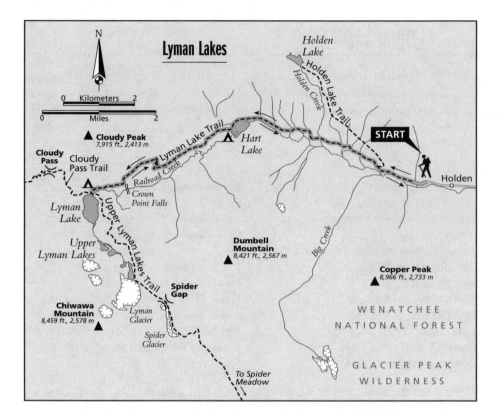

largest wilderness area, encompasses 576,865 acres of very rugged mountains, vast ice fields, deep river valleys, and the state's only totally protected volcano. The usual mosquitoes and biting flies are present from early to midsummer. Even with their remote locations, you can expect people at Lyman and Hart Lakes, but there are also many isolated nooks where you can find solitude with a modicum of effort. Fishing for cutthroat trout is only fair in silty Lyman Lake but more productive in Hart Lake. No camping or fires are allowed within 200 feet of Lyman Lake.

The shuttle bus from Lucerne to Holden Village will be waiting when you disembark the boat. On your way out on the trail, remember that you'll need to return to the village in time to catch the 1:45 P.M. bus back down to Lucerne. It's also best to make boat reservations for the return trip in advance.

Beautifully situated Holden Village is a historic mining-village-turned-nondenominational-retreat. Once the site of Washington's largest copper mine, Holden was home to as many as 600 people during its heyday in the 1930s. The town boasted a movie theater, bowling alley, and baseball diamond. Ore was transported to Lucerne and Chelan on barges and then shipped to Tacoma for processing. Today's Holden is operated by the Lutheran Church and offers showers, three good meals a day at a reasonable price, and a campground at the end of the road. There's also a small store and hiker's hut with equipment rental, where you're asked to register before you begin your hike. Set aside some time to explore.

To find the trail from Holden Village, walk 1 mile up the road to the trailhead at the west end of town, past intriguing old homesites and the town's baseball diamond.

The trail undulates for the first mile to a junction with northwest-bound Holden Lake Trail. It continues up the U-shaped valley of Railroad Creek through cotton-woods, giant willows, and mixed conifer forest. Much of the valley was burned in a 1896 fire purposely set by miners. The understory is diverse, including bracken fern, pachistima, red-osier dogwood, Sitka alder, wild rose, thimbleberry, serviceberry, false Solomon's seal, and Douglas maple.

En route up the broad valley, you'll be able to look south and see various U-shaped waterways surrounded by broken peaks, a contrast to the rounded contours of brush-and-forest-covered slopes on the north side of the canyon. To the west, crags associated with the Bonanza Peak massif will also catch your attention.

After passing a swampy clearing at the head of the first long bench in the valley, the route ascends brushy slopes to a point overlooking Hart Lake, resting at the east end of the next long bench in the glacial valley. To the west, Crown Point Falls cascades impressively at the head of the bench.

You'll pass a small camping area above Hart Lake, partially shaded by small cottonwoods. Then you'll cross a boulder-filled stream. The ford may be difficult before August during most years.

Beyond Hart Lake the route climbs steadily above Crown Point Falls to the third in a series of benches. After leveling off you'll pass an interesting jumble of granite slabs. Notice how the rock peels away like leaves of lettuce in a process known as exfoliation.

Soon the way passes a mine shaft and then a grass-floored subalpine meadow. From this point on, huckleberries are abundant, reaching their peak in late September.

The route briefly climbs to the next bench, passes a signed southbound spur to Upper Lyman Lakes, and reaches a junction at large, milky-green Lyman Lake. The right fork climbs 1 mile to Cloudy Pass, while the left fork leads to campsites on the lake's west shore. Other good campsites in subalpine fir forest are located north of the lake.

Keep in mind that no camping or fires are allowed within 200 feet of Lyman Lake. Backpackers should use the more durable sand flats near the trail for campsites rather than the fragile heather areas above the lake. Water draining from Lyman Glacier is not potable due to an abundance of suspended silt.

From the west shore, views across the lake basin are dizzying, featuring the highest nonvolcanic summit in the state, 9,511-foot Bonanza Peak. This peak is composed of resistant gneiss (metamorphosed granite) while its neighbor north of the lake, 7,915-foot Cloudy Peak, is composed of granite, much of which was stripped away by the ancient Lyman Glacier more than 10,000 years ago.

Numerous optional side trips are possible from a Lyman Lake base camp. With a car shuttle, experienced hikers might consider the route past Upper Lyman Lakes over Spider Gap to the Chiwawa River, which requires crossing a small glacier and knowledge of ice ax use.

Another possibility is to follow the trail for a mile, climbing 850 feet, to Cloudy Pass (above timberline). From the pass, you can see the icebound north slopes of mighty Glacier Peak and look down the rugged South Fork Agnes Creek. Or spend a full day hiking another 6 miles west to scenic Image Lake, one of the most photographed as well as most frequently visited spots in the wilderness.

▶ Olympic and Cascade weather can turn rapidly wet and cold at any time of year. Even on the sunniest of days, always be prepared for changing weather by bringing rain gear and warm, noncotton clothing to avoid hypothermia.

For a more extended trip, backpack down the South Fork Agnes Creek to the Stehekin River, a total of about 28 miles, where you can catch a shuttle bus to the boat dock in Stehekin at the head of Lake Chelan.

A side trip to the fascinating Lyman Glacier is a must. Follow the trail signed for Upper Lyman Lakes, climbing over a low meadow-covered ridge to the upper basin, accompanied by a chorus of waterfalls falling from snowfields and glaciers high on Bonanza and Dumbell Peaks. Scattered islands of subalpine fir dot the lower end of this basin, while Lyall larch grow only on hummocks above the glacier-scooped bowl. The trail passes the remains of an old cabin above the two lowest lakes in Upper Lyman Lakes Basin.

Since the end of the Little Ice Age in the early part of the twentieth century, many glaciers have begun an unsteady retreat—advancing and retreating, but mostly retreating. You'll soon come upon evidence of Lyman Glacier's farthest advance of the last hundred years in a very fresh terminal moraine, a load of rock debris deposited at the tip of the glacier. On the east walls of the basin is a line of red rocks carried from the red peak above and deposited along the side of the glacier's path—a lateral moraine, which illustrates the depth of the glacier. Small trees pioneering that moraine lie below a distinct line of larger trees that escaped the advance of ice.

Proceed southward through the raw landscape, passing a third lake and climbing over a larger terminal moraine created by the latest major advance of the glacier. One more lake lies at the foot of the glacier. The lower part of the glacier is riddled with crevasses, and you can sit and watch chunks of ice break off and fall into the lake below. You'd be hard pressed to find a more dramatic spot to take a rest and call it a day.

Key Points

0.0 Start on the gravel road at the west end of Holden Village, just past the hiker's hut.

0.8 Pass the ballpark fields and a camping area on the left (south) of the road, after which the road reverts to trail.

1.4 Arrive at a junction with the Holden Lake Trail leading right (north) 4 miles to Holden Lake. Continue straight ahead on the main trail.

2.5 Cross a wooden footbridge over the stream that originates from Holden Lake.

3.0 Pass a boggy marsh to the south of the trail.

4.4 Arrive at a junction trail leading left (south) to Hart Lake (use the designated trail) and to campsites on the right (north) side of the trail. Three designated, partially shaded, good-sized campsites are available here.

4.5 Rock-hop across a boulder-filled stream, a potentially difficult crossing during high snowmelt.

5.2 Arrive at the forested Rebel camp to the left (south) of the trail, where you'll find additional camps.

6.2 Begin climbing switchbacks up to lower Lyman Lake.

8.3 Arrive at the lower Lyman Lake outlet and the signed junction trail to Upper Lyman Lakes. Just beyond is a signed junction leading right (north) to Cloudy Pass. Bear left. The first set of camps can be found here to the right (north) of the trail, with additional camps beyond.

16.8 Arrive back at Holden Village.

Hike Information

Local information

Chelan Chamber of Commerce, (800) 4-CHELAN, www.lakechelan.com.

Accommodations

Lake Chelan State Park campground, located between Fields Point and Chelan, (509) 687-3710, www.parks.wa.gov.

Holden Village B&B, near the Fields Point Landing, (509) 687-9695.

Restaurants

BC McDonalds, Chelan, WA, (509) 682-1354.
Peter B's Bar and Grill, (509) 682-1031.

23 Crater Lakes

Hike this 8.4-mile out-and-back day trip or backpack to a scenic lake basin in the Sawtooth Range east of Lake Chelan in the Okanogan National Forest. The lake offers a good base camp for trout fishing, or for further roaming of the lakes and peaks in this rugged and lesser-known range.

Start: At Eagle Lakes Trailhead 431.
Length: 8.4 miles out-and-back.
Approximate hiking time: 4 hours.
Difficulty rating: Moderate, due to modest length and elevation gain.
Trail surface: Dirt trail.
Elevation gain: 2,209 feet.
Land status: National forest, federal wilderness area.
Nearest town: Twisp, WA.
Other trail users: Equestrians, motorcycles on first 0.8 mile of trail.
Canine compatibility: Dog friendly.

Trail contacts: Okanogan/Wenatchee National Forest, Methow Valley ranger station, (509) 996-4003, www.fs.fed.us/r6/oka.
Schedule: July through mid-October.
Fees/permits: Parking at the trailhead requires a $5.00 day pass or $30.00 annual Northwest Forest Pass. You can purchase a pass at www.fs.fed.us/r6/feedemo or by calling (800) 270-7504.
Maps: USGS Martin Peak 7.5-minute quad; USDA Forest Service Okanogan National Forest map.

Finding the trailhead: From Pateros on the Columbia River, follow Washington Route 153 northwest for 17.2 miles to the Gold Creek Road and turn left, following the west bank of the Methow River upstream. The river road continues northwest, leading back to Washington Route 20 in 1.6 miles. Travelers from Winthrop can reach this point in 21.5 miles. Turn left again after 0.8 mile, where a sign indicates the Crater Creek Trailhead, among other destinations. After 1 mile continue straight ahead onto Forest Service Road 4340, and remain on this road past subsequent junctions. Avoid a left fork after another 1.75 miles. Turn left onto Forest Service Road 300 at 1.5 miles beyond the end of the pavement, marked by a Crater Creek Trailhead sign, a total of 5.7 miles from the river. Follow this switchbacking road for 4.4 miles to the trailhead parking area, signed for the Eagle Lakes Trail. *DeLorme Washington Atlas & Gazetteer* page 99, C6.

The Hike

Washington's backcountry areas are wonderlands of remote valleys, many filled with alpine lakes and tarns. Repeated episodes of glaciation have carved and gouged the mountain landscape into sharp crests and pointed peaks that rise above broad cirques and U-shaped valleys.

Although this glacier-created scenery is widespread throughout the state, each region has its own unique character based on rock type, vegetation, climate, and other factors.

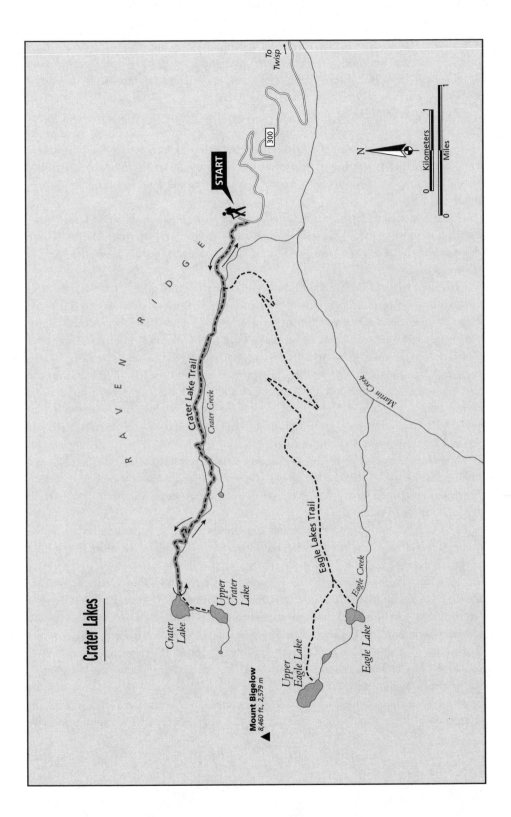

Crater Lakes

START

To Twisp

300

R A V E N R I D G E

Crater Lake Trail

Crater Creek

Martin Creek

Eagle Lakes Trail

Eagle Creek

Crater Lake

Upper Crater Lake

Mount Bigelow
8,460 ft., 2,579 m

Upper Eagle Lake

Eagle Lake

N

Kilometers

Miles

0   1

0   1

The Sawtooth Range east of Lake Chelan is one of the easternmost subranges of the Cascades. Its forests are open and dry, and its rugged granite peaks attain heights upward of 8,000 feet, rising above a series of cirque basins on the northeast slope of the range.

This rewarding hike to lower Crater Lake and, with a short scramble, an upper lake will lead you through the upper reaches of an east-side drainage to a peak-rimmed lake basin. The basin is covered in timberline forests of Engelmann spruce, Lyall larch, white-bark pine (trees almost exclusive to the east side of the Cascades), and subalpine fir. Campsites are numerous, and fishing for trout in both lakes is productive.

From the trailhead, proceed on an easy grade through an open, grass-floored forest. You'll soon reach a viewpoint that offers glimpses into the Martin Creek drainage to the southwest and the Crater Creek drainage in the west; the latter is your destination.

The trail bridges Crater Creek, and you'll reach a junction. Thus far, motorcycles are allowed to use this trail, and they can continue up the left fork to the Eagle Lakes, 4 miles distant. But you'll turn right onto the Crater Lake Trail. Although this trail is beyond the boundaries of the Lake Chelan–Sawtooth Wilderness, it remains closed to motor vehicles, thankfully leaving the razzing bikes behind you.

The trail climbs moderately through a spruce-fir forest with limited views for the first few miles, crossing the blue pools of Crater Creek on a bridge—a good place to top off a water bottle. Then it executes three steep switchbacks, where you may pause to enjoy a fine view to the pine- and grass-covered hills of the Methow Valley and beyond to the Columbia Basin.

Ahead, the canyon opens up as the trail briefly reaches the level ground of the first in a series of the steplike benches so typical of glacial valleys. Views are good up the canyon to rugged granite peaks. A small unseen tarn lies at the head of the bench at an elevation of 6,200 feet.

The trail presently leaves that bench and climbs steeply at times to another bench at 6,800 feet. This second bench features a lovely meadow and a campsite frequented by horsepackers.

Now in subalpine forest, the trail climbs gently to 6,841-foot Crater Lake. This scenic lake is shallow but supports a stable population of pan-sized trout. There's a large campsite at the trail's end; more campsites, lesser used, are located along the eastern shore amid timberline forest. Beyond is a backdrop of rugged, craggy peaks shaped by glacial plucking and frost wedging. Mount Bigelow, 8,460 feet, rises southwest of the basin, shining brightly with the morning sun but somber gray in the waning daylight hours.

An even more secluded lake lies above, reached by a sketchy trail that climbs up from the southeast shore of Crater Lake for 0.3 mile. Set on a bench surrounded by

Crater Lake.

stunted timber and encircled by high peaks, this lake is an excellent choice for the solitude seeker. Like the lower lake, it boasts a healthy population of pan-sized trout. Blue gentian, pink heather, and white heather are among the alpine cushion plants present at the 6,969-foot lake.

Another tiny lake lies 500 feet above on an alpine bench below Peak 8174. You can reach it by a tough but rewarding scramble. Many of the peaks encircling this basin can be reached in the same way.

From the lakes, notice the south slopes of Raven Ridge, densely covered with stunted white-bark pines. These trees contrast with the cold-tolerant larches, spruces, and firs that prefer the cooler, glacier-scoured basin.

Descend the way you came back to the trailhead.

Key Points

0.0 Start at the west end of the trailhead parking area at the trailhead sign for the Horsehead Pass, Martin Creek, and Crater Creek Trails.

0.7 Arrive at a junction where hiker and horse trails split. Stay to the right on the hiker trail, crossing Crater Creek on a bridge.

0.8 Arrive at a junction, turning right (west) onto Crater Lake Trail 416.

1.5 Cross Crater Creek on a wooden bridge.

3.6 Climb through a large boulder field on switchbacks.

4.2 Arrive at Crater Lake. A large camp is located at the trail's end, with more camps around the east side of the lake.

8.4 Arrive back at the trailhead and parking area.

Hike Information

Local information

Twisp Visitor Information Center, (509) 997-2926, www.twispinfo.com.
Methow Valley Sports Trail Association, (509) 996-3287, www.mvsta.com.

Local events/attractions

Winthrop Rhythm and Blues Festival (summer), **Winthrop Octoberfest** (fall), (509) 996-2125, www.methow.com.

Accommodations

Methow Valley Inn B&B, Twisp, WA, (509) 997-2253, www.methowvalleyinn.com.
USDA Forest Service Foggy Dew campground, (509) 996-4003.

Restaurants

Fiddlehead Bistro, Twisp, WA, (509) 997-0343.
Duck Brand Hotel and Cantina, Winthrop, WA, (509) 996-2192.

24 Island Lake

This moderate 10.6-mile round-trip backpack offers a sampling of the scenic, lake-dotted Alpine Lakes Wilderness. You'll also have access to eleven lakes cupped in forest below rocky peaks. Island Lake makes a good base for further roaming in this accessible area, only an hour's drive from Seattle.

Start: At the Trail 1039 Trailhead at the end of Forest Service Road 9030.
Length: 10.6 miles out-and-back.
Approximate hiking time: 5–6 hours.
Difficulty rating: Moderate, due to modest elevation gain and a well-graded trail.
Trail surface: Dirt trail.
Elevation gain: 1,940 feet.
Land status: Federal wilderness area.
Nearest town: North Bend, WA.
Other trail users: None.
Canine compatibility: Leashed dogs are permitted.
Trail contacts: Mount Baker-Snoqualmie National Forest, North Bend Ranger District, (360) 888-1421, www.fs.fed.us/r6/mbs.

Schedule: Best hiked from July through October.
Fees/permits: Parking at the trailhead requires a $5.00 day pass or $30.00 annual Northwest Forest Pass. You can purchase a pass at www.fs.fed.us/r6/feedemo or by calling (800) 270-7504. Permits are required for overnight stays in the Alpine Lakes Wilderness; pick one up for free at the trailhead.
Maps: USGS Bandera 7.5-minute quad; USDA Forest Service Alpine Lakes Wilderness map and Mount Baker-Snoqualmie National Forest map.

Finding the trailhead: Follow Interstate 90 to Exit 45, where a sign indicates the Lookout Point Road, 14.5 miles east of North Bend. Take the exit, cross north (left) over the freeway, and turn northwest onto FR 9030. The pavement ends after 0.4 mile. Proceed another 0.4 mile to a junction and turn right. Drive this often rough and narrow dirt road 2.3 miles to its end at the trailhead. *DeLorme Washington Atlas & Gazetteer* page 64, A4.

The Hike

In the southwestern corner of the Alpine Lakes Wilderness, the landscape is covered in heavy forest, and few peaks rise above timberline. Elevations are generally lower than in much of the rest of the wilderness, meaning that this lake–dotted region opens up for hiking earlier than many areas that remain snowbound until later in the season.

The destination of this hike is the lake basin on the north side of Bandera Mountain. The Talapus Lake Trailhead is only an hour's drive from Seattle, and the area hosts more than its share of hikers on some weekends. But this trail offers access to better than eleven lakes, so solitude seekers can usually find an isolated spot, even among these crowds. If you can make it away, weekdays are the optimal time to visit—you're more likely to have a lake or two to yourself.

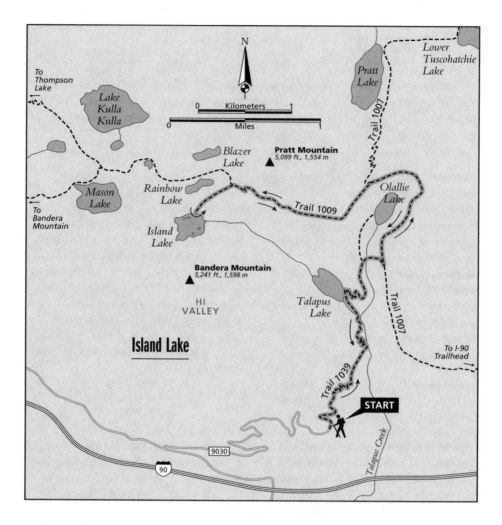

Wood fires are prohibited at Talapus, Olallie, and Melakwa Lakes, all of which are accessed from this well-maintained and easy-to-follow trail. In general, it's a good idea to use a stove when possible in this heavily hiked area where wood may be scarce.

The trail begins as an old logging road and proceeds into second-growth timber and, after 0.25 mile, into a virgin forest of western hemlock, western red cedar, and Douglas fir. You'll enter the Alpine Lakes Wilderness and very soon cross the outlet just below Talapus Lake. Notice the huge green leaves of the skunk cabbage growing in a marshy area near the wilderness boundary. You aren't likely to see its yellow-and-green-flowering head during summer, since it blooms quite early in spring.

Talapus Lake offers a scenic destination for a short day hike, especially for families with small children. Fishing is fair, and a few campsites, shaded by hemlock, fir, and cedar, dot the lower east shore. Bandera Mountain rises nearly 2,000 feet above the west side of the lake.

The trail leads upward under a canopy of silver fir and western hemlock to the Olallie Lake Trail. The 3,800-foot lake lies 0.5 mile up that short spur trail. You'll climb through forest above Olallie, catching only a brief glimpse of the egg-shaped lake before reaching a ridgetop junction. Here you can descend northward toward Pratt Lake and continue east to Lower Tuscohatchie Lake. Trails lead beyond to Kaleetan Lake, nestled under the impressive spire of 6,259-foot Kaleetan Peak, and east to 4,500-foot Melakwa Lake, also surrounded by precipitous peaks.

If you bear left on the ridge, you'll soon begin a westward traverse along the flower-filled south slopes of Pratt Mountain. Wildflowers along this sunny stretch include Indian paintbrush, lupine, and tiger lily, accompanied by bear grass as well as bracken fern.

The trail climbs a bit before dropping to a junction with the trail to Island Lake. The left fork leads to sheltered campsites at Island Lake, located at 4,250 feet in a cirque carved into the north flank of Bandera Mountain. The lake makes a good base camp for further exploration. Bandera and Pratt Mountains are easy scrambles for experienced hikers, both featuring far-reaching views. Closer at hand are Rainbow Lake, just over a timbered rise north of Island Lake, and a small tarn less than a mile west along the trail, both an easy stroll from an Island Lake camp.

Key Points

0.0 Start at the north side of the parking lot for the Trail 1039 Trailhead.

2.0 Cross the lake's outlet and arrive at Talapus Lake, off to the left (west) of the trail.

2.4 Reach the junction with the Olallie Lake Trail, which leads left (north) for 0.7 mile to Olallie Lake. Turn right.

3.2 Reach another junction with Trail 1007 and turn left (north). The right fork leads 2.1 miles to another trailhead off I-90 at Exit 47.

3.8 Reach a junction where Trail 1007 leads right (north) to Pratt Lake. Turn left (west) onto Trail 1009.

4.9 Reach a junction for the trail heading left (south) 0.4 mile to Island Lake.

5.3 Arrive at the north side of Island Lake.

10.6 Arrive back at the trailhead.

Hike Information

Local information

Upper Snoqualmie Valley Chamber of Commerce, (425) 888-4440, www.snovalley.org.

Accommodations

The Roaring Fork at North Bend B&B, North Bend, WA, (425) 888-4834, www.theroaring river.com.

USDA Forest Service Tinkham campground, (360) 888-1421.

Restaurants

Robertiello's Ristorante Italiano, North Bend, WA, (360) 888-5700.

25 Granite Mountain

This 9.6-mile out-and-back hike is a quick jaunt off Interstate 90 and easily accessible from the Seattle area. While not an easy hike, its open upper slopes make for a scenic outing from early June on, when its open south slopes melt free of snow. The fire lookout at the summit is still in use, making for a rewarding destination, along with the 360-degree views.

Start: At the Pratt Lake Trailhead off I-90.
Length: 9.6 miles out-and-back.
Approximate hiking time: 5½–6 hours.
Difficulty rating: Difficult, due to elevation gain.
Trail surface: Dirt trail.
Elevation gain: 3,770 feet.
Land status: Federal wilderness area.
Nearest town: North Bend, WA.
Other trail users: None.
Canine compatibility: Leashed dogs are permitted.

Trail contacts: Mount Baker–Snoqualmie National Forest, North Bend Ranger District, (360) 888-1421, www.fs.fed.us/r6/mbs.
Schedule: Late June through October.
Fees/permits: Parking at the trailhead requires a $5.00 day pass or $30.00 annual Northwest Forest Pass. You can purchase a pass at www.fs.fed.us/r6/feedemo or by calling (800) 270-7504.
Maps: USGS Snoqualmie Pass quad; USDA Forest Service Mount Baker–Snoqualmie National Forest map.

Finding the trailhead: From Seattle, drive I-90 east from Seattle to Exit 47, turn left (north), and cross back over the freeway. Turn left, driving 0.5 mile to the Pratt Lake Trailhead parking lot. *DeLorme Washington Atlas & Gazetteer* page 65, A5.

The Hike

For being so accessible from the Seattle metropolitan area, Granite Mountain can feel like a world away. Though strenuous and occasionally crowded on weekends, this mountain hike will reward you with delightful gardens of granite splashed with wildflowers, sweeping views of Mount Rainier and teardrop alpine lakes, and a historic Cascade Mountain fire tower.

Granite Mountain is located in the heart of the region's self-named Mountains to Sound Greenway, straddling I–90. The summit sits just west of the crest of the Cascade Range and south of the rugged Alpine Lakes Wilderness. The steep trail gains nearly 3,800 feet from trailhead to summit, and its south-facing, open slopes can be scorching on hot summer days. And although its south slopes largely melt free of snow by early summer when many of the region's other mountain trails are still buried, you should be wary of an avalanche gully at about the 4,000-foot elevation mark that may pose crossing dangers until June.

The first mile of trail meanders gently through cool forest to a junction near a small creek, then turns right and starts a challenging grind up a series of switchbacks.

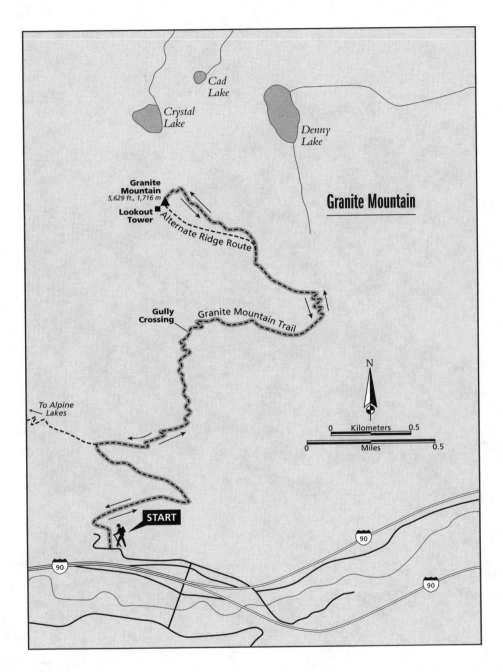

At about 2 miles from the trailhead, forest gives way to views down the valley, jumbled slabs of rock, and lush carpets of grass and wildflowers. Here the trail opens to views of a sea of peaks to the south, east, and west. You'll also reach the avalanche gully that may contain snow until June.

The remainder of the trail winds up through increasingly open and pleasant meadows, crossing a few small creeks cascading down avalanche-carved gullies. Fragrant white spikes of bear grass carpet upper slopes in summer, along with other alpine flowers, heather, and thistle, while blueberries abound in fall.

When you've reached the base of the summit ridge, you'll have two options for reaching the summit. The main trail traverses around the north side of the summit ridge and through a small basin. This route is often snowbound well into summer, making a scramble up the rocky ridge (your second option) appealing. While shorter, this scramble will require rock-hopping and should not be attempted with children.

From the summit at 5,629 feet, you'll find 360-degree views of snowy peaks, including the massive Mount Rainier and the glacier-carved peaks of the Alpine Lakes Wilderness, verdant valleys, and sparkling blue lakes. For even better views and a close-up view inside a classic and still-operational Cascade fire lookout, climb the summit tower. If you're lucky, you'll catch a summer volunteer on duty to let you take a peek inside.

Key Points

0.0 Start at the north end of the parking area for Pratt Lake Trail 1007.

0.3 Cross a stream on a small footbridge.

1.2 Arrive at a trail junction. The trail straight ahead continues toward Pratt Lake. Turn right (east) onto Granite Mountain Trail 1016.

2.1 Enter the Alpine Lakes Wilderness.

2.5 Cross an avalanche gully—a potentially dangerous crossing if it's still snow filled.

3.0 Break out into open meadows.

4.1 Arrive at a saddle with views of the back side of the summit fire lookout. If the trail remains snow covered, you can scramble across the summit ridge from here to the summit.

4.7 Proceeding on the trail, arrive at the summit lookout.

9.4 Arrive back at the trailhead and parking lot.

Hike Information

Local information
Upper Snoqualmie Valley Chamber of Commerce, (425) 888-4440, www.snovalley.org.

Accommodations
The Roaring Fork at North Bend B&B, North Bend, WA, (425) 888-4834, www.theroaringriver.com.

USDA Forest Service Tinkham campground, (360) 888-1421.

Restaurants
Robertiello's Ristorante Italiano, North Bend, WA, (360) 888-5700.

◄ *Trail near the summit of Granite Mountain.*

Honorable Mentions

North Cascades

H14 Mount Constitution

The not-so-wild 2,409-foot summit of Mount Constitution is the apex of the San Juan Islands. The view from the top, said by one early visitor to be the "finest marine view in North America," takes in the ocean, many islands, and the mountains of two countries. Most visitors drive the steep, narrow, tortuous paved road to the summit, but a few take the rewarding—albeit strenuous—hike from the North End campground on Cascade Lake. Views are magnificent and far-ranging, including Vancouver Island; the cities of Vancouver, British Columbia, and Bellingham, Washington; the British Columbia Coast Range; Mount Baker; Twin Sisters Mountain; the North Cascades; and many of the San Juan Islands. The Olympics raise snowy peaks far above the Strait of Juan de Fuca in the southwest, and even Mount Rainier can be seen on a clear day.

To get there from the Orcas ferry landing, follow the main road north and then east through Eastsound Village, turning right toward Rosario and Moran State Park after 9.2 miles. The park entrance arch is 13 miles from the ferry landing. Continue through the arch to the Cascade Lake swim area and the trailhead for Mount Constitution. The signed Mount Constitution Trail begins on the north side of the road just east of the campground registration booth. For more information, contact Moran State Park, (360) 376–2326, www.parks.wa.gov. *DeLorme Washington Atlas & Gazetteer* page 108, C2.

H15 Obstruction Pass Beach

To experience the San Juan Islands, you must climb their mountains, explore their forests, and walk their beaches. This short but rewarding hike to the campground and narrow beach at Obstruction Pass Park, administered by the Washington Department of Natural Resources (DNR), is a fine addition to anyone's Orcas Island itinerary. Offshore views reach as far as the snow-covered Olympics, more than 50 miles away. More immediate views include Obstruction Island beyond narrow Obstruction Pass.

To get there from the Orcas ferry landing, follow the main road north and then east through Eastsound Village, turning right toward Rosario and Moran State Park after 9.2 miles. Enter Moran State Park, passing Cascade Lake and the trailhead for Mount Constitution, and bear right 0.9 mile beyond the campground registration booth toward Olga, where the Mountain Lake Road forks left. Turn left after another 2 miles at Café Olga, signed for Doe Bay and Obstruction Pass. Travel 0.5

mile and turn right toward Obstruction Pass. You'll reach another junction within 0.9 mile, indicated by a trailhead sign. Turn right onto this dirt road, which leads to the road's end and the trailhead after 0.8 mile. You'll have traveled a total of 5.1 miles from Cascade Lake. For more information, contact the DNR at (360) 856–3500 or www.wa.gov/dnr. *DeLorme Washington Atlas & Gazetteer* page 108, C2.

H16 Tomyhoi Lake

The North Fork Nooksack River country contains some of the most uniquely scenic mountains in all the North Cascades. Mile-long Tomyhoi Lake rests in a deep valley in the heart of the Chilliwack Range, encircled by some of the highest, most impressive peaks in the range. This fish-filled lake lies at nearly the same elevation as the trailhead, but to get there you must negotiate a steep trail over timberline Gold Run Pass. Most visitors simply take a day hike to the pass for the memorable view.

Follow the Mount Baker Highway (Washington Route 542) east from its junction with Washington Route 547 at Kendall, passing the ranger station after 10.5 miles. Continue another 12.4 miles to the Twin Lakes Road, immediately beyond a highway maintenance station. Turn left here and follow this steep and narrow gravel road, avoiding a left turn after 2.8 miles, to the trailhead, signed for Tomyhoi Lake Trail, 4.5 miles from the highway at the switchback just below a sign that reads END OF MAINTAINED ROAD. For more information, contact the Mount Baker–Snoqualmie National Forest, Mount Baker Ranger District, (360) 856–5700, www.fs.fed.us/r6/mbs. *DeLorme Washington Atlas & Gazetteer* page 111, A3.

H17 Copper Ridge

This exceptionally scenic hike climbs over Hannegan Pass and into the wilds of the Chilliwack Range. As you hike along scenic Copper Ridge, you'll cross timberline parks not commonly found in the North Cascades. There are continuous vistas of some of the state's most rugged peaks—Shuksan, Baker, Challenger, and the Picket Range—as well as dramatic views north to craggy summits stretching into Canada.

Follow the Mount Baker Highway (Washington Route 542) east from Kendall for 23 miles to eastbound Forest Service Road 32, signed for Hannegan Pass Trail. Follow this road, ignoring right-forking Forest Service Road 34 (but not the glorious view of Mount Shuksan) at 1.3 miles. You'll reach the camping area and trailhead at the road's end, 5.2 miles from the highway. For more information, contact the Mount Baker–Snoqualmie National Forest, Mount Baker Ranger District, (360) 856–5700, www.fs.fed.us/r6/mbs. *DeLorme Washington Atlas & Gazetteer* page 110, A4.

H18 Anderson Butte Lookout Site, Watson and Anderson Lakes

East of Baker Lake and adjacent to the western boundary of North Cascades National Park lies the 14,300-acre Noisy-Diobsud Wilderness, which protects the drainages of Noisy and Diobsud Creeks. These short hikes start high and stay high, providing access to three fishable lakes. The broad vistas from the Anderson Butte Lookout are breathtaking.

From Washington Route 20, 14.5 miles east of Sedro Woolley or 15 miles west of Rockport, turn north onto the Baker Lake Road. Follow this highway through the Grandy Creek drainage, turning right after 11.9 miles at a Baker Lake sign. Shortly after the snowy cone of Mount Baker comes into view, turn right onto Forest Service Road 1106 where a sign points to Baker Dam and the Kulshan campground, 13.4 miles from WA 20. Pavement quickly ends on FR 1106, and you'll reach a junction just beyond the Kulshan campground after 0.9 mile. Avoid the left and right forks and bear straight ahead toward the Watson Lake Trail. The road crosses Baker Dam and reaches another junction 2 miles from the Baker Lake Road. Turn left here onto Forest Service Road 1107. This good but sometimes narrow dirt road climbs steadily, offering superb views of Mount Baker (for passengers only). Avoid a left fork 10.5 miles from the Baker Lake Road. You'll reach the trailhead spur road just before milepost 10, after 11.6 miles. Turn left here and drive 0.5 mile up the spur road to the trailhead. For more information, contact the Mount Baker–Snoqualmie National Forest, Mount Baker Ranger District, (360) 856–5700, www.fs.fed.us/r6/mbs. *DeLorme Washington Atlas & Gazetteer* page 110, C4.

H19 Thornton Lakes

This scenic but strenuous hike is unusual for North Cascades National Park in that it leads to three subalpine lakes. Lakes are otherwise few and far between in the park, and very few have established trails leading to them. This strenuous 10.5-mile out-and-back hike will take you to three bodies of water below soaring Mount Triumph. Take the side trip to Trappers Peak for even more scenery.

Follow the North Cascades Highway (Washington Route 20) east from Marble-mount for 11 miles to the signed Thornton Creek Road, just past milepost 117. Turn left (northwest) and follow this very steep and rough gravel road as it switchbacks 4.9 miles to it's end. Parking is limited to about five or six vehicles. For more information, contact North Cascades National Park's Wilderness Information Center at (360) 873–4500, www.nps.gov/noca. *DeLorme Washington Atlas & Gazetteer* page 111, C6.

H20 Maple Pass

This 6.5-mile loop starts just across the road from the hike to Cutthroat Pass (Hike 12) and provides easy access to a scenic but popular pass with big views of glaciers and peaks. Lake Ann makes a good side trip from the trail, although no camping is allowed at the lake.

Follow the North Cascades Highway (Washington Route 20) to Rainy Pass, 50.2 miles east of Marblemount or 43 miles west of Winthrop. The trail starts at the Rainy Pass picnic area on the south side of the road. For more information, contact

Okanogan National Forest, Methow Valley Ranger District, (509) 996–4003, www.fs.fed.us/r6/oka. *DeLorme Washington Atlas & Gazetteer* page 112, D3.

H21 McAlester Lake

This backpack trip leads through rain-shadow forests at the headwaters of Bridge Creek, a major tributary to the Stehekin River. The destination is a beautiful sub-alpine lake boasting a healthy trout population. If you're seeking a longer wilderness trek, you can continue on, taking the Rainbow Creek–Bridge Creek loop or making a point-to-point hike to Stehekin at the head of Lake Chelan.

This obscure trailhead lies in a grassy clearing on the north side of the North Cascades Highway (Washington Route 20), 1.2 miles east of Rainy Pass or 3.4 miles west of Washington Pass, and just west of milepost 159. If you're eastbound, you'll find the trailhead after crossing Bridge Creek (signed) for the second time. If you're westbound, you'll find it just before crossing Bridge Creek for the first time. The trail begins on the south side of the highway, opposite the parking area. For more information, contact North Cascades National Park's Wilderness Information Center at (360) 873–4500, www.nps.gov/noca. *DeLorme Washington Atlas & Gazetteer* page 98, A3.

H22 Blue Lake

Few short hikes from the North Cascades Highway rival Blue Lake for fabulous scenery and ease of access. Nestled in a high cirque in the shadow of the granite dome of Liberty Bell Mountain and Early Winters Spires, Blue Lake offers a peaceful, scenic destination for a one- to two-hour hike. The lake hosts a good population of pan-sized trout. The good trail maintains a steady, moderate grade throughout its length, making the hike suitable for most hikers, even families with young children.

Follow the North Cascades Highway (Washington Route 20) 54 miles east from Marblemount or 39 miles west from Winthrop to the signed Blue Lake Trailhead parking area, located on the south side of the highway. The trailhead lies 0.8 mile west of Washington Pass and 3.8 miles east of Rainy Pass. For more information, contact Okanogan National Forest, Methow Valley Ranger District, (509) 996–4003, www.fs.fed.us/r6/oka. *DeLorme Washington Atlas & Gazetteer* page 112, D3.

H23 Cedar Creek Falls

Cedar Creek, born on the flanks of the towering granite crags of Silver Star, North Gardiner, and Gilbert Mountains, flows 9 miles through a rugged and lonely canyon 3,000 to 4,000 feet deep. Scenery ranges from lofty, ice-encrusted summits to peaceful forests of Douglas fir and ponderosa pine. The length of the canyon, the grandeur of its scenery, and its remoteness combine to make Cedar Creek an attractive backpacking destination. Actually a double waterfall, Cedar Creek plummets over two 32-foot granite ledges—just two of several waterfalls in the canyon's lower reaches—2 miles from the trailhead.

From Washington Route 20 (the North Cascades Highway), 17.7 miles west of Winthrop and 2.6 miles west of the Early Winters Information Station, or 13.4 miles east of Washington Pass, turn south onto Forest Service Road 200, signed for the Cedar Creek Trail. This one-lane dirt road, rough in places, leads another 0.9 mile to the large trailhead parking area. For more information, contact Okanogan National Forest, Methow Valley Ranger District, (509) 996–4003, www.fs.fed.us/r6/oka. *DeLorme Washington Atlas & Gazetteer* page 112, D5.

H24 Goat Peak

If Goat Peak did not boast incredible views from its summit, the hike would nonetheless be a worthwhile excursion, passing among wind-flagged forests and stands of Lyall larch that flame with autumn color. But it's the views that attract hikers to this prominent peak. Ranging from the green fields of the Methow Valley to the rolling ridges of the Okanogan Cascades and from the bare 8,000-foot summits of the Pasayten Wilderness to the great ice-encrusted peaks of the North Cascades, the vista from Goat Peak is truly breathtaking.

From the North Cascades Highway (Washington Route 20), 17 miles east of Washington Pass or 17.5 miles west of Winthrop, turn north toward Mazama. After 0.4 mile turn right, drive southeast for 2 miles to the Goat Creek Road, and turn left. This one-lane dirt road, rough in places, climbs steadily for 2.7 miles to a junction. Turn left again; a sign indicates that the Goat Peak Lookout Trail is 9 miles ahead. This good dirt road leads 6.2 miles to signed Forest Service Road 200. Bear right here and proceed another 3 miles to the small trailhead parking area on the ridge at a three-way junction. For more information, contact Okanogan National Forest, Methow Valley Ranger District, (509) 996–4003, www.fs.fed.us/r6/oka. *DeLorme Washington Atlas & Gazetteer* page 112, D5.

H25 Billy Goat Loop

Pasayten country is big, lonely country, unlike any other wildland in the state. Although punctuated by a few sharp peaks, its landscape is primarily gentle and rolling. This weeklong, 50-mile backpack trip tours fishable lakes, subalpine forests and parkland, alpine ridges and cirque basins, and eight passes, two of which must be recrossed on the return trip. Travelers are few and far between in this country.

From Washington Route 20 at the west end of Winthrop, turn northwest onto the West Chewuch Road, just west of the bridge over the Chewuch River. This paved road follows the valley of the Chewuch River for 9.6 miles to a junction with left-forking Forest Service Road 5130. Turn left here where the sign indicates Billy Goat and Buck Lake. Avoid several signed spur roads as you follow the winding pavement of FR 5130 up the Eightmile Creek drainage. The pavement ends after 5.3 miles, but the dirt portion of FR 5130 remains wide and smooth, except for the final rough mile to the trailhead, 16.6 miles from the Chewuch River and 26.2 miles from Winthrop. For more information, contact Okanogan National Forest, Methow Valley Ranger District, (509) 996–4003, www.fs.fed.us/r6/oka. *DeLorme Washington Atlas & Gazetteer* page 112, B6.

H26 Black Lake

Most hikes into the Pasayten Wilderness require a backpack of several days to a week or more to appreciate the unique landscapes of this eastern Cascades wild area. But the short hike to Black Lake, one of the gems of the Pasayten, can be enjoyed either as a day hike or as a weekend backpack. In addition to good fishing, this 0.8-mile-long lake rests in a beautiful setting; its forest- and rock-rimmed shores lie at the foot of lofty ridges soaring more than 3,000 feet above. The low elevation of the lake gives this hike a longer season than most other trails in the Pasayten.

From Washington Route 20 at the west end of Winthrop, turn northwest onto the West Chewuch Road, just west of the bridge over the Chewuch River. This paved road follows the valley of the Chewuch River for 9.6 miles to a junction with left-forking Forest Service Road 5130. Continue straight ahead on the paved West Chewuch Road. This road turns to one-lane pavement after another 1.4 miles. After another 10.3 miles and immediately after bridging Lake Creek, turn left onto the one-lane dirt road and drive 2.5 miles to the trailhead parking area. For more information, contact Okanogan National Forest, Methow Valley Ranger District, (509) 996–4003, www.fs.fed.us/r6/oka. *DeLorme Washington Atlas & Gazetteer* page 112, B7.

H27 Tiffany Lake

The Tiffany Mountain massif is the highest, and arguably the most scenic, feature of the Okanogan Cascades beyond the boundaries of the Pasayten Wilderness. The stroll to Tiffany Lake—downhill all the way—is a fine choice for families with small children. The lake rests in the forested valley between the cliffs of Tiffany Mountain and the alpine slopes of Rock Mountain. More adventurous hikers have several side-trip opportunities, including the ascent of Rock or Middle Tiffany Mountains for far-ranging vistas, and a scramble to the timberline tarns of Little Tiffany Lakes.

From Washington Route 20 at the west end of Winthrop, turn northwest onto the West Chewuch Road, following it for 6.9 miles along the Chewuch River. Then turn right, bridge the small river, and immediately turn left (north) onto paved Forest Service Road 37. Follow FR 37 along the east bank of the Chewuch River for 7.6 miles, bearing right at the end of the pavement. After another 5.8 miles turn left off FR 37 and onto Forest Service Road 39. This gravel road, rough in spots, leads to Freezeout Pass (Hike 14 begins here). From Freezeout Pass, continue on FR 39 for another 4.1 miles to the Tiffany Spring campground. Parking is available at the campground entrance, and the signed trail begins on the opposite side of the road. For more information, contact Okanogan National Forest, Methow Valley Ranger District, (509) 996–4000, www.fs.fed.us/r6/oka. *DeLorme Washington Atlas & Gazetteer* page 114, C1.

H28 Lake Byrne

The White Chuck and North Fork Sauk are among the most popular routes into the west side of the vast Glacier Peak Wilderness, part of Washington's largest continuous roadless area. But the Lost Creek Ridge Trail takes the high route, thousands of feet above those deep river valleys, to scenic Lake Byrne in the shadow of Glacier Peak. This strenuous route can also be turned into a point-to-point hike by descending to the White Chuck River from the lake and exiting via the White Chuck Trailhead.

From Washington Route 530 in Darrington (28 miles east of Arlington), turn south onto the Mountain Loop Highway where WA 530 makes a right-angled bend. Pavement ends 8.9 miles from Darrington at a four-way junction. If you plan to return via the White Chuck River, you should turn left at this junction and follow Forest Service Road 23 east for 11 miles to the White Chuck Trailhead. Otherwise, continue southeastward on winding dirt Forest Service Road 20 along the east and northeast banks of the Sauk River. At 15.6 miles from Darrington, turn left onto Forest Service Road 49 (North Fork Sauk Road) where a sign points to the Lost Creek Ridge Trail, 3 miles ahead on the north side of the road, just past milepost 3. For more information, contact the Mount Baker–Snoqualmie National Forest, Verlot Public Service Center, (360) 691–7791, www.fs.fed.us/r6/mbs. *DeLorme Washington Atlas & Gazetteer* page 97, D7.

H29 Green Mountain

Come climb this 6,500-foot summit to vast meadows that give the mountain its well-fitting name. Along the way you'll find a spectacular show of flowers in early season, and blueberries later on. There's also a lookout on top, with views of Glacier Peak and beyond. (**Note:** The lookout, flown out for repair, is scheduled to return in 2004 or 2005.)

Drive the Suiattle River Road 19 miles to Green Mountain Road 2680. Turn left and drive 5 miles to the road's end and trailhead. For more information, contact the Mount Baker–Snoqualmie National Forest, Verlot Public Service Center, (360) 691–7791, www.fs.fed.us/r6/mbs. *DeLorme Washington Atlas & Gazetteer* page 97, B7.

H30 Trails of the Chiwawa River Valley: Carne Mountain, Buck Creek Pass, Spider Meadow

The Chiwawa River Valley offers access to spectacular country on the eastern side of the Glacier Peak Wilderness. Follow the 19.2-mile out-and-back trip to Buck Creek Pass for an in-your-face view of Glacier Peak, or follow the trail to Spider Meadow, from which experienced hikers can climb over Spider Gap and the small Spider Glacier to Lyman Lakes (Hike 22). Day hikers will find inspiration trekking through high meadows to the rocky perch of Carne Mountain, with spectacular views of Mount Maude and beyond.

All three hikes are accessible by following U.S. Highway 2, 20 miles east of Stevens Pass and turning left toward Lake Wenatchee. Bear right toward Fish Lake and turn left onto Forest Service Road 62, which becomes the Chiwawa River Road (Forest Service Road 6200). Follow this road to the Phelps Creek Road (Forest Service Road 6211), and turn right. You'll reach the trailhead at the end of this dirt road. For more information, contact the Wenatchee National Forest, Leavenworth Ranger District, (509) 548–6977, www.fs.fed.us/r6/wenatchee. *DeLorme Washington Atlas & Gazetteer* page 98, D1.

H31 Stehekin-Area Trails: McGregor Mountain, Chelan Lakeshore Trail, Rainbow Loop

The Stehekin area, just "uplake" on Lake Chelan from the jumping-off point for the Lyman Lakes Trail (Hike 22), offers a scenic base for miles and miles of hiking trails of all types. Ready for 144 switchbacks? Then try the grueling climb of more than 6,000 feet to the summit of McGregor Mountain. Or if you're looking for an early-season backpack, try the 18-mile trail along the southeast shore of Lake Chelan. You'll find scenic lakeside camps along the way and can arrange pickup and drop-off transportation with the boat servicing the lake.

To get there, drive U.S. Highway 2 to the town of Chelan. Here you'll have to catch the boat up the lake to Stehekin (see www.ladyofthelake.com for the latest boat schedules). For more information, contact North Cascades National Park's Wilderness Information Center at (360) 873–4500, www.nps.gov/noca. *DeLorme Washington Atlas & Gazetteer* page 99, B3.

H32 Heather Lake

North of Stevens Pass, the crest of the Cascade Range stays fairly low in elevation for nearly 20 miles to the Glacier Peak Wilderness boundary, allowing substantial moisture from Pacific storms to fall east of the crest. Thus forests here maintain a moist, "west-side" character. This scenic overnighter travels through such forests to Heather Lake, the second largest lake in the 103,591-acre Henry M. Jackson Wilderness. The Cascade crest forms a timbered backdrop for many hemlock-sheltered campsites near the lake's outlet.

To get there, drive east from Stevens Pass on U.S. Highway 2 for 19.5 miles to the Lake Wenatchee turnoff (Washington Route 207). Turn left and follow this paved road, ignoring the left fork to the Nason Creek campground and the two right forks to Plain (Washington Route 209) and the Chiwawa Loop Road. WA 207 follows the north shore of Lake Wenatchee, passing a ranger station and reaching a junction 2 miles beyond. Bear left onto Forest Service Road 65 where the White River Road forks right. Bear right after 6 miles; a sign here points to the Little Wenatchee Ford campground. Turn left onto Forest Service Road 6700 where a sign points to US 2. Cross the Little Wenatchee River and, after 0.4 mile, turn right onto Forest Service Road 6701/400. (This junction can be reached by driving 12.2 miles north from US 2 at a junction signed for Smithbrook 4 miles east of Stevens Pass.) Follow this good dirt road for 4.7 miles, and then turn left onto Forest Service Road 400, signed for the Heather Lake Trail. This good dirt road leads through a patchwork of young forest virgin timber for 2.2 miles to the small parking area at the end of the road. For more information, contact the Wenatchee National Forest, Leavenworth Ranger District, (509) 548–6977, www.fs.fed.us/r6/wenatchee. *DeLorme Washington Atlas & Gazetteer* page 81, B8.

H33 Alpine Lookout

This day hike traverses a portion of a major east–west divide separating the upper Wenatchee River from Nason Creek and U.S. Highway 2. Views of the Wenatchee River drainage, including such major tributaries as the White and Chiwawa Rivers, in addition to the snowy cone of Glacier Peak, make the Alpine Lookout a popular and rewarding destination. There's also a good chance you'll see mountain goats along the ridge. A quick 0.5-mile hike leads to the squat lookout tower set on a rocky 6,200-foot bump on Nason Ridge, where views are seemingly endless.

Follow US 2 eastbound from Stevens Pass for 17.2 miles to a roadside rest area and the southbound Coulter Creek Road. Proceed 0.2 mile to a hard-to-spot junction with northbound Forest Service Road 6910, just east of milepost 82, and turn left. The dirt road enters an area of residences, bridges Nason Creek, and passes under power lines before climbing timbered slopes. Ignore a closed, right-forking road after 3.1 miles, and bear right onto Forest Service Road 6910/170 after 4.4 miles. Signs at both junctions point to TRAIL. This spur road executes a tight right-hand switchback before reaching the signed Round Mountain Trail after 0.2 mile. For more information, contact the Wenatchee National Forest, Leavenworth Ranger District, (509) 548–6977, www.fs.fed.us/r6/wenatchee. *DeLorme Washington Atlas & Gazetteer* page 82, B2.

H34 Mad River–Lost Lake Loop

The Entiat Mountains are high, jagged, and snowcapped to the north but gentle and timber covered to the south, dotted with many large grassy meadows. The forests in the southern Entiats are open, with very little understory. This hike along the upper Mad River in the southern Entiats proceeds through a rolling, meadow-dotted landscape in one of the largest roadless nonwilderness areas in the state.

Drive U.S. Highway 2 west from Leavenworth 14.6 miles to the Lake Wenatchee turnoff (Washington Route 207), or drive 19.5 miles east of Stevens Pass. Ignore eastbound Washington Route 209 to Plain at 3.6 miles, and turn right onto the Chiwawa Loop Road in another 0.6 mile, just after crossing the Wenatchee River. Follow this paved county road (Chelan County Road 22), ignoring turnoffs to Fish Lake, Chiwawa River, and Trinity, to a bridge over the Chiwawa River about 4.6 miles from WA 207. Half a mile beyond, where the road bends south, lies a hard-to-spot junction signed for northbound travelers only (LOWER CHIWAWA, MAVERICK

SADDLE). Turn north here onto Forest Service Road 6100; the pavement ends in 0.1 mile. After 1.6 miles is the Deep Creek campground and a junction. Turn right onto Forest Service Road 6101, avoiding several spurs and always following signs to Maverick Saddle. This good dirt road gets rougher as you approach the Deer Camp campground, where you turn left (north), still on FR 6101, 4.6 miles from the county road. The road becomes steep, narrow, and even rougher for the next 2.7 miles to Maverick Saddle and a junction with southbound Forest Service Road 5200 and the northbound spur to the Mad River Trail. Park at the saddle. For more information, contact the Wenatchee National Forest, Leavenworth Ranger District, (509) 548–6977, www.fs.fed.us/r6/wenatchee. *DeLorme Washington Atlas & Gazetteer* page 82, B4.

H35 Snow Lake/Prusik Pass

The Enchantment Lakes Basin is perhaps the most scenic hiking area in the state. Numerous lakes—some forested, some alpine—lie on benches that proceed in stair-step fashion down the U-shaped drainage of Snow Creek. Jagged, broken alpine peaks surround the basin, attracting climbers from throughout the state to challenge the stable granitic rock. And for a few days to a week each October, the abundant Lyall larch in the upper basin put on an unforgettable display of orange and gold. The hike to the upper basin isn't easy, and you'll need to reserve a permit well ahead of time to camp, but the memorable reward is certainly well worth the effort.

To get there from U.S. Highway 2 at the west end of Leavenworth (33.4 miles east of Stevens Pass), turn south onto the signed Icicle Creek Road. Follow this paved road past several rural residences and then west up Icicle Creek. You'll reach the large parking area on the south side of the road after 4.2 miles. For more information, contact the Wenatchee National Forest, Leavenworth Ranger District, (509) 548–6977, www.fs.fed.us/r6/wenatchee. *DeLorme Washington Atlas & Gazetteer* page 82, D3; page 67, A2.

H36 Mount Dickerman

This strenuous hike gains almost 4,000 feet in just over 4 miles to the summit. The difficulty seems to thin out the crowds, many of which head to Mount Pilchuck (Hike 21) just down the road to the west. From the summit, you'll catch views of Big Four Mountain to the south, the peaks around the Monte Cristo area, and Glacier Peak.

Drive the Mountain Loop Highway 16.5 miles from the Verlot Public Service Center to a small sign and parking area on the north side of the road. For more information, contact the Mount Baker–Snoqualmie National Forest, Verlot Public Service Center, (360) 691–7791, www.fs.fed.us/r6/mbs. *DeLorme Washington Atlas & Gazetteer* page 97, D5.

H37 Blanca Lake

This 8-mile out-and-back hike leads to a sparkling turquoise lake at the foot of the Columbia Glacier and Kyes Peak beyond. The trail mercilessly grinds its way up several switchbacks before beginning its descent to the picturesque lake, where you'll find scenic camps and good fishing.

Drive U.S. Highway 2 to the left turnoff to Index and follow the North Fork Skykomish River Road for 14 miles to Forest Service Road 63. Turn left onto Forest Service Road 63 and drive 2 miles to the Blanca Lake Trailhead and parking area. For more information, contact the Mount Baker–Snoqualmie National Forest, Skykomish Ranger District, (360) 677–2414, www.fs.fed.us/r6/mbs. *DeLorme Washington Atlas & Gazetteer* page 81, A6.

H38 Tuck and Robin Lakes

The rocky basin of Tuck and Robin Lakes is often called the Little Enchantments for its likeness to the spectacular Enchantment Lakes Basin. You'll hike up a steep, rough trail to Tuck Lake, surrounded on all sides by granite ledges. Higher up are the snowfields and tarns of Robin Lake with a head-on view of the massive and glacier-covered Mount Daniel.

Take Interstate 90 east to the Salmon La Sac exit. Follow the road north to Salmon La Sac and continue another 12.5 miles to the road's end and trailhead. For more information, contact the Wenatchee National Forest, Cle Elum Ranger District, (509) 674–4411, www.fs.fed.us/r6/wenatchee. *DeLorme Washington Atlas & Gazetteer* page 81, D8.

H39 Rachel Lake/Rampart Lakes

The route to Rachel and Rampart Lakes follows a rugged trail, but despite its rigors this is a popular weekend hike. Numerous campsites, shaded by hemlocks and firs, dot the eastern shore of this 0.5-mile-long lake. You'll reach Rampart Lakes, set on a bench just west of Rampart Ridge, by way of a 1-mile trail from Rachel Lake, gaining about 600 feet of elevation en route. Views of jagged summits and the timberline setting make camping amid these lakes scenic and memorable.

To get there, proceed to Exit 62 off Interstate 90, 48 miles west of Ellensburg and 30 miles east of North Bend. Drive northeast toward Kachess Lake via paved Forest Service Road 49. Turn left onto Forest Service Road 4930 after about 5 miles. A sign here and at subsequent junctions indicates the Rachel Lake Trail. This good dirt road leads to a brief section of pavement, which in turn leads to the trailhead parking area on the south side of the road, opposite the trailhead proper, 8.8 miles from I-90. For more information, contact the Wenatchee National Forest, Cle Elum Ranger District, (509) 674–4411, www.fs.fed.us/r6/wenatchee. *DeLorme Washington Atlas & Gazetteer* page 65, A6.

South Cascades

Washington's South Cascades region is a volcanic wonderland best defined by its three volcanoes—Mount Saint Helens, Mount Adams, and Mount Rainier—that soar from surrounding plains of forest-covered basalt and andesite. But beyond these three snowy giants, you'll find a landscape different than the rugged peaks in the North Cascades. A legacy of forty million years of volcanism has left behind a region of cinder cones, lava flows, and granitic outcroppings, now covered by lush forests and dotted with lakes. And while tranquility has returned, the devastating 1980 eruption of Mount Saint Helens was a grim reminder that volcanism still plays an active role in shaping this unique landscape.

Mount Rainier's massive 14,410-foot summit, the highest in the state, towers over western Washington, its ice-mantled summit the state's more popular icon. With more than twenty-six glaciers tumbling from its flanks, much of the mountain's upper slopes are better left for experienced mountaineers, thousands of whom attempt to climb the mountain each year. Visitors to Mount Rainier National Park will find plenty of hiking opportunities, however, among the park's deep forests, sprawling gardens of heather, alpine lakes, and tumbling waterfalls. Hikes to Comet Falls/Van Trump Park and Upper Palisades Lake provide just a small sample of the park's vast alpine areas, while the hike to the Carbon River surveys some of the park's best old-growth forests, ending at an up-close look at the lowest-elevation glacier in the lower forty-eight states.

While Mount Rainier is young in geologic time, underlying the mountain are layers of dark andesite lava flows, light-colored sedimentary rocks, and granitic magma, all produced by episodes of volcanic activity that predate Mount Rainier by millions of years. Many of these harder underlying layers are exposed as craggy outcroppings in places like the Tatoosh Range on the south side of the mountain. The hike to Tatoosh Lakes will take you through the heart of the often overlooked Tatoosh Wilderness, where you'll get a good feel for its rugged terrain of rocky spires, alpine lakes, and meadows.

The north side of Mount Saint Helens, a region devastated by the 1980 eruption, is a startling contrast to the green forests and meadows of Mount Rainier. Here the hike to Norway Pass will take you through a seemingly timber-flattened wasteland to a dead-on view over Spirit Lake and into the mountain's crater. But look closer and you'll see the remarkable process of an ecosystem in recovery, as pioneer plants and wildlife actively reclaim the area.

About 50 miles east of Mount Saint Helens is Mount Adams, the state's second highest peak. While its hulking, snowy mass is arguably as impressive as Mount Rainier, Mount Adams's more remote location means that you'll find far fewer crowds here. The trail to Foggy Flat, following a portion of the Pacific Crest Trail along the broad, gentle north slopes of the mountain, will lead you to flower-filled slopes and beyond into the raw volcanic high country of the Mount Adams Wilderness.

Finally, the more subtle scenery of this region shouldn't be overlooked. Hikes along the Lewis River and in the Indian Heaven Wilderness make for scenic weekend outings and provide good trout-fishing opportunities. Come in fall to Indian Heaven and you'll also find some of the best berry picking around. And last but not least, don't forget to keep an eye out over your shoulder for the ever-elusive bigfoot, rumored to roam this part of the state.

26 Carbon Glacier

Hike through grand moss-covered forest to one of the largest glaciers in the lower forty-eight states, mantling the northwest slopes of Mount Rainier. Along the way you'll cross an impressive suspension bridge over a rocky, glacier-gouged channel of the Carbon River, carrying torrents of milky meltwater from the glacier just above.

Start: At the Ipsut Creek campground and Carbon River Trailhead.
Length: 7 miles out-and-back to the glacier viewpoint.
Approximate hiking time: 4 hours.
Difficulty rating: Moderate, due to modest elevation gain and length.
Trail surface: Dirt trail, suspension bridge.
Elevation gain: 1,275 feet.
Land status: National park.
Nearest town: Buckley, WA.
Other trail users: None.

Canine compatibility: Not dog friendly.
Trail contacts: Mount Rainier National Park, (360) 569-2211, www.nps.gov/mora.
Schedule: June through October.
Fees/permits: A $10 fee is collected at the park entrance. A free permit is required for backcountry camping; call (360) 569-HIKE for reservations and information.
Maps: USGS Mowich Lake 7.5-minute quad; Mount Rainier National Park quad; Mount Rainier National Park map.

Finding the trailhead: Follow Washington Route 165 first south then east from Buckley to the Carbon River Road. Turn left where a sign here indicates the Carbon River ranger station. The trailhead parking area, often packed on weekends, is 23 miles from Buckley at the Ipsut Creek campground. An entry fee of $10 can be paid either at the park entrance or at the Wilderness Information Center in the nearby crossroads of Wilkeson. This road frequently washes out, so it's a good idea to call ahead for conditions. *DeLorme Washington Atlas & Gazetteer* page 48, A2.

The Hike

Ancient glaciers were largely responsible for creating the lakes and jagged peaks that attract thousands of backcountry enthusiasts to Washington's Cascade Range each year. Several of those glaciers yielded to a warming trend that began about 10,000 years ago, and many present-day Washington glaciers are mere remnants of a recent cooling trend, known as the Little Ice Age, which began around A.D. 1500 and ended in the early twentieth century.

Today heavy precipitation in the Cascade Range nurtures the single largest system of glaciers in the contiguous United States. Mount Rainier alone contains more than twenty-six glaciers, most of which emanate from its lofty summit ice cap.

The Carbon Glacier begins its journey in the shadow of the largest rock face on Mount Rainier—the 3,000-foot-high Willis Wall, just below 14,112-foot Liberty Cap, the mountain's northwest summit—and flows northwestward into the moist forests of the Carbon River (so named because of coal seams near the towns of Wilkeson and Carbonado in the Cascade foothills). Descending to an elevation of

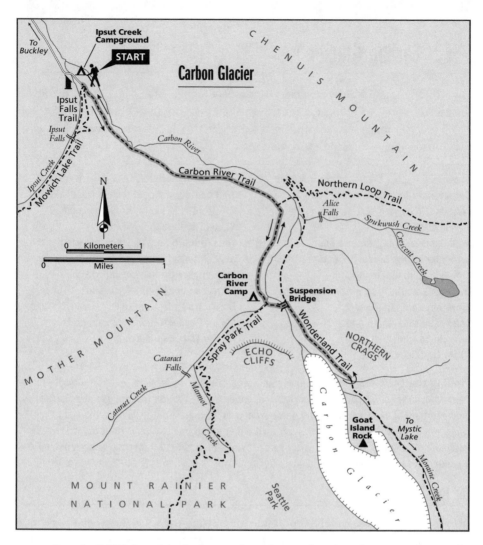

approximately 3,500 feet, this glacier reaches a lower elevation than any other in the United States outside of Alaska.

This easy hike passes through lush forest en route along a portion of Mount Rainier's famed Wonderland Trail to the snout of the Carbon Glacier. Although glaciers and dense forests make for scenic contrast, they both originate from the same source—abundant moisture, caused, in this case, by storms blowing in from the Pacific Ocean.

From the trailhead at the Ipsut Creek campground, take the right-forking trail and proceed into a mossy forest of western hemlock, western red cedar, and Douglas fir.

Flowing through a boulder-strewn bed, the milky, braided Carbon River—the milkiness is caused by fine particles of "glacial flour" ground from the bedrock by the movement of the ice—is always close at hand. Its flow fluctuates widely, depending on temperature, time of year, and weather conditions.

The Northern Loop Trail, which can be used for the return trip, originates across the river after 2 miles. For now, bear right and follow above the river for 0.9 mile to the right-forking Spray Park Trail, reached just after crossing a clear, nonglacial stream. The Carbon River camp (no wood fires) lies nearby, tucked away past an area of recent blowdown.

Stay on the main trail, and you'll soon reach the impressive large suspension bridge that spans the riverbed. The rock anchoring the bridge cables bears visible scratches from the abrasion of the ancient Carbon Glacier.

On the opposite side of the bridge is a junction. Take the left fork to loop back to the trailhead. To continue toward the glacier, turn right, climbing steadily to the snout of the glacier, buried under rock debris at the base of a precipitous wall of andesite known as the Northern Crags.

Stop and experience this raw landscape in action, listening to the tumble of boulders and rush of water below you as ice and rock grind together. There's no particular destination beyond here; you can either just turn around once reaching the glacier, or you can continue upward along the steep trail for a better look at the glacier and access to the glorious alpine country of Moraine Park, or off-trail (and difficult) wanderings to Elysian Fields, Vernal Park, and beyond.

Key Points

0.0 Start on the Carbon River (Wonderland) Trail at the west end of the trailhead parking lot.

0.3 Arrive at a junction where the Ipsut Falls Trail leads to the right (southwest). Continue left (south) toward the Carbon Glacier.

0.4 Reach a junction for a right-leading trail to Mowich Lake. Continue on to the left.

2.0 Reach a junction with the Northern Loop Trail leading left (east) 4.6 miles to Windy Gap and 6.5 miles to Lake James. Continue forward.

2.8 Pass a trail leading right for the Carbon River camp, with campsites just off the trail.

2.9 Cross clear, nonglacial Cataract Creek on a log footbridge and pass a junction with the right-leading Spray Park Trail to the Cataract Valley camp in 1.6 miles, Seattle Park in 3.2 miles, and Spray Park in 5.3 miles. Continue to the left.

3.1 Cross the Carbon River on a suspension bridge. Just across bridge is another junction. To the left (north) the trail leads to Windy Gap and Lake James and offers an alternative return to the trailhead. Turn right (south) to reach the Carbon Glacier.

3.5 Reach the viewpoint of the Carbon Glacier along the trail.

7.0 Arrive back at the trailhead and parking lot.

Hike Information

Local information

A Pocket Field Guide to the Plants and Animals of Mount Rainier by Joe Dreimiller.

Accommodations

Mount Rainier National Park Ipsut Creek campground, (360) 569-2211.
Mountain View Inn, Buckley, WA, (360) 829-1100, www.mtviewinn.com.

27 Upper Palisades Lake

This day hike or overnight trip offers access to a string of seven subalpine lakes and tarns on the dry side of Mount Rainier National Park. Along the way the up-and-down trail passes through meadows splashed with wildflowers in summer and the columnlike formations of The Palisades.

Start: Upper Palisades Lake Trail, opposite the Sunrise Point parking area.
Length: 5.8 miles out-and-back.
Approximate hiking time: 3½ hours.
Difficulty rating: Moderate, due to modest up-and-down terrain and length.
Trail surface: Wide and well-graded forest and meadow trail.
Elevation gain: 640 feet in, 900 feet out.
Land status: National park.
Nearest town: Buckley, WA.
Other trail users: None.

Canine compatibility: Not dog friendly.
Trail contacts: Mount Rainier National Park, (360) 569–2211, www.nps.gov/mora.
Schedule: Mid-July through mid-October.
Fees/permits: A $10 fee is required to enter Mount Rainier National Park. A free permit is required for backcountry camping; call (360) 569–HIKE for reservations and information.
Maps: USGS White River Park 7.5-minute quad; Mount Rainier National Park quad; Mount Rainier National Park map.

Finding the trailhead: From Washington Route 410 in Mount Rainier National Park, 3.4 miles north of Cayuse Pass and 40 miles southeast of Enumclaw, turn west onto the road signed for the White River and Sunrise. Follow this paved road 13 miles to the large parking area and Sunrise vista point, located where the road makes a horseshoe bend from east to west. *DeLorme Washington Atlas & Gazetteer* page 48, A3.

The Hike

This easy, scenic hike on the dry side of Mount Rainier National Park offers access to seven subalpine lakes on the eastern flank of the Sourdough Mountains. Campsites and water are abundant—as are mosquitoes during early summer. Equally attractive as a day hike or weekender, this trail has something for nearly everyone—peaks to climb, lakes to fish, flower gardens to enjoy, and solitude to relish amid subalpine grandeur.

From Sunrise Point, follow the trail along Sunrise Ridge northeastward through an open hemlock-fir forest. Views are immediately sweeping to the north, east, and south. The trail doubles back on a lower contour and, after 0.5 mile, reaches the junction with a short side trail to Sunrise Lake, the first in a series of timberline lakes dotting the upper reaches of White River Park.

Bear right at this junction and proceed across talus and into the basin toward Clover Lake. On the way you'll pass wildflowers such as buttercups, glacier lilies, and

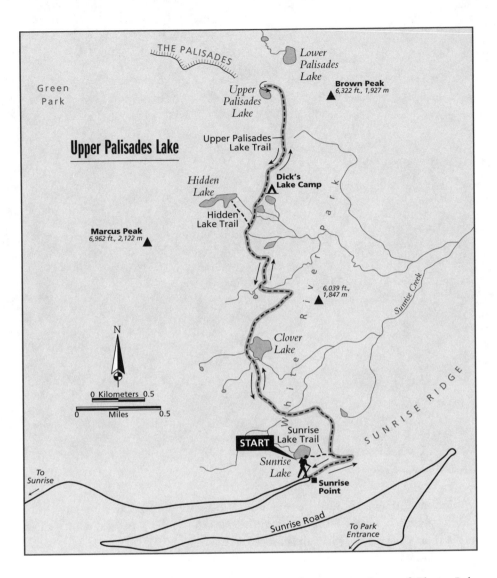

Upper Palisades Lake

western mountain pasqueflowers. The trail skirts the western shore of Clover Lake and passes a short, plainly visible right-leading spur trail to the lakeshore. The main trail climbs a low ridge before descending steadily into the next basin, flanked by increasingly thick stands of mountain hemlock and subalpine fir.

Cross the floor of this basin, under the shadow of 6,962-foot Marcus Peak, to a signed junction about a mile north of Clover Lake. The left fork, an unmaintained trail, climbs quickly to the hanging valley in which Hidden Lake rests. (Hidden Lake is closed to camping.) Green Park is an easy jaunt over the ridge from the lake.

Upper Palisades Lake.

Continue straight ahead at this junction, hop across Hidden Lake's outlet stream, and shortly reach a right-forking trail to the Dick's Lake camp (stoves only), located in the timber between two small lakes below the trail.

Bearing left, you'll make another brief ascent, but the trail soon levels off in a beautiful flower-filled meadow next to a clear, meandering stream. Jagged summits loom above you immediately to the west.

The trail then climbs to a saddle overlooking Upper Palisades Lake, nestled in a tiny cirque below the volcanic crags of The Palisades. This ridge of andesite, some geologists believe, was formed by molten magma associated with the Tatoosh Pluton that flowed on the surface, rather than cooling underground, as did the main body of the Tatoosh Range. The rocks of the Tatoosh Pluton predate Mount Rainier and make up the foundation upon which the comparatively young volcano was built.

A faint trail branches right here toward 6,322-foot Brown Peak, the bump on the ridge 0.3 mile to the east. You'll turn left, skirting the east shore of Upper Palisades Lake to the trail's end at the lake's north shore. Campsites are limited at the lake, but there is ample opportunity for cross-country camping. Return to the trailhead via the same route.

Key Points

0.0 Start at the Upper Palisades Trailhead just north across the road from the Sunrise Point parking area.

0.5 Arrive at a junction. To the left (west), the trail leads 0.1 mile to Sunrise Lake. Turn right (northeast) toward Upper Palisades Lake.

1.1 Pass a short spur trail to the shore of Clover Lake.

1.5 Arrive at a saddle and continue forward, ignoring right- and left-forking trails.

2.0 Arrive at a junction for the signed (but unmaintained) Hidden Lake Trail. Continue forward on the Upper Palisades Lake Trail.

2.1 Pass a signed trail off to the right leading to Dick's Lake camp. Continue forward on the Upper Palisades Lake Trail.

2.6 Reach a signed junction for Upper Palisades Lake and camp. Turn left (northeast) toward the lake, visible just off the trail. Ignore an unsigned trail to the right leading up the ridge.

2.9 Arrive at the north end of Upper Palisades Lake.

5.8 Arrive back at the trailhead and parking lot.

Hike Information

Local information
A Pocket Field Guide to the Plants and Animals of Mount Rainier by Joe Dreimiller.

Local events/attractions
King County Fair, second and third weeks of July, Enumclaw, WA, www.kingcountyfair.com.

Accommodations
Mount Rainier National Park White River campground, (360) 569-2211.

King's Motel, Enumclaw, WA, (360) 825-1626.

Restaurants
Cynthia's Pony Express Café, Enumclaw, WA, (360) 825-2055.

28 Comet Falls and Van Trump Park

Follow this 4.8-mile out-and-back day hike along a scenic stream-filled gorge to a series of spectacular waterfalls, including the 300-foot-high Comet Falls. Beyond the falls you'll find timberline gardens of flowers and meadows on the south slopes of Mount Rainier, where you can wander for views and more views, or just sit and stare up at the icy summit flanks above you.

Start: At the Comet Falls Trailhead parking area.
Length: 4.8 miles out-and-back.
Approximate hiking time: 3 hours.
Difficulty rating: Moderate, due to elevation gain.
Trail surface: Dirt trail.
Elevation gain: 1,700 feet to Comet Falls, 2,000 feet to Van Trump Park.
Land status: National park.
Nearest town: Ashford, WA.
Other trail users: None.

Canine compatibility: Not dog friendly.
Trail contacts: Mount Rainier National Park, (360) 569-2211, www.nps.gov/mora.
Schedule: Mid-July through mid-October.
Fees/permits: A $10 fee is required to enter Mount Rainier National Park. A free permit is required for backcountry camping; call (360) 569-HIKE for reservations and information.
Maps: USGS Mt. Rainier West 7.5-minute quad; Mount Rainier National Park quad; Mount Rainier National Park map.

Finding the trailhead: Drive east from the Nisqually entrance to Mount Rainier National Park (at the southwestern corner of the park) and follow the road along the Nisqually River for 10 miles. Park in the small parking area on the northwest side of the road just beyond milepost 10. Or drive 23.5 miles west from the Stevens Canyon entrance to find the trailhead. *DeLorme Washington Atlas & Gazetteer* page 48, B2.

The Hike

This trail leads to Van Trump Park in Mount Rainier National Park, a hanging valley resplendent with summer wildflowers. Along the way you'll pass some of the park's most beautiful waterfalls and enjoy excellent views of Mount Rainier with its south-slope glaciers.

From the trailhead, the route climbs toward Van Trump Creek. You'll enjoy a good view southward across the canyon of the Nisqually River to jagged Tatoosh Range summits. After just 0.25 mile the trail bridges the creek above a spectacular, roaring cataract. Rarely out of sight and always within sound of the tumultuous creek, you'll climb steadily through a forest of Alaska yellow cedar, silver fir, and hemlock.

After 1.4 miles the trail crosses a creek amid the roar of thundering water via a foot log and handrail. Round a bend in the trail and you'll confront one of the most

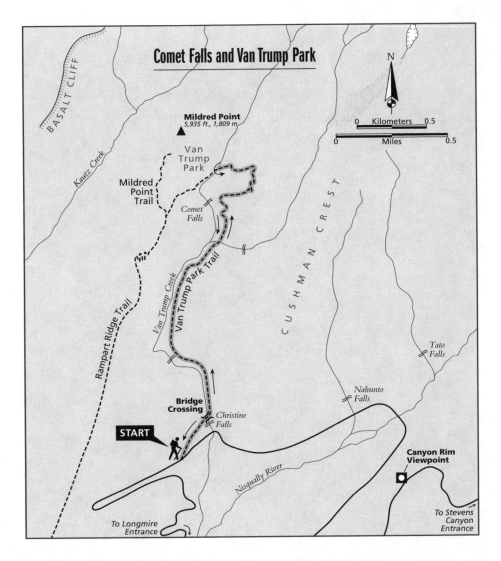

Comet Falls and Van Trump Park

Mildred Point
5,935 ft., 1,809 m

Van Trump Park

Mildred Point Trail

Comet Falls

BASALT CLIFF

Kautz Creek

Rampart Ridge Trail

Van Trump Creek

Van Trump Park Trail

CUSHMAN CREST

N

0   Kilometers   0.5

0   Miles   0.5

Tato Falls

Nahunto Falls

Bridge Crossing

Christine Falls

START

Canyon Rim Viewpoint

Nisqually River

To Longmire Entrance

To Stevens Canyon Entrance

impressive displays of water in the park—thunderous Comet Falls plunging 320 feet from the hanging valley of Van Trump Park. The falls make a scenic end to a quick hike, or you can continue upward where forests give way to the meadowy shoulders of Mount Rainier.

To reach the glorious alpine country above you, you'll climb steeply for 1 mile to the ridge above, with meadows and more meadows to explore, along with over-the-shoulder views of Mount Adams and Mount Saint Helens. From here you can ascend the ridge and wander off-trail northward toward Van Trump Glaciers, quickly trading flower meadows for rock and ice. Or head for 5,935-foot Mildred Point, the

hill rising immediately northwest of Van Trump Park, with a head-on view of the Kautz Glacier. In either case Mount Rainier looms directly above, and you'll certainly get a stiff neck if you gaze upward toward Point Success—the south summit—for too long.

After enjoying the meadows, retrace your route to the trailhead.

Key Points

0.0   Start at the north side of the small parking area on the northwest side of the road.

0.2   Cross Van Trump Creek on a high bridge.

1.4   Arrive at a footbridge across a stream; the main trail crosses the bridge to Comet Falls. An unsigned spur trail to the right (east) leads to another waterfall just visible from the main trail.

1.6   Reach the base of Comet Falls.

2.2   Arrive at a signed junction for Van Trump Park. To the right (north), the Van Trump Park Trail leads 0.2 mile to its end amid meadows. The left trail leads 1 mile to Mildred Point and 3.1 miles to the Wonderland Trail.

2.4   Arrive at Van Trump Park.

4.8   Arrive back at the trailhead and parking lot.

Hike Information

Local information

A Pocket Field Guide to the Plants and Animals of Mount Rainier by Joe Dreimiller.

Local events/attractions

Cascadian Dinner Train, Elbe, WA, (360) 569-2588, www.mrsr.com.

Accommodations

Whittaker's Bunkhouse, Ashford, WA, (360) 569-2439.

Mount Rainier Cougar Rock campground, (360) 569-2211.

Restaurants

Alexander's Country Inn, Ashford, WA, (360) 569-2300.

◀ *Comet Falls plunges from the flanks of Mount Rainier.*

29 Tatoosh Ridge/Tatoosh Lakes

This 7.8-mile out-and-back hike climbs to a high meadow and two lakes in the heart of the Tatoosh Wilderness just south of Mount Rainier National Park. From Tatoosh Ridge, you'll gaze out at the rocky summits of the Tatoosh Range and the snowy mass of Mount Rainier. Upper and Lower Tatoosh Lakes lie nestled in a deep cirque and make a pleasant destination for a day hike, and camping nearby offers opportunity to extend your trip to a weekend or longer.

Start: At the Tatoosh Trail 161 Trailhead.
Length: 7.8 miles out-and-back to Tatoosh Lakes.
Approximate hiking time: 4 hours.
Difficulty rating: Strenuous, due to steep terrain and elevation gain.
Trail surface: Forest and meadow trail.
Elevation gain: 1,800 feet.
Land status: Federal wilderness area.
Nearest town: Packwood, WA.
Other trail users: Equestrians.
Canine compatibility: Leashed dogs are permitted.

Trail contacts: Gifford Pinchot National Forest, Cowlitz Valley Ranger District, (360) 494-0600, www.fs.fed.us/gpnf.
Schedule: July through early October.
Fees/permits: Parking at the trailhead requires a $5.00 day pass or $30.00 annual Northwest Forest Pass. You can purchase a pass at www.fs.fed.us/r6/feedemo or by calling (800) 270-7504.
Maps: USGS Packwood 15-minute quad; Tatoosh Wilderness map.

Finding the trailhead: From U.S. Highway 12 in Packwood, turn northwest onto Skate Creek Road 52, opposite the ranger station, and drive 4 miles to eastbound Forest Service Road 5270, signed for Tatoosh Trail. Follow this dirt road 6 miles, bear right at a fork onto Forest Service Road 5272, and reach the trailhead after another mile. Parking is limited to turnouts alongside the road. *DeLorme: Washington Atlas & Gazetteer* page 48, C3.

The Hike

The Tatoosh Range is composed of a large body of granodiorite, an erosion-resistant granitic rock. Ancient glaciers, however, have carved deep cirques and jagged peaks out of this rock, and geologists believe that the Tatoosh Range in pre–Mount Rainier times (more than one million years ago) bore a strong resemblance to the mountains you'll find here today. The range is part of the ancient Cascade landscape upon which Mount Rainier was built. Luckily, the north half of this unique landscape lies partly within Mount Rainier National Park, while the southern half is protected from development by the Tatoosh Wilderness.

This scenic day hike or overnighter will lead you into the heart of the Tatoosh Wilderness to broad, sloping alpine meadows, peaks, vista points, and two gemlike alpine lakes cupped in a deep basin. The price you'll pay is a strenuous ascent, which

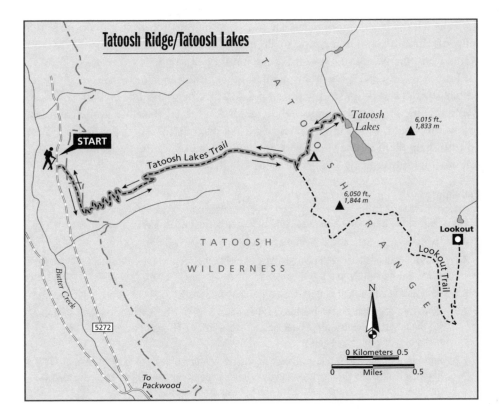

may seem longer than the altitude gain suggests. Carry plenty of water, as little is available en route. And, par for the course in the Cascades, mosquitoes and biting flies may annoy you in early to midsummer.

From the trailhead, the splendid view up the canyon to craggy Tatoosh summits and icebound Mount Rainier is just a sample of the scenery to come. The trail begins in a shady forest of western hemlock, silver fir, and Douglas fir, wasting little time in beginning the relentless ascent. A traverse above a Butter Creek tributary soon follows, across wildflower-brightened slopes covered in silver fir and Alaska yellow cedar. Ahead loom the grassy western slopes of the Tatoosh Range.

Finally, amid flower-filled meadows, the trail switchbacks past a spring and reaches a junction. Trails lead north and south, presenting you with two options.

For a quick side trip, take the trail heading south for 0.5 mile across meadowed slopes and through stands of Alaska yellow cedar, mountain hemlock, and subalpine fir to another west-trending ridge offering fine views of Mount Adams, Mount Saint Helens, and the tip of Mount Hood in the south. For even better views, continue following this faint trail southeastward, and then turn north for another 0.75 mile to Peak 6318, former site of the Tatoosh Lookout.

To reach the lakes, you'll follow the trail heading north from the junction. In 0.5 mile of climbing you'll reach a small notch, where excellent views of Mount Rainier and the northern Tatoosh Range unfold before you.

From here, the path, becoming fainter, quickly descends north and east, crosses a small stream, and drops steeply through forest to Upper and Lower Tatoosh Lakes, separated only by a small isthmus. While there are a few small camps in the basin just below the notch, camping is presently not allowed at the lakes themselves in an effort to help them recover from past damage. Instead, enjoy the beautiful alpine setting for the day, retracing your steps to the trailhead.

Key Points

0.0 Start at the trailhead on the east side of Forest Service Road 5272.

0.1 Pass a sign for the Tatoosh Wilderness boundary.

2.7 Pass a small unsigned trail heading east at a sign that reads TRAIL ABANDONED. Continue to follow the main trail up a switchback.

2.8 Pass and ignore a faint path leading off to the northwest.

3.0 Reach a signed junction with Tatoosh Lakes Trail 161B, turn left (north), and begin climbing the ridge. (**Note:** As an optional side trip, take Trail 161B right (south), traversing meadows, to the lookout site.)

3.2 Arrive at a notch with expansive views before descending steeply to Tatoosh Lakes. Ignore a faint north-leading trail along the ridge, instead descending steeply east toward the lakes. Camps can be found in the sandy saddle below the notch.

3.9 Arrive at Tatoosh Lakes.

7.8 Arrive back at the trailhead and parking area.

Hike Information

Accommodations
Hotel Packwood, Packwood, WA, (360) 494-5431.
USDA Forest Service Summit Creek campground, (360) 494-0600.

Restaurants
Club Café, Packwood, WA, (360) 494-5977.

30 Bear Creek Mountain

Start at a high trailhead on the dry east side of the Goat Rocks Wilderness and hike 7.2 miles out-and-back to this rocky peak with sweeping views of the Goat Rocks Peaks, Mount Rainier, and beyond. Much of the hike is through open country, passing through subalpine forests and meadows, before climbing the open, rocky slopes to the mountain's summit.

Start: At the Bear Creek Mountain Trailhead at Section 3 Lake.
Length: 7.2 miles out-and-back.
Approximate hiking time: 4 hours.
Difficulty rating: Moderate, due to modest length and elevation gain.
Trail surface: Meadow trail and rocky climb to the summit.
Elevation gain: 1,320 feet.
Land status: Federal wilderness area.
Nearest town: Packwood, WA.
Other trail users: Equestrians.
Canine compatibility: Leashed dogs are permitted.

Trail contacts: Wenatchee National Forest, Naches Ranger District, (509) 653-2205, www.fs.fed.us/r6/wenatchee.
Schedule: Mid-July through September.
Fees/permits: Parking at the trailhead requires a $5.00 day pass or a $30.00 annual Northwest Forest Pass (www.fs.fed.us/r6/feedemo or call 800-270-7504). Self-issued free permits are available at the trailhead for day and overnight use.
Maps: USGS White Pass 15-minute quad; USDA Forest Service Goat Rocks Wilderness map.

Finding the trailhead: From U.S. Highway 12, 8 miles east of White Pass and 47 miles west of Interstate 82 in Yakima, turn southwest onto the paved Tieton Road (Forest Service Road 12), signed for Clear Lake. Follow the pavement around the west and south shores of Clear Lake (sometimes dry) for 5.4 miles, then turn right just beyond Cold Creek onto gravel Forest Service Road 1205 toward Pinegrass and Section 3 Lake. Ignore a right-hand spur at 2.4 miles. After 2.6 miles bear right where Forest Service Road 742 forks left and uphill. Turn left after another 2.1 miles onto Forest Service Road 757, where a sign indicates the Bear Creek Mountain Trail. Continue straight ahead to a sign pointing to your trail after another 0.7 mile; bear right and, after 1.4 miles, turn right again onto an unsigned road (Forest Service Road 1204) that climbs a hill. This road is rough, narrow, and rutted, passable to passenger cars with high clearance. The trailhead parking area is at Section 3 Lake, after another 2.4 miles or 14.8 miles from US 12. *DeLorme Washington Atlas & Gazetteer* page 49, D6.

The Hike

Beginning at one of the highest-elevation trailheads in Washington's Cascades, this scenic day hike leads through timberline forests, across meadows filled with flowers for most of summer, and ascends a glacier-carved cirque to end atop an alpine peak where glorious views unfold of the snowy Goat Rocks, Mount Rainier, and Mount

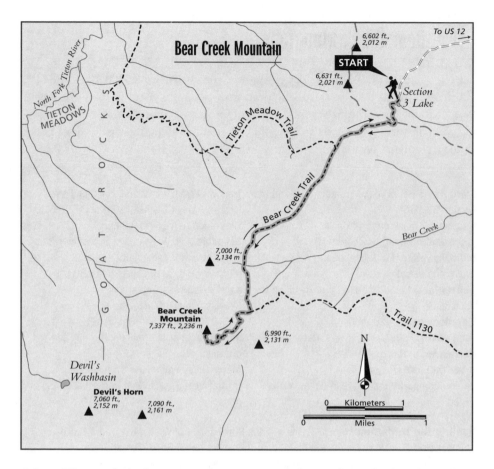

Adams. The scenic basins traversed en route and the small creeks that drain them may invite an overnight stay, which makes this area a particularly good choice for families introducing their children to high-mountain backpacking.

For the adventurous and experienced backpacker, Devil's Washbasin, a small lake located 1.5 difficult cross-country miles from Bear Creek Mountain, offers a dramatic destination and good fishing for cutthroat trout.

From the trailhead, the trail curves gently uphill past Section 3 Lake (not much more than a frog-filled pond) and into a timberline forest of subalpine fir and mountain hemlock. The dark volcanic spires of Pinegrass Ridge jut skyward just west of the trail and above you.

Soon you'll pass the wilderness boundary, beyond which the trail curves southwest onto sunny slopes where trailside trees thin enough to offer glimpses of the rocky massif of Bear Creek Mountain to the south.

After 0.5 mile cross the runoff of three springs watering a verdant, sloping meadow enlivened by the brilliant colors of paintbrush, lupine, bog orchid, and elephant-head. The trail ahead traverses above a small tarn, passes through another flower-speckled meadow and crosses a spring's runoff, then opens up into a more expansive but dry meadow. Soon thereafter it meets the Tieton Meadow Trail, forking right 0.8 mile from the trailhead.

Bear left, crossing more lovely meadows, and proceed into increasingly smaller groves of subalpine fir, mountain hemlock, white-bark pine, and Alaska yellow cedar. Upon entering the spacious cirque beneath Bear Creek Mountain, cross several small streams while winding among stunted trees and flower-filled meadows. You'll encounter another junction 1.7 miles from the last; bear right and begin your final steep ascent toward the summit.

Views expand with every step as you labor up the steep, rocky, and sandy trail. Snow patches may obscure the trail until late summer in some years. Eventually the trail crests the ridge just east of the rocky peak, where views of the massive bulk of Mount Adams to the south greet you. Follow the ridgeline trail as it winds upward among ground-hugging trees to the boulder-strewn summit just above.

The vast panorama that unfolds is breathtaking. The caldera formed by the peaks of Goat Rocks and the great icy cones of Mount Adams and Mount Rainier dominate the view from south to west. Northward beyond Fifes Peaks, Norse Peak, and the forested cinder cone landscape of the William O. Douglas Wilderness, peaks as far away as Mount Daniel near Snoqualmie Pass are visible.

Northeastward, the horizon is punctuated by the Stuart Range, and eastward the forested plateaus of the Cascades fade into the hazy distance of the Yakima Valley.

When you've soaked in the views, simply retrace your steps to the trailhead.

Key Points

0.0 Start on Trail 1130 on the west side of the parking lot.

0.3 Enter the Goat Rocks Wilderness.

0.8 Arrive at a junction where Tieton Meadow Trail 1128 heads off to the west (right). Continue straight ahead.

2.5 Arrive at a junction where Trail 1130 turns and heads left (east). Turn right on Trail 1130A toward the summit.

3.6 Reach the rocky, open summit ridgetop.

7.2 Return to the trailhead and parking lot.

Hike Information

Accommodations
Hotel Packwood, Packwood, WA, (360) 494-5431.
USDA Forest Service Summit Creek campground, (360) 494-0600.

Restaurants
Club Café, Packwood, WA, (360) 494-5977.

31 Norway Pass

This 4.6-mile out-and-back day hike surveys the destruction and subsequent natural revegetation of an area in the Mount Saint Helens National Volcanic Monument caught in the crosshairs of the 1980 eruption that devastated this region. The entire hike is open, winding through former forests obliterated by the blast. From Norway Pass, you'll get head-on views into the crater of the mountain, across Spirit Lake. Climb another mile to the summit of Mount Margaret for even better views.

Start: At the Boundary Trail 1 Trailhead.
Length: 4.6 miles out-and-back.
Approximate hiking time: 2–3 hours.
Difficulty rating: Easy, due to short distance and modest elevation gain.
Trail surface: Dirt trail.
Elevation gain: 908 feet.
Land status: National monument.
Nearest town: Randle, WA.
Other trail users: None.
Canine compatibility: Not dog friendly.
Trail contacts: Gifford Pinchot National Forest, Mount Saint Helens National Volcanic Monument, (360) 247-3900 or (360) 449-7800, www.fs.fed.us/gpnf.

Schedule: Late June through mid-October.
Fees/permits: Parking at the trailhead requires a $5.00 day pass or $30.00 annual Northwest Forest Pass. You can purchase a pass at www.fs.fed.us/r6/feedemo or by calling (800) 270-7504. Overnight camping permits are required; call (360) 247-3900.
Maps: USGS Spirit Lake SE 7.5-minute quad; Mt. St. Helens and Vicinity quad; Mount Saint Helens National Volcanic Monument visitor map.

Finding the trailhead: Forest Service Road 99, branching west from Forest Service Road 25 at a point 22 miles south of Randle and 44 miles from Cougar, is the main thoroughfare into Mount Saint Helens National Volcanic Monument. Follow FR 99 west from its junction with FR 25 (both are paved) for 9 miles to Forest Service Road 26 and turn right; continue 0.9 mile to the Norway Pass Trailhead parking area.

The Goat Mountain Trailhead (see Honorable Mentions section) can be reached by continuing north on FR 26 for another 3.7 miles, then turning west just north of Ryan Lake and following Forest Service Road 2612 west for 0.4 mile to the trailhead parking area. *DeLorme Washington Atlas & Gazetteer* page 33, B7.

The Hike

From the large parking area, Norway Trail will lead you steadily upward through the otherworldly post-eruption landscape, among flattened trees and standing snags stripped of all bark and branches by the intense blast from the volcano. The trail passes many small trees, mostly hemlock and silver fir that miraculously survived the blast because they were insulated by a deep blanket of snow. More than twenty years

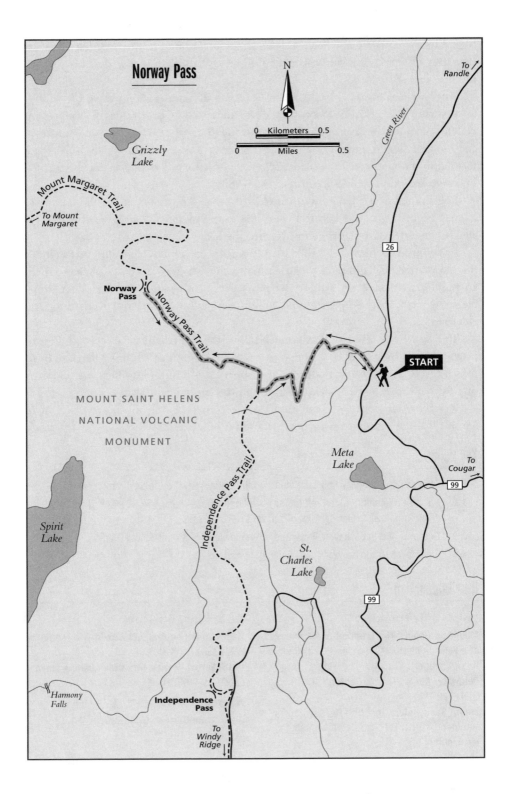

Norway Pass

N

Kilometers

Miles

Green River

To
Randle

26

Grizzly
Lake

Mount Margaret Trail

To Mount
Margaret

Norway
Pass

Norway Pass Trail

START

MOUNT SAINT HELENS

NATIONAL VOLCANIC

MONUMENT

Meta
Lake

To
Cougar

99

Spirit
Lake

Independence Pass Trail

St.
Charles
Lake

99

Harmony
Falls

Independence
Pass

To
Windy
Ridge

later, a host of other plants have also returned, including pink fireweed, a common colonizer of recovering landscapes. The trail is dry and exposed, and can be hot on summer days.

After a series of switchbacks, the route levels off and heads northwest to 4,508-foot Norway Pass and a head-on view of the blown-away north side of Mount Saint Helens. At times the lava dome building in the crater is visible, but clouds of steam and blowing dust frequently obscure it. You may also notice the small glacier that's formed in the crater as it's cooled. This is the Northwest's youngest glacier, formed since the last eruptive activity in the mid-1980s.

Logjammed Spirit Lake lies just below the pass. The slopes above the lake were swept bare of logs and debris following the eruption, perhaps by a giant wave created when a debris avalanche crashed into the lake.

In addition to fireweed, other plant pioneers are rapidly spreading throughout the devastated area, adding a green patina to the ash-gray landscape. Among them are raspberry, huckleberry, wild strawberry, valerian, false Solomon's seal, alder, thimbleberry, ferns, grasses, penstemon, lupine, avalanche lily, pearly everlasting, and elderberry.

The trail from Norway Pass connects with the Truman Trail, allowing hikers to climb another mile to even grander views at the summit of Mount Margaret, or to return to FR 99 at Windy Ridge via the Spirit Lake Basin. This offers the opportunity for a more extended backpack through this unique landscape.

Retrace your steps to the trailhead while contemplating the snowy summit of Mount Rainier visible to your north. Could it be next?

Key Points

0.0   Start at the Boundary Trail 1 Trailhead on the north side of the paved parking area.

1.2   Arrive at a junction. To the left (south) is Independence Ridge Trail 227A, leading 1.3 miles to Trail 227. Turn right (north) toward Norway Pass.

2.3   Descend to a gap, Norway Pass, and dramatic views of Mount Saint Helens.

4.6   Arrive back at the trailhead and parking area.

Hike Information

Local information

Mount St. Helens: The Eruption and Recovery of a Volcano by Rob Carson and Geff Hinds (photographer).
Coldwater Ridge Visitor's Center, (360) 274-2996.
Mount Saint Helens Institute (classes and seminars), (360) 891-5095, www.mtsthe lensinstitute.org.

Accommodations

Hampton House Bed and Breakfast, Randle, WA, (360) 497-3180.
USDA Forest Service Iron Creek campground, (360) 494-0600.

Restaurants

Big Bottom Bar and Grill, Randle, WA, (360) 497-9982.

A DAY IN HISTORY

The May 8, 1980, eruption of Mount Saint Helens may be a distant memory in the minds of many, but its effects are still starkly evident on the landscape. This eruption came as little surprise to some geologists. They knew that the volcano had been extremely active since the last ice age due to the lack of glacial scarring. The existing mountain stood on a violent predecessor that probably produced catastrophic eruptions.

With the energy of 21,000 atomic bombs, the blast and subsequent collapse of the north side of the mountain triggered a huge debris avalanche that obliterated or severely burned 230 square miles of forest. Pumice and gases heated to more than 1,000 degrees Fahrenheit barreled down the mountain at up to 670 miles an hour, burying many areas under 150 feet of mud and debris. Bark was ripped from trees as far as 15 miles away. By the time it was over, the mountain had lost 1,300 feet of elevation, ash covered parts of three states, and more than fifty people had lost their lives.

Given the widespread and catastrophic devastation, scientists studying the recovery of ecosystems around the mountain have noted remarkable recovery in some areas. Over time, erosion of ash has uncovered plant roots, and seeds have blown in from surrounding meadows and forests. Trees such as red alder and black cottonwood have begun to recolonize some areas, as have shrubs like willow. Even in the most devastated blast zones, prairie lupines have started to come back, fixing nitrogen for future arrivers. By 2200 visitors to Mount Saint Helens may well find forests much like they existed before the eruption. That's assuming that the mountain does not erupt again, which is far from certain.

32 Tumac Mountain and Twin Sisters Lakes

On this hike in the William O. Douglas Wilderness, you'll hike to the summit of the young volcanic cone of Tumac Mountain and across a volcanic plateau dotted with dozens of lakes ranging from deep, several-acre gems to shallow, marshy ponds. Spending a night at Twin Sisters Lakes will allow you more time to explore the geologically unique southern half of this wilderness area.

Start: On the Twin Sisters Trail at the Deep Creek campground.
Length: 9.6 miles out-and-back.
Approximate hiking time: 5 hours out-and-back.
Difficulty rating: Moderate, due to modest length and elevation gain.
Trail surface: Forest and meadow trail.
Elevation gain: 1,890 feet.
Land status: Federal wilderness area.
Nearest town: Yakima, WA.
Other trail users: Equestrians.
Canine compatibility: Leashed dogs are permitted.

Trail contacts: Wenatchee National Forest, Naches Ranger District, (509) 653-2205, www.fs.fed.us/r6/wenatchee.
Schedule: July through October.
Fees/permits: Parking at the trailhead requires a $5.00 day pass or $30.00 annual Northwest Forest Pass. You can purchase a pass at www.fs.fed.us/r6/feedemo or by calling (800) 270-7504.
Maps: USGS White Pass and Bumping Lake 15-minute quads; USDA Forest Service Wenatchee National Forest map; William O. Douglas Wilderness map.

Finding the trailhead: Proceed to the junction of the Bumping River Road and Washington Route 410, 23.1 miles east of Chinook Pass and 44 miles west of the Interstate 84/U.S. Highway 12 junction north of Yakima. Turn left (southwest) onto the Bumping River Road at a sign pointing to Bumping Lake, Camp Fife, and Goose Prairie. Follow the Bumping River Road past several campgrounds to the end of the pavement at 11.3 miles and continue straight ahead on the Deep Creek Road (1808) at 13.6 miles. After an additional 7.1 miles, you'll reach the road's end and trailhead at the Deep Creek campground. Parking is available along the road. The trail begins on the northwest side of the road at the Twin Sisters Trail sign. *DeLorme Washington Atlas & Gazetteer* page 49, C6.

The Hike

The volcanic Tumac Plateau, littered with dozens of lakes and ponds, stands in stark contrast to the jagged peaks and glaciers of Mount Rainier to the west, the alpine range of Nelson Ridge to the east, and the craggy headwaters of the Bumping River to the north. The glacier that overrode this lava plateau left behind an intriguing landscape of lakes as evidence of its passing, ranging from deep lakes of many acres to tiny, shallow ponds. Together they provide interesting insight into a range of plant communities and various stages of ecological succession as the lakes slowly transform to meadow. The abundant water also makes a productive breeding ground for

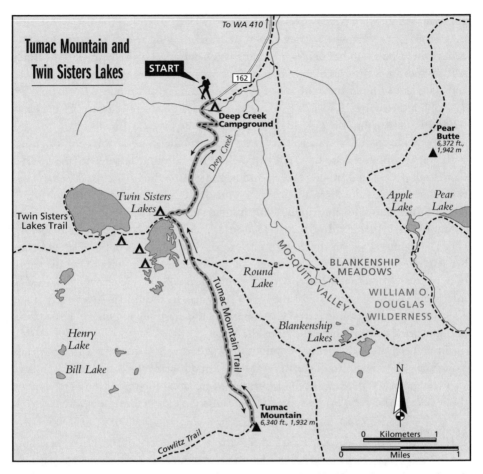

Tumac Mountain and
Twin Sisters Lakes

To WA 410

START

Deep Creek
Campground

Deep Creek

Twin Sisters
Lakes

Twin Sisters
Lakes Trail

Pear
Butte
6,372 ft.,
1,942 m

Apple
Lake

Pear
Lake

Round
Lake

MOSQUITO VALLEY

BLANKENSHIP
MEADOWS

WILLIAM O.
DOUGLAS
WILDERNESS

Blankenship
Lakes

Henry
Lake

Bill Lake

Tumac Mountain Trail

N

Tumac
Mountain
6,340 ft., 1,932 m

Cowlitz Trail

0   Kilometers   1

0   Miles   1

mosquitoes well into the month of August, and you're likely to share the trail with horses throughout the hiking season.

Experienced either as a day hike or an overnighter—with a layover at Twin Sisters Lakes, Mosquito Valley, or Pear and Apple Lakes—this interesting trip is an excellent introduction to the southern half of the William O. Douglas Wilderness.

The gently graded trail heads south, climbing through a forest of silver fir, mountain hemlock, and Alaska yellow cedar for just over 2 miles to the edge of the plateau at Little Twin Sisters Lake. Fishing for trout can be productive here and at other deep lakes on the plateau.

To reach the young volcanic cone of Tumac Mountain, turn left at the lake. You'll reach another junction after 0.4 mile. The left fork leads past (true-to-its-name) Mosquito Valley and beyond to beautiful Blankenship Meadows in 1.5 miles. A glance at your topographic map will reveal a network of trails on the plateau that can be arranged into a variety of loop trips.

Bear right at the junction toward your goal, visible on the nearby horizon to the southeast. The nearly level trail crosses subalpine meadows, discontinuous timber, and abundant wildflowers. Many small subalpine fir trees are invading the flat, wet meadows, growing in sites where snow lingers and the growing season is short. Botanists believe there are a number of reasons for the regeneration of typically treeless sites such as these meadows. A series of dry winters, light frost conditions, an adequate seed crop, and abundant summer moisture may have created the right conditions for these trees to establish themselves. It's likely that many of the meadows on the Tumac Plateau and other sites throughout the Cascades eventually will be overtaken by forest.

The grade increases on the northwest ridge of the cone as the trail junctions with the westbound Cowlitz Trail just below the summit, leading to the Pacific Crest Trail (PCT) in 2 miles. Stay left and negotiate one final switchback across volcanic slopes carpeted with heather to reach the 6,340-foot summit of Tumac Mountain, a former lookout site fringed with stunted subalpine fir.

From the top, the entire Tumac Plateau and dozens of lakes spread out before you. The alpine ridge on the eastern edge of the plateau hosts the highest peaks in the wilderness. To the south across miles of heavily forested mountains are the summits of the Goat Rocks, Mount Adams, and Mount Saint Helens. To the west is inescapable Mount Rainier and the Tatoosh Range; to the north, American Ridge rises above the Bumping River Canyon, with the startling jumble of Fifes Peaks pointing stark volcanic pinnacles into the sky.

From here, there are plenty of options for wandering. You can hike a 10-mile loop along Trail 44 (Cowlitz Trail), north on the PCT and back to the Sand Ridge Trail and Twin Sisters Lakes. The most popular campsites are along the trail at the north end of the smaller of the Twin Sisters Lakes. Some camps are closed for restoration.

Key Points

0.0 Start at the signed trailhead for the Twin Sisters Trail (980) on the northwest side of the road.

2.2 Arrive at a plateau above Twin Sisters Lakes and a junction with Sand Ridge Trail 1104. Turn left (southeast) onto the Sand Ridge Trail toward Tumac Mountain. Trails from here also lead toward Mosquito Valley, Pear and Apple Lakes, and Twin Lakes. (**Note:** Campsites at Twin Sisters Lakes make a good base for further exploration.)

2.6 Reach the junction of the Sand Ridge and Tumac Mountain Trails. Bear right (south) toward Tumac Mountain on Trail 944.

4.8 Arrive at the summit of Tumac Mountain.

9.6 Arrive back at the trailhead.

Hike Information

Accommodations
USDA Forest Service Deep Creek campground, (509) 653–2205.
Alta Crystal Resort Cabins, (800) 277–6475, www.altacrystalresort.com.

Restaurants
Grant's Brewery Pub, Yakima, WA, (509) 575–2922.

33 Foggy Flat (Mount Adams)

This 13.4-mile out-and-back day hike or backpack in the Mount Adams Wilderness leads from peaceful forests and lava flows to the fields of wildflowers and the ice-covered flanks of Washington's second tallest volcano. From a base camp in the scenic meadows of Foggy Flat, the intriguing volcanic landscape of Mount Adams invites exploration. By leaving a car at the Killen Creek Trailhead, you can return via a pleasant semi-loop along the Pacific Crest Trail (PCT) and descend through meadows and more meadows along the Killen Creek Trail.

Start: At the Potato Hill Trailhead along the PCT.

Length: 13.4 miles out-and-back, or a 14.4-mile semi-loop returning on the Killen Creek Trail.

Approximate hiking time: 6–7 hours.

Difficulty rating: Moderate, due to modest elevation gain and gentle grade.

Trail surface: Dirt trail.

Elevation gain: 1,800 feet.

Land status: Federal wilderness area.

Nearest town: Packwood, WA.

Other trail users: Equestrians.

Canine compatibility: Leashed dogs are permitted.

Trail contact: Gifford Pinchot National Forest, Mount Adams Ranger District, (509) 395-3400, www.fs.fed.us/gpnf

Schedule: July through September.

Fees/permits: Parking at Potato Hill is free. If you're planning to camp on the slopes above 7,000 feet between June 1 and September 30, you'll need a Cascade Volcano Pass, available at ranger stations in Randle and Trout Lake, at www.fs.fed.us/gpnf or self-issued at the Killen Creek Trailhead. The cost is $15 for a weekend pass or $30 for an annual pass.

Maps: USGS Green Mtn., Glaciate Butte, and Mt. Adams East 7.5-minute quads (**Note:** A portion of the Muddy Meadows Trail between the PCT and the Highline Trail is not shown on the quads); USDA Forest Service Mount Adams Wilderness map; Gifford Pinchot National Forest map.

Finding the trailhead: From Trout Lake, follow mostly paved Forest Service Road 23 for 24.4 miles to Forest Service Road 2329 (0.5 mile north of Baby Shoe Pass) and turn right. Ignoring several signed junctions, follow this one-lane road, paved for the first 1.5 miles and graveled thereafter, for 10.2 miles to the junction with paved Forest Service Road 5603. Turn right and drive another 1.7 miles to the PCT Trailhead parking area on the south side of the road, beneath the tall cinder cone of Potato Hill. (**Note:** The road beyond this point across the Yakima Reservation is closed to public traffic.)

Or from Packwood and Randle, follow Forest Service Road 25 south for a mile, then turn onto FR 23. Drive another 17.4 miles, then turn onto the one-lane paved Forest Service Road 21. After 4.8 miles turn right onto graveled Forest Service Road 56. After 3 miles bear right onto FR 5603, reaching the trailhead after another 6.8 miles, or 32.9 miles from Packwood and Randle. *DeLorme Washington Atlas & Gazetteer* page 34, B4.

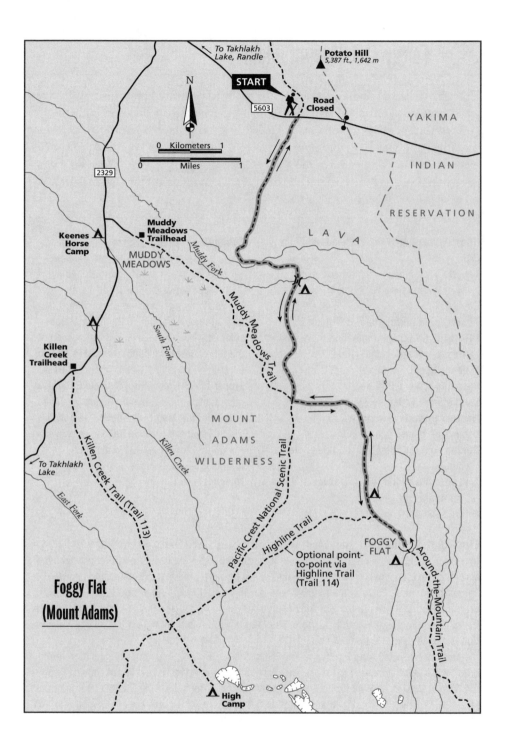

**Foggy Flat
(Mount Adams)**

The Hike

Mount Adams, Washington's second highest mountain, may take second place in many respects to Mount Rainier, Washington's largest and best-known volcano, but it offers solitude and a wilderness experience unavailable in the popular Mount Rainier National Park to the north.

Mount Adams itself is broad and asymmetrical—far from being simply one volcano, geologists believe it's composed of a series of andesite cones overlying one another, building over time to its bulky, ice-covered summit today. And unlike its sibling volcanoes under the nervous watch of scientists, Mount Adams is considered dormant; what little activity that presently exists (steam and hydrogen sulfide gas emissions from the summit area) appears to be diminishing.

This highly scenic and pleasant long day trip, better done as a two- to three-day backpack, surveys nearly the full range of scenery in the Mount Adams Wilderness, from open pine forests to stunted subalpine fir, from flower-filled meadows to broken lava flows, and from clear spring-fed streams to glacial torrents. And while many hikers visiting the north side of Mount Adams access the area via the more popular Killen Creek Trail to the west, you're more likely to find solitude here. A worthwhile side trip on the Highline Trail from Foggy Flat climbs above timberline to the very foot of Mount Adams, where broken glaciers, fresh moraines, hidden tarns, and vast lava fields invite seemingly endless off-trail exploration opportunities for experienced hikers and mountaineers.

The trail maintains a gentle to moderate grade along most of its length but is sandy with Mount Saint Helens fallout. Carry a good insect repellent—mosquitoes can be troublesome from the Muddy Meadows Trail to timberline.

The southbound Pacific Crest Trail begins opposite the trailhead below the conical Potato Hill. Obtain a backcountry permit at the Trout Lake ranger station or be sure to fill one out at the register box located a few yards down the trail. The initial 1.6 miles of the trail is a pleasant, gentle descent. Lupine and bear grass grow among the open forests of young lodgepole pines, and trees frame glimpses of massive Mount Adams ahead of you. Descend along the western margin of an impressive recent lava flow to your left, soon thereafter reaching the cold, vigorous waters of Lava Springs and the wilderness boundary. A good campsite lies just above and east of the spring.

Beyond the spring, the trail ascends at a gentle grade, skirting the southern edge of the lava flow and then fording a silty stream before curving southeast to bridge the torrent of Muddy Fork, laden with glacial silt. From here, you'll enter a peaceful forest of tall silver firs and hike moderately uphill for about 0.75 mile before crossing through a patch of burned forest with charred, sun-bleached snags.

The trail ahead enters a pine, fir, and hemlock forest, passing amid beautiful meadows speckled with wildflowers before it reaches a four-way junction 2.5 miles

The volcanic wonderland of Mount Adams above Foggy Flat.

from Lava Springs. Turn left (east) at the junction onto the Muddy Meadows Trail, climbing a gentle to moderate grade through forests and meadows for 1.25 miles to the Green Timber camp. You'll find good campsites here near a small stream.

The forest thins above the camp as the trail winds upward over old glacial moraines to the junction with the Highline Trail, 1.9 miles from the PCT. Turning left (southeast), the Highline Trail descends briefly before climbing, sometimes steeply, past small meadows and timberline forest for 0.9 mile to the lovely green spread of Foggy Flat. Enlivened by myriad wildflowers, rimmed by subalpine forest and rubbly moraines, watered by a cold, clear creek, and backdropped by the north face of Mount Adams, Foggy Flat makes an immensely scenic base camp for forays toward the ice-clad flanks of Mount Adams, only a short distance away via the Highline Trail. Look for campsites well back into the forest and avoid camping too close to the fragile meadow.

From here, you can simply retrace your steps, or plan a return using a car shuttle by following the Highline Trail west to Killen Creek, descending via Killen Creek Trail 113. While the trip will add about a mile to your total mileage, the scenery along the way, with sprawling meadows and still more views of Mount Adams, is well worth the added effort.

Key Points

0.0 Start on PCT 2000 at the Potato Hill Trailhead on the north side of the road.

1.4 Cross Lava Springs and a sign marking the boundary of the Mount Adams Wilderness.

1.7 Cross a stream with large camps on the left (east) side of the trail.

2.3 Cross South Fork Muddy Creek on a large bridge.

3.9 Reach a junction with Highline Trail 113 and turn left (east). The trail to the right leads to Muddy Meadows, while the PCT continues straight ahead to a junction with Highline Trail 114.

5.8 Reach a junction with Highline Trail 114 and turn left (east) toward Foggy Flat. (**Note:** To return from Foggy Flat via Killen Creek, follow the right-leading (west) section of the Highline Trail from here to Killen Creek Trail 113, where you'll turn right (north) and descend to the Killen Creek Trailhead.)

6.7 Reach Foggy Flat, a large, flat meadow area with camps just west of a stream.

13.4 Arrive back at the trailhead.

Hike Information

Accommodations

Hotel Packwood, Packwood, WA, (360) 494-5431.
USDA Forest Service Takhlakh Lake and Horseshoe Lake campgrounds, (509) 395-3400.

Restaurants

Club Café, Packwood, WA, (360) 494-5977.

HIKING WASHINGTON'S VOLCANOES

There's little that matches the feeling of standing high on the snowy flanks of one of Washington's five volcanoes. And while most routes to their upper slopes require glacier travel and mountaineering skills, each of the three South Cascades volcanoes offer routes accessible without the use of roped glacier travel. On Mount Rainier a strenuous hike from Paradise across the Muir Snowfield leads hikers to Camp Muir, base camp for the mountain's most popular climbing route. Using the South Spur route on Mount Adams, strong hikers can reach the summit of the state's second highest volcano in a day or two. The barren southern slopes of Mount Saint Helens offer access to the summit and crater rim, with dizzying views into the depths of the mountain's blasted-out crater.

None of these trips, however, is easy, and their hazards shouldn't be underestimated. Mountain weather can change rapidly—with sunny skies turning to whiteout conditions within minutes, travel can become hazardous, particularly on Mount Rainier, where hikers have perished by straying onto the heavily crevassed Nisqually Glacier. Other potential hazards include rockfalls, dehydration, altitude sickness, or just plain exhaustion. But with preparedness and a healthy dose of caution, you'll be able to experience the landscape of rock, snow, and ice that makes Washington's volcanoes unique.

34 Lewis River

This day hike or backpack follows the last remaining primitive section of the Lewis River in the Gifford Pinchot National Forest. Along the way you'll pass through grand old-growth forest of stately Douglas fir, western hemlock, and western red cedar, always within sight or sound of the rushing river. Two trailheads offer the option of either doing a shorter 5.4-mile out-and-back hike or a longer 9.4-mile one-way trip by leaving a car at the upper trailhead.

Start: At the Lewis River Trailhead of Forest Service Road 9039.
Length: 5.4 miles out-and-back, 9.4 miles point-to-point.
Approximate hiking time: 3 hours for shorter trip, 5 hours for longer point-to-point trip.
Difficulty rating: Easy, due to gentle terrain.
Trail surface: Dirt trail.
Elevation gain: 100 feet for shorter hike, 600 feet for longer hike.
Land status: National forest.
Nearest town: Carson, WA; Cougar, WA.
Other trail users: Equestrians, mountain bikes.
Canine compatibility: Leashed dogs are permitted.

Trail contacts: Gifford Pinchot National Forest, Mount Saint Helens National Volcanic Monument, (360) 247-3900, www.fs.fed.us/gpnf.
Schedule: March through mid-December.
Fees/permits: Parking at the trailhead requires a $5.00 day pass or $30.00 annual Northwest Forest Pass. You can purchase a pass at www.fs.fed.us/r6/feedemo or by calling (800) 270-7504.
Maps: USGS Burnt Peak 7.5-minute quad (the Spencer Butte 7.5-minute quad is required for the upper portion of the river); USDA Forest Service Gifford Pinchot National Forest map.

Finding the trailhead: Follow Forest Service Road 90 east from Cougar for 23.1 miles (4.75 miles east of the Lewis River bridge) to the hard-to-spot junction with left-forking (westbound) Forest Service Road 9039. Turn here, following gravel FR 9039 for 0.7 mile to the bridge over the Lewis River. Parking is on the south side of the bridge, while the trail begins on the north side of the river. *DeLorme Washington Atlas & Gazetteer* page 34, D1.

The Hike

Born on the icy flanks of Mount Adams and draining a vast region of the southern Cascades, the Lewis River cuts a deep swath through the mountains on its journey to the lower Columbia River.

Excessive logging has marred this densely forested region, and logging roads follow the Lewis River for much of its length. However, this easy trail follows the river for 9.4 miles along its middle reaches. This area is being preserved by the Forest Service and has been identified for eventual designation as a federal Wild and Scenic River. Its primitive condition lets you experience what many of the region's forests were before logging.

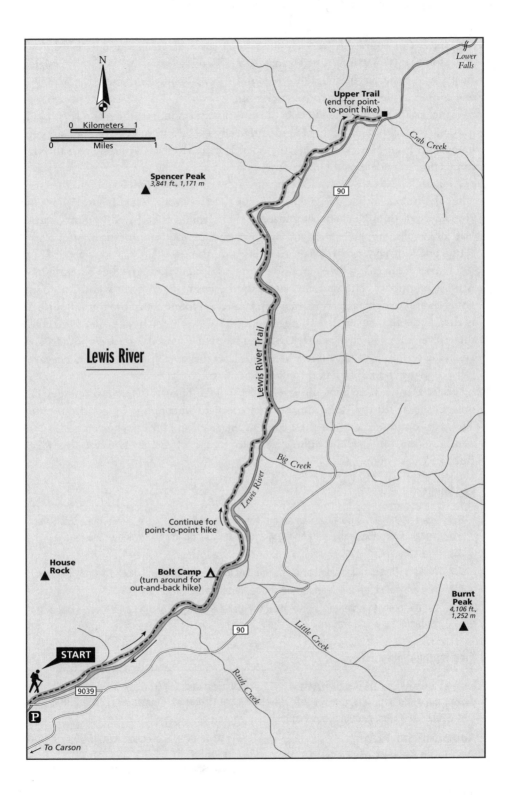

N

0 Kilometers 1

0 Miles 1

Spencer Peak
3,841 ft., 1,171 m

Upper Trail
(end for point-
to-point hike)

*Lower
Falls*

Crab Creek

90

Lewis River

Lewis River Trail

Big Creek

Lewis River

Continue for
point-to-point hike

**House
Rock**

Bolt Camp
(turn around for
out-and-back hike)

**Burnt
Peak**
4,106 ft.,
1,252 m

90

Little Creek

START

Rush Creek

9039

P

← *To Carson*

Hikers can enjoy this leisurely hike along the wide river through a lush low-elevation forest of western red cedar, Douglas fir, western hemlock, and bigleaf maple where the varying hues of green in the ferns, epiphytes draping the branches, and mosses along the trail are mesmerizing.

Anglers are also attracted here by the promise of landing rainbow and large Dolly Varden trout, although fishing is presently only catch-and-release. The season generally runs from May 30 through October 31. The river is also home to a thriving population of endangered bull trout.

The trail heads northeast from the bridge, passing a spur trail leading to the river. After 0.3 mile, another unsigned trail joins the river route on the left. Follow the riverside trail through shady virgin forest. The ground is carpeted by ferns, vanilla leaf, and oxalis; thimbleberries and raspberries offer good summertime snacking en route. The lush understory makes camping almost impossible.

The river alternates between noisy rapids and calm, slow stretches where fishing is most productive. The trail also alternates between the riverbank and the forest, which has all the characteristics of a temperate rain forest. Since the forest floor here is already densely covered with vegetation, it's difficult for new plants to establish themselves. The best chance a tree seedling has to get started is on a slightly decayed fallen log or stump, called a nurse log. Plants also may establish footholds on decayed parts of living trees, such as on broken branches.

Large Rush Creek joins the river from the southeast at 2.1 miles, and after 2.7 miles hikers reach the Bolt camp shelter, a lean-to surrounded by good campsites. The trail continues along the west bank of the river, and hikers who've arranged for transportation can trek the entire 9.4 miles to FR 90 below Lower Lewis River Falls, a pleasant endpoint.

Key Points

0.0 Start at the gravel parking area on the south side of FR 9039 just before the Lewis River bridge. Cross the bridge and find Lewis River Trail 31 on the north side of the road.

2.1 Cross Rush Creek.

2.7 Arrive at Bolt camp, a good turnaround point for an out-and-back day hike along the river.

5.4 Arrive back at the trailhead for the shorter out-and-back hike.

9.4 For the point-to-point trip, arrive at FR 90 and the bridge over the Lewis River, a good endpoint for a one-way trip.

Hike Information

Local events/attractions
Carson Hot Springs Resort, Carson, WA, (509) 427-8292, www.carsonhotspringsresort.com.

Accommodations
USDA Forest Service Paradise Creek campground, (509) 427-3200.
Lone Fir Resort, Cougar, WA, (360) 238-5210.

Restaurants
Big River Grill, Stevenson, WA, (509) 427-4888.
El Rio, Stevenson, WA, (509) 427-4479.

35 Cultus Creek Loop

This 6.9-mile trip makes a loop into the heart of the scenic Indian Heaven Wilderness and offers a healthy sampling of the area's lakes, forests, and meadows. As a day hike or overnighter, this moderately difficult trip offers a good introduction for novice campers and backpackers. Camps at many of the lakes make a good base for further excursions to remote lakes or along the Pacific Crest Trail (PCT). Come here in fall and you'll also find some of the best berry picking around.

Start: At the Cultus Creek campground.
Length: 6.9-mile loop.
Approximate hiking time: 3½ hours.
Difficulty rating: Moderate, due to modest length and elevation gain.
Trail surface: Forest and meadow trail.
Elevation gain: 1,450 feet.
Land status: Federal wilderness area.
Nearest town: Trout Lake, WA.
Other trail users: Equestrians.
Canine compatibility: Leashed dogs are permitted.
Trail contacts: Gifford Pinchot National Forest, Mount Adams Ranger District, (509) 395-3400, www.fs.fed.us/gpnf.

Schedule: Best hiked July through October.
Fees/permits: Parking at the trailhead and campground requires a $5.00 day pass or $30.00 annual Northwest Forest Pass. You can purchase a pass at www.fs.fed.us/r6/feedemo or by calling (800) 270-7504. Camping permits can be purchased at ranger stations.
Maps: USGS Lone Butte 7.5-minute quad; USDA Forest Service Gifford Pinchot National Forest map; Indian Heaven Wilderness map.

Finding the trailhead: From Trout Lake (20 miles north of White Salmon off Washington Route 14), follow Washington Route 141 east for about 8 miles to the Peterson Prairie campground. Turn north onto gravel Forest Service Road 24, following signs indicating Sawtooth Berry Fields. After about 9 miles you'll reach the Cultus Creek campground. You'll find parking just west of FR 24 at the north end of the campground, or at the south end of the campground near Trail 33. *DeLorme Washington Atlas & Gazetteer* page 34, D2.

The Hike

The Indian Heaven Wilderness sits astride the crest of the Cascade Range south of Mount Adams. Several prominent mile-high peaks rise above a densely forested, gently rolling high plateau dotted with dozens of small lakes waiting for exploration. You'll be able to sample many of these lakes in this moderate loop through the middle of the wilderness, and the gentle terrain here makes it a good destination for families and children. If you're an angler, be sure to bring along your fishing rod.

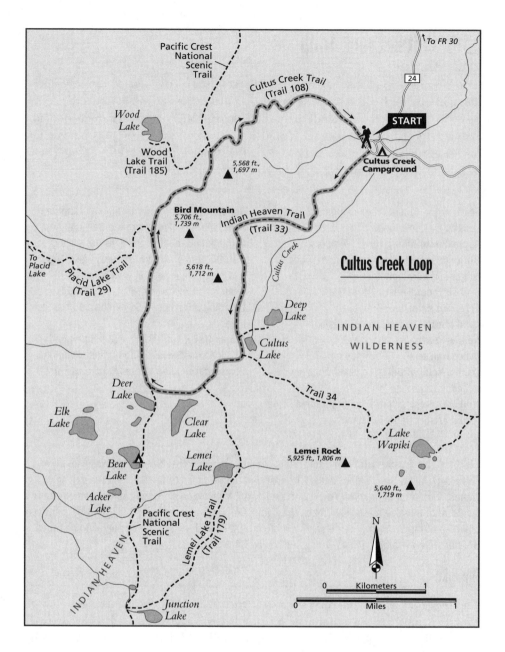

Weekend trips are probably the best way to enjoy this small 20,650-acre wilderness. Besides fishing, this area is renowned for its huckleberry thickets, and berry picking is a popular activity in August and September. You'll also find that horse-packing is common here. And where there is so much water, you'll also have to endure mosquitoes, which reach their peak during July.

Looking north toward imposing Mount Adams.

To begin the hike, walk southeastward along the campground loop road to the sign marking the beginning of Trail 33.

The trail immediately begins climbing steadily southwestward through a forest of hemlock, spruce, and fir. After 0.75 mile the trail approaches Cultus Creek but quickly jogs north, climbing away from the creek. After getting most of your climbing behind you in the first mile, you'll enjoy a good rest stop with a fine view to the north, including Sawtooth Mountain, Mount Adams, Goat Rocks, and Mount Rainier.

From here to Cultus Lake, the route traverses a subalpine basin that an ancient glacier carved into the slopes of Bird Mountain, its rocky cliffs visible above you off to the right of the trail.

After hiking 2.5 miles from the trailhead, you'll reach a junction at the outlet of 5,050-foot Cultus Lake with a left-forking trail leading a short distance to scenic Deep Lake.

The main trail continues forward, passing Cultus Lake and soon climbing over a 5,100-foot saddle amid hemlocks and firs. You'll soon reach a junction for the Lemei Lake Trail, branching left amid pink heather, bear grass, and avalanche lilies. Bear right on the main trail, quickly descending past a talus field to Clear Lake. Like most lakes in Indian Heaven, Clear Lake has no inflow or outflow. A good view of craggy Lemei Rock is available from the trail west of the lake.

Beyond Clear Lake the trail descends through increasing forest to join the Pacific Crest Trail above Deer Lake immediately after crossing an early-season creek. Fair campsites are located on benches below the trail, but the best campsites in the area are located at Bear Lake, 0.6 mile to the south along the PCT.

Turn right (north) onto the PCT, gently traversing the west slopes of Bird Mountain through a subalpine forest. Numerous early-season creeks cross the trail, most of which offer possible camping. Ignore stretches of the abandoned Cascade Crest Trail that frequently cross the PCT and are visible at times paralleling the main trail. Avalanche lilies are common here in early summer.

The trail eventually leads northeast, passes above a shallow tarn (possible campsites), and continues through a jumble of volcanic boulders to the signed Wood Lake Trail, branching left.

You will come to a junction 2.1 miles from Deer Lake. Turn right here onto Cultus Creek Trail 108, quickly reaching a saddle at 5,237 feet. Experienced hikers may want to leave the trail and follow the crest of the Cascades south for 0.75 mile to 5,706-foot Bird Mountain for an all-encompassing view.

Back at the saddle, follow the trail as it descends steadily for 1.5 miles to the trailhead. Abundant huckleberries and views of Mount Adams are major distractions along the final segment of this scenic slice of Indian Heaven.

Key Points

0.0 Start on Indian Heaven Trail 33 at the south end of the Cultus Creek campground and parking area.

1.1 Arrive at a switchback with expansive views toward Mount Adams and the Goat Rocks.

2.5 Arrive at an intersection with Deep Lake Trail 33A to the left. (**Note:** The short 0.1-mile trail to Deep Lake makes a good side trip.) Continue straight ahead past Cultus Lake on the main trail.

2.7 Reach a junction with Lemei Trail 34 to the left. Continue forward on the main trail.

3.1 Arrive at a junction with Lemei Lake Trail 179 heading off to the left, leading 1.5 miles to PCT Trail 2000. Continue forward on Indian Heaven Trail 33.

3.4 Pass Clear Lake and arrive at a junction with the PCT. To the left, the trail passes Deer Lake and, in 0.6 mile, Bear Lake, with good campsites. Continue forward on what becomes the PCT.

4.4 Arrive at a junction with Placid Lake Trail 29 to the left (west). Continue forward (north) on the PCT.

5.4 Wood Lake Trail 185 cuts back to the left (southwest), while the PCT continues straight ahead. Turn right off the PCT onto Cultus Creek Trail 108.

6.9 Arrive back at the trailhead at the north end of the Cultus Creek campground.

Hike Information

Accommodations

USDA Forest Service Cultus Creek campground (at the trailhead), (509) 395-3400.
Kelly's B&B, Trout Lake, WA, (509) 395-2488, www.thefarmbnb.com.

Restaurants

Serenity's, Trout Lake, WA, (509) 395-2500.
KJ's Bear Creek Café, Trout Lake, WA, (509) 395-2525.

36 Falls Creek Falls

This pleasant 3.4-mile out-and-back day hike leads you through low-elevation forest to one of the most impressive waterfalls accessible by trail in the Gifford Pinchot National Forest. Thundering Falls Creek Falls, the endpoint of this short hike, plunges more than 200 feet, surrounded by lush fern- and moss-draped cliffs.

Start: At the trailhead for the Falls Creek Trail (Trail 152A).
Length: 3.4 miles out-and-back.
Approximate hiking time: 2 hours.
Difficulty rating: Easy, due to short length.
Trail surface: Dirt trail.
Elevation gain: 950 feet.
Land status: National forest.
Nearest town: Carson, WA.
Other trail users: Mountain bikes.
Canine compatibility: Leashed dogs are permitted.

Trail contacts: Gifford Pinchot National Forest, Wind River Work Center, (509) 427-3200, www.fs.fed.us/gpnf.
Schedule: Mid-April through October.
Fees/permits: Parking at the trailhead requires a $5.00 day pass or $30.00 annual Northwest Forest Pass. You can purchase a pass at www.fs.fed.us/r6/feedemo or by calling (800) 270-7504.
Maps: USGS Wind River 7.5-minute quad; USDA Forest Service Gifford Pinchot National Forest map.

Finding the trailhead: Follow the Wind River Road north from Carson off Washington Route 14, passing the left turnoff to Government Mineral Springs after 15 miles. Bear right here, and after another 0.7 mile turn right where a sign indicates the Falls Creek Trail. Follow this gravel road, avoiding two signed turnoffs and left-branching Forest Service Road 610 after 1.6 miles. Two miles from the Wind River Road, turn right onto Forest Service Road 3062/057 where a sign points to Trail 152A. You will reach the turnaround at the trailhead within 0.3 mile. *DeLorme Washington Atlas & Gazetteer* page 24, A1.

The Hike

To hikers familiar with the southern Cascades, *waterfalls* and *Columbia Gorge* are synonymous. But the trails to those waterfalls, mostly on the Oregon side and a short drive from Portland off Interstate 84, can be less than peaceful on weekends, filled with throngs of tourists and locals alike out for a quick jaunt.

Washington's Falls Creek Falls, with a three-tiered descent of about 200 feet, are well off the beaten track, and are the rewarding destination of this pleasant, easy day hike above the Wind River.

From the trailhead, the trail briefly follows an old road, passing through second-growth Douglas fir. Soon, however, the route narrows and enters a virgin forest of

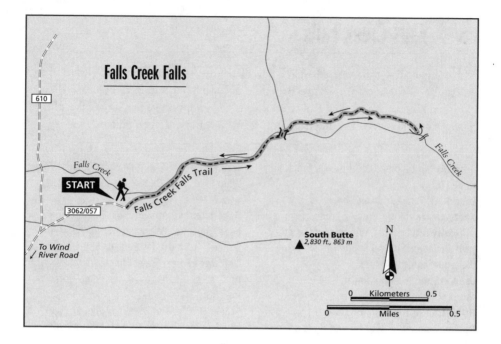

Falls Creek Falls

610

Falls Creek

START

3062/057

Falls Creek Falls Trail

Falls Creek

To Wind River Road

South Butte
2,830 ft., 863 m

N

| 0 | Kilometers | 0.5 |

| 0 | Miles | 0.5 |

Douglas fir and western larch. The needles of the larch, the only deciduous conifer in the state of Washington, turn fiery gold in fall. It's found typically on the drier eastern slopes of the Cascades, but the western slopes of the southern Cascades are comparatively dry, and the valley of lower Falls Creek provides a suitable habitat for drought-tolerant trees such as the larch.

Tumultuous Falls Creek, always close at hand but often inaccessible as you hike along the trail, is interrupted at times by many deep, inviting pools. The trail proceeds through giant western hemlocks and Douglas firs to a well-designed and interesting bridge across the creek after 0.4 mile. You'll find a small campsite on a bench just above the bridge, beside the trail. Beyond this point, giant red cedar trees join the forest, and the trail begins climbing moderately.

The terrain becomes increasingly rocky, crossing a boulder-filled gully on a bridge as an overpowering roar fills the air. Suddenly the falls appear—one of the most dramatic displays of water in Washington's southern Cascades.

The trail ends opposite the lower fall amid mossy, spray-dampened boulders—a cool spot on even the hottest summer days. From the falls, retrace the route to the trailhead.

Falls Creek Falls. ▶

Key Points

0.0 Start at the north side of the small parking area for the Falls Creek Trail.

0.4 Cross a suspension bridge over Falls Creek.

1.4 Cross another bridge over a boulder-filled streambed.

1.7 Reach Falls Creek Falls.

3.4 Arrive back at the trailhead.

Hike Information

Local events/attractions

Carson Hot Springs Resort, Carson, WA, (509) 427-8292, www.carsonhotspringsresort.com.

Accommodations

USDA Forest Service Paradise Creek or Beaver Creek campgrounds, (877) 444-6777 (reservations).

Skamania Lodge, Stevenson, WA, (509) 427-7700.

Restaurants

Big River Grill, Stevenson, WA, (509) 427-4888.

El Rio, Stevenson, WA, (509) 427-4479.

Honorable Mentions

South Cascades

H40 Fish and Crag Lakes

North of the Bumping River, the Cascade crest sheds its blanket of timber and rises to craggy heights. Many timberline lakes rest in shady, east-facing cirques below the 6,000-foot-plus peaks. This fine weekender visits several mountain lakes at the headwaters of the Bumping River in the William O. Douglas Wilderness. Crag Lake itself makes a good base camp for exploring the lakes to the north along the Cascade crest. The Three Lakes—two of which lie within Mount Rainier National Park—are an easy 2-mile jaunt west of Crag Lake.

Drive Washington Route 123 to its junction with eastbound Forest Service Road 44 (Carlton Creek Road), 0.25 mile south of the Mount Rainier National Park boundary, about 54 miles southeast of Enumclaw and 9.5 miles northeast of Packwood. Follow gravel FR 44 northeastward (there are some steep and narrow stretches) for 7.1 miles to the trailhead at a permanent roadblock. Park here, where a spur road descends to Carlton Creek. For more information, contact the Wenatchee National Forest, (360) 494–0600, www.fs.fed.us/r6/wenatchee. *DeLorme Washington Atlas & Gazetteer* page 49, B5.

H41 Little Crow Basin

North of Chinook Pass and northeast of Mount Rainier, the Cascade crest loses elevation, and its contours become more rounded and heavily forested. This is a ridge-line hike much of the way, and the lack of appreciable elevation gain, broad vistas, and colorful wildflowers combine to make it a very attractive weekend trip. Much of the crest route passes through the site of an old burn. Wildflowers are common in sunny openings, including lupine, phlox, yarrow, wild strawberry, waterleaf, glacier lily, buttercup, yellow violet, and senecio. You can return to the trailhead by following the Pacific Crest Trail south over the ridge into the alpine bowl of Big Crow Basin.

Drive east from Chinook Pass on Washington Route 410 for 22.5 miles, or west 40.5 miles from Yakima to Little Naches River Road (Forest Service Road 19) and turn northwest, following the course of the Little Naches. Turn left onto Forest Service Road 1902 after 2.6 miles, quickly crossing the river via a bridge. At this and subsequent junctions, follow signs indicating Raven Roost. Follow this good dirt road for 12 miles to an excellent viewpoint, from which you can see Mount Rainier in the southwest and Fifes Peaks in the south, just beyond the short spur road to Raven Roost (an even better vista point). Dispersed camping is available at this junction. Trailhead parking is available at Raven Roost. For more information, contact the Mount Baker–Snoqualmie National Forest, (206) 470–4060, www.fs.fed.us/r6/mbs/index.html. *DeLorme Washington Atlas & Gazetteer* page 65, D5.

H42 Grand Park

The trail to Grand Park starts at the highest trailhead in Mount Rainier National Park and travels through an alpine environment before descending through subalpine forests and flower fields to beautiful Grand Park. There you'll find a flower-filled meadow nearly 2 miles long and 0.75 mile wide, as well as an interesting perspective of the north side of Mount Rainier.

To get there from Washington Route 410 in Mount Rainier National Park, 3.4 miles north of Cayuse Pass and 40 miles southeast of Enumclaw, turn west onto the road signed for the White River and Sunrise. Follow this paved road 15.5 miles to the huge parking area at Sunrise Lodge. For more information, contact Mount Rainier National Park, (360) 569–2211, www.nps.gov/mora. *DeLorme Washington Atlas & Gazetteer* page 48, A3.

H43 Burroughs Mountain

This ridge running along the northeast flanks of Mount Rainier National Park walks a line between heaven and earth through glorious alpine country in the icy shadows of the Emmons Glacier on Mount Rainier. The 7-mile out-and-back trail is strenuous, and snow may cover portions of the trail all year. Along the way to the 7,300-foot ridgetop you'll pass Shadow and Frozen Lakes.

To get there, drive 43 miles from Enumclaw east on Washington Route 410 to the White River entrance of Mount Rainier National Park. Drive to the Sunrise Road and follow it 17 miles west to the large parking lot and visitor center at the road's end. The trailhead is on the south side of the parking lot. For more information, contact Mount Rainier National Park, (360) 569–2211, www.nps.gov/mora. *DeLorme Washington Atlas & Gazetteer* page 48, A3.

H44 Round Pass to Gobblers Knob

This day hike or overnighter offers a tremendous vista from the lookout atop 5,485-foot Gobblers Knob, an easy downhill stroll to Goat Lake within tiny (3,050 acres) Glacier View Wilderness, and solitude seldom enjoyed within the national park. Perhaps no other vantage point offers such a commanding look at the immense hulk of Mount Rainier.

Drive east from the Nisqually entrance for 0.8 mile and turn northeast onto the unpaved West Side Road. Due to a washout, the road is closed at the 3-mile point; hikers must walk the final 4 miles of the road to reach the old Round Pass Trailhead. The National Park Service is still deciding the future of this road, so check with park headquarters on its status before beginning the hike. For more information, contact Mount Rainier National Park, (360) 569–2211, www.nps.gov/mora. *DeLorme Washington Atlas & Gazetteer* page 48, B1.

H45 Grove of the Patriarchs

Walk softly through this cathedral-like grove of giants on the southeast side of Mount Rainier National Park. This short trail, just over 1 mile and easily walked in less than an hour, will nevertheless make you feel dwarfed amid 1,000-year-old Douglas firs, western red cedars, and hemlocks, some with trunks more than 30 feet in diameter.

Drive 41 miles from Enumclaw east on Washington Route 410 to Washington Route 123. Follow WA 123 south for 11 miles to the Stevens Canyon entrance to the park. The trailhead is just west of the entrance station. For more information, contact Mount Rainier National Park, (360) 569–2211, www.nps.gov/mora. *DeLorme Washington Atlas & Gazetteer* page 48, B4.

H46 Stevens Canyon Road to Snow Lake

Resting in a deep cirque in the shadow of the highest Tatoosh Range summit, Snow Lake offers an easy and highly scenic destination for day hikers and beginning backpackers. This hike is an excellent choice for families with small children. The trail climbs to the western shore of emerald-green Snow Lake, elevation 4,700 feet, fed by the milky meltwater of Unicorn Glacier. Lovely waterfalls enter the basin from three sides.

To get there, proceed 15.5 miles west from the Stevens Canyon entrance to the trailhead on the south side of the road, indicated by a small, metal destination-and-mileage sign. Or drive 18 miles east from the Nisqually entrance to the first trailhead east of Louise Lake. For more information, contact Mount Rainier National Park, (360) 569–2211, www.nps.gov/mora. *DeLorme Washington Atlas & Gazetteer* page 48, B3.

H47 Mount Aix

The trail up Mount Aix is far from easy—particularly with little water along the way—but the rewards for reaching this 7,766-foot summit are worth the effort. You'll climb more than 4,000 feet in 5 long miles to the windy, rocky summit, where you'll find airy views of the Goat Rocks, Mount Rainier, and Mount Adams.

Drive 47 miles from Enumclaw on Washington Route 410 to Chinook Pass and drive 19 miles east to the Bumping Road (Forest Service Road 18). Turn right and follow the road to the pavement's end, where it becomes Forest Service Road 1800. Proceed to a junction and stay left on the Deep Creek Road (Forest Service Road 1808). Drive 1.5 miles to the Mount Aix Trailhead just before the Copper Creek bridge. For more information, contact the Wenatchee National Forest, (509) 653–2205, www.fs.fed.us/r6/wenatchee. *DeLorme Washington Atlas & Gazetteer* page 49, B5.

H48 Walupt Creek Loop

Lakes, broad vistas, rushing streams, and timberline forests combine to make this weekender a fine introduction to the scenic Goat Rocks Wilderness, one of Washington's oldest primitive areas. Camp at 5,710-foot Sheep Lake to enjoy a superb view of Mount Adams across the water. Nearby Nannie Peak beckons with the promise of more far-flung views.

From Packwood, drive U.S. Highway 12 west for 2.5 miles or go 13 miles east from Randle to southeast-bound Johnson Creek Road 21. Drive this good dirt road, following signs for Walupt Lake, for 15.5 miles to eastbound Forest Service Road 2160. Enjoy an excellent view here of Mount Adams in the south and the Goat Rocks in the northeast. This gravel road with paved sections leads 4 miles to the trailhead at the campground on the north shore of Walupt Lake. For more information, contact Gifford Pinchot National Forest, (360) 497–1100 or www.fs.fed.us/gpnf. *DeLorme Washington Atlas & Gazetteer* page 35, A5.

H49 Badger Lake

A series of north–south ridges about 15 miles west of Mount Adams, capped by craggy summits more than a mile high, constitute the Dark Divide Roadless Area, the largest unroaded area not formally designated as wilderness in the Gifford Pinchot National Forest. This highly scenic area deserves protection so that it may be enjoyed by future generations. Here you can climb to the rocky summit of 5,664-foot Badger Peak, where you'll get far-ranging views of the South Cascades. Badger Lake, which may remain frozen until early July, makes a fine base camp from which to explore this seldom-visited area.

For more information, contact the Wenatchee National Forest, (509) 653–2205, www.fs.fed.us/r6/wenatchee. *DeLorme Washington Atlas & Gazetteer* page 34, B1.

H50 Holdaway Butte

Holdaway Butte, only a minor bump on the lofty ridge dividing Yellowjacket and McCoy Creeks, doesn't compare to the spectacular craggy summits that dominate the Dark Divide Roadless Area. What it does offer is a short hike to expansive views of not only the Dark Divide country but also much of Washington's southern Cascades. The rugged McCoy Peak ridge stretches away to the north, its steep slopes plunging more than 3,000 feet into the canyons of Yellowjacket and McCoy Creeks. From the south to the northwest are several prominent Dark Divide peaks: Hat Rock, Craggy Peak, Shark and Kirk Rocks, Badger Peak, and the curious splintered crag of Pinto Rock. Mount Saint Helens and the tall peaks of the Mount Margaret country rise on the western skyline. The blocky crest of Juniper Ridge to the east foregrounds a grand view of the immense ice dome of Mount Adams.

From Randle, proceed south on signed Forest Service Road 25 for 1 mile, then turn left onto Forest Service Road 23, drive another 7.9 miles to Forest Service Road 28, and turn right (south). After another mile, turn left onto unpaved Forest Service Road 29 at Yellowjacket Ponds Recreation Site; the sign points to Boundary Trail. Follow this good one-lane gravel road, with turnouts, as it steadily ascends southward high above McCoy Creek. The final 3 miles are narrow and rocky. After 15 miles you reach the Boundary Trail at McCoy Pass, where there is limited parking in roadside turnouts. For more information, contact Gifford Pinchot National Forest, (360) 497–1100, www.fs.fed.us/gpnf. *DeLorme Washington Atlas & Gazetteer* page 34, B2.

H51 Goat Mountain and Deadman's Lake

Goat Mountain, rising beside the Green River just north of the blast zone, narrowly escaped the full force of the 1980 eruption of Mount Saint Helens. This trail alternates between unscathed forest and heat-killed trees and offers startling views into the heart of the blast zone. You'll enjoy a well-earned view where the trail finally crests Goat Mountain: Mount Rainier rises to the north, while Mount Adams rises above the partially devastated forests of Strawberry Mountain to the east. Mount Hood is visible far to the south, across the barren landscape where virgin timber once stood. And finally, the source of all the destruction, the truncated mass of Mount Saint Helens, rises above the glacier-carved north slope of the Mount Venus–Mount Whittier ridge.

Forest Service Road 99, branching west from Forest Service Road 25, 22 miles south of Randle and 44 miles from Cougar, is the main thoroughfare into Mount Saint Helens National Volcanic Monument. Follow FR 99 west from its junction with FR 25 (both are paved) for 9 miles to Forest Service Road 26, turn right, and continue for 0.9 mile to the Norway Pass Trailhead parking area. The Goat Mountain Trailhead can be reached by continuing north on FR 26 for another 3.7 miles, then turning west just north of Ryan Lake and following Forest Service Road 2612 westward for 0.4 mile to the trailhead parking area. For more information, contact Gifford Pinchot National Forest, (360) 497–1100, www.fs.fed.us/gpnf. *DeLorme Washington Atlas & Gazetteer* page 33, A7.

H52 Plains of Abraham

Perhaps one of the most surreal experiences to be had on the trail in Washington can be found here, on the broad, barren pumice Plains of Abraham on the east side of Mount Saint Helens. Here the flanks of the mountain, still largely barren more than twenty years after the blast, are in full view, and you can watch the clouds mysteriously swirl around the summit. At 8.2 miles out-and-back, it's a moderate day hike, but plan to stay overnight on the plains and be lulled by the sound of waterfalls rushing from the mountain's bare, rocky slopes. Views are spectacular from the first step.

From Randle, drive 8 miles south on Forest Service Road 25 and cross the Cispus River. Just beyond the river, turn right onto Forest Service Road 26. Continue about 15 miles to Forest Service Road 99, turn right, and continue to the road's end and trailhead at the Windy Ridge viewpoint. For more information, contact Mount Saint Helens National Volcanic Monument, (360) 247–3900, www.fs.fed.us/gpnf/mshnvm. *DeLorme Washington Atlas & Gazetteer* page 33, C8.

H53 Spencer Butte

Considerable effort is normally required to reach mountain peaks and enjoy their panoramic vistas. But by following the short, easy trail to Spencer Butte, virtually anyone can gaze out upon hundreds of square miles of mountain country, from Mount Adams and Mount Saint Helens to Oregon's Mount Jefferson. The trail, deep in crunchy pumice from the 1980 eruption of Mount Saint Helens, ascends the western slopes of Breezy Point through young trees and reaches the high point of the ridge at an elevation of 4,247 feet. Looking to the west, you'll see the east side of squat Mount Saint Helens, lined by the paths of numerous 1980 mudflows. To the east, slopes fall steadily away into the deep canyon of the Lewis River. Mount Adams, often cloud capped in early summer, looms boldly on the eastern horizon. To the south, beyond miles of patchy forests, Mounts Hood and Jefferson appear as distant, hazy mirages.

Follow Forest Service Road 90 east from Cougar past Yale Lake and Swift Reservoir for 18.2 miles to northbound Forest Service Road 25, signed for Mount Saint Helens, and turn north. Follow this road for 5.3 miles to the junction with eastbound Forest Service Road 93 just beyond the Muddy River and bear right onto FR 93. Follow this one-lane paved road with turnouts for 7.5 miles to the sign for the Spencer Butte Trailhead. For more information, contact Gifford Pinchot National Forest, (360) 497–1100, www.fs.fed.us/gpnf. *DeLorme Washington Atlas & Gazetteer* page 34, C1.

H54 Summit Prairie

This scenic hike leads through forests past small meadows beneath the volcanic cliffs of Table Mountain and a former lookout site with grand views of four ice-clad volcanoes, vast forests, and the rugged peaks of the Dark Divide Roadless Area. Brilliant summer blossoms of mariposa, tiger lily, lupine, and red columbine may momentarily distract you from the tremendous views. Prominent features to the south include Lemei Rock and Bird Mountain in the Indian Heaven Wilderness, while beyond rises Mount Hood.

From Trout Lake, proceed 1.25 miles north toward Randle and the prominently signed Forest Service Road 23. Follow this road northwest (the pavement ends after 22 miles) for 25 miles to Forest Service Road 2334—signed for Council Lake and the Boundary Trail—and turn left. That spur road can also be reached from Randle by following signed Forest Service Road 25 south for 8 miles to FR 23, which you follow for another 25 miles to the above-mentioned junction, 0.9 mile south of signed Baby Shoe Pass. Follow wide gravel FR 2334 for 1.2 miles and bear left where the spur to Council Lake forks right. After another 2.3 miles, turn right onto a much narrower dirt road, which is signed for the Boulder Trail. This is an unmaintained dirt road that is often rutted and possibly blocked by blowdowns. Proceed about 0.1 mile to a junction with a right-forking spur road. Park at the small turnout on the north side of the road. For more information, contact Gifford Pinchot National Forest (360) 497–1100, www.fs.fed.us/gpnf. *DeLorme Washington Atlas & Gazetteer* page 34, B3.

H55 Horseshoe Meadow

This hike offers access to the western base of Mount Adams and the Round-the-Mountain Trail. Using Horseshoe Meadow as a base camp, you'll find numerous possible cross-country routes that invite further exploration to many alpine meadows, glacial valleys, and cinder cones on the flanks of Mount Adams. Keep an eye out for the black-tailed deer and Roosevelt elk that inhabit the area.

To get there from Trout Lake, head north toward Randle. After 1.25 miles bear left onto Forest Service Road 23. Turn right onto gravel Forest Service Road 521, 14 miles from Trout Lake, and reach the Pacific Crest Trail after 0.3 mile. You can also reach the trailhead by following mostly paved Forest Service Road 90 up the Lewis River to FR 23, about 49 miles from Cougar. Then follow FR 23 south for 6 miles to Forest Service Road 521, and another 0.3 mile to the trailhead. For more information, contact the Wenatchee National Forest, (509) 653–2205, www.fs.fed.us/r6/wenatchee. *DeLorme Washington Atlas & Gazetteer* page 34, C4.

H56 **Observation Peak**

This hike in the Trapper Creek Wilderness, one of the state's smallest wilderness areas and far from overbearing peaks and crowded hiking trails, allows you to contemplate nature in both its simplicity and its complexity. A hike in these hushed forests also encourages introspection. From the observation peak's summit, Mount Adams, Mount Rainier, Mount Saint Helens, and miles of eruption-flattened forest dominate the view from northeast to northwest. Mount Hood rises majestically beyond Columbia Gorge in the south. And in the east a few prominent Cascade crest peaks rise out of the forest in Indian Heaven country.

To get there from the Carson turnoff on Washington Route 14, about 47 miles east of Vancouver, follow the paved Wind River Road northward through the forested Wind River Valley for about 15 miles (passing the turnoff to the Wind River ranger station after 9.5 miles) to the Government Mineral Springs turnoff and bear left. Cross the Wind River, then turn right after 0.4 mile. A sign here points to the Trapper Creek Wilderness Trailhead opposite the left-forking Little Soda Springs Road. Follow dirt Forest Service Road 5401 for 0.4 mile to the parking area at the trailhead. For more information, contact Gifford Pinchot National Forest, (360) 497–1100, www.fs.fed.us/gpnf. *DeLorme Washington Atlas & Gazetteer* page 23, A8.

Northeast Washington

ortheast Washington is often called the "forgotten corner" of the state, and for good reason. Relatively few Pacific Northwest hikers, particularly from west of the Cascades, know much about this vast, remote area stretching from Washington Route 97 east to the Idaho border. Thanks to its anonymity, this region of rolling mountain ranges interspersed with fertile valley ranches and farms offers something you'll not easily find in more populated parts of the state—solitude. Hundreds of miles of trails access the Kettle River Range, the Selkirk Mountains farther to the east, and the old-growth forests of the Salmo-Priest Wilderness in the far northeast corner of the state. It's not uncommon to have a trail to yourself here, and backcountry campsites are typically plentiful, even on the most popular summer weekends.

The highlands of northeastern Washington rise just east of the Cascade Range and north of the Columbia Basin, extending east and north into northern Idaho and southern British Columbia. Three mountain ranges sweep from north to south through the area and are separated by deep valleys. These ranges—the Okanogan, Kettle Highlands, and Selkirks—are considered the western foothills of the Rocky Mountains, rising gently up to heights of 8,000 feet.

The Okanogan Highlands in the western part of the region were once a separate small continent adrift in the Pacific Ocean. The Columbia River now traces the eastern and southern borders of this former continent; the Okanogan River, its western margin. As it drifted east and merged with the main North American continent, a line of volcanoes, such as Mount Bonaparte in the Okanogan National Forest, formed fifty to seventy-five million years ago along its crest, with steam and basalt rising above the colliding landmasses. Most of the route between Tonasket and Republic crosses this Okanogan Dome, a mass of granite about 20 miles wide shrouded in a mantle of gneiss between 5 and 10 miles wide.

Farther to the east lies the ponderosa pine country of the 1.1-million-acre Colville National Forest. Just east of the town of Republic, the forested Kettle Highlands rise to elevations of more than 7,000 feet. The Kettle Dome occupies a large area in the Kettle Highlands and is another large mass of intrusive granite mantled with gneiss, similar to the Okanogan Dome to the west. The Sherman Pass National Forest Scenic Byway (Washington Route 20) takes you through the heart of the Kettle Crest and over the highest paved pass in the state. The peaks along this crest, including Sherman Peak, are a complex mixture of old continental crust and younger granite. Granite appears in roadside cuts on either side of Sherman Pass, and you'll find both granite and gneiss exposed on the rocky summits of the highlands south of Sherman Pass. This area was also severely burned in the 1988 White Mountain fire, providing a close-up view of a forest ecosystem in the process of dynamic renewal.

East of the Kettle Crest and Columbia River, the Selkirk Mountains unfold in broad, forested ridges culminating in peaks rising more than 7,000 feet, such as Abercrombie Mountain and the summits north of Grassy Top Mountain. This portion of the region contains the oldest sedimentary and metamorphic rocks in the state. Here you'll also find the region's only federal wilderness area, the 41,335-acre Salmo-Priest Wilderness, where wildlife such as the endangered woodland caribou, along with the grizzly bear, wolverine, black bear, cougar, elk, lynx, pine marten, and moose, outnumber hikers for much of the year. Lush valley bottom forests line the South Salmo River, flowing through the heart of this wild and remote area.

South of the Selkirks, the higher hills around Spokane, including Mount Kit Carson in Mount Spokane State Park, are outposts of the northern Rocky Mountains. Most of these hills consist of granite and granodiorite and are closely related to the Idaho Batholith, a large mass of granite extending through central Idaho and into western Montana. Mount Spokane State Park is located near the center of the Spokane Dome, a large mass of younger granite that intruded ancient continental crustal rocks about one hundred million years ago.

Farther to the west, lava flows of the Columbia Plateau lap onto the older granite of the Okanogan subcontinent in the area around Grand Coulee Dam. The area's geological formations are remnants of intense volcanic activity that blanketed the area with deep layers of basalt, followed by cataclysmic ice age floods that cut down through the basalts, carving deep canyons, or coulees. In Northrup Canyon you'll get glimpses of this geologic transition zone, where granite and basalt meet. Lake Roosevelt, extending for 130 miles behind Grand Coulee Dam, was created from the immense Columbia River Basin project, which tamed the wild, free-flowing Columbia River for irrigation and hydropower. Named for President Franklin Roosevelt, the Lake Roosevelt National Recreation Area is now one of the largest recreation draws in Washington.

37 Mount Bonaparte

The Mount Bonaparte Trail climbs 3.2 miles through forest to a historic fire look-out, still active today and open to visitors, perched on the western edge of Washington's Okanogan Mountains. Climb the lookout at the broad, rocky summit for sweeping 360-degree views north into Canada, west to the Sawtooth Range, and east toward the Kettle Crest.

Start: From the Mount Bonaparte Trailhead 306 off Forest Service Road 300.
Length: 6.4 miles out-and-back from the upper trailhead.
Approximate hiking time: 3½ hours.
Difficulty rating: Moderate, due to moderate length, modest elevation gain, and well-graded trail.
Trail surface: Dirt trail.
Elevation gain: 2,778 feet.
Land status: National forest.
Nearest town: Tonasket, WA.

Other trail users: Equestrians, mountain bikes, motorcycles.
Canine compatibility: Dog friendly.
Trail contacts: Okanogan National Forest, Tonasket Ranger District, (509) 486–2186, www.fs.fed.us/r6/oka.
Schedule: Late June through early October.
Fees/permits: None required.
Maps: USGS Mt. Bonaparte 15-minute quad; USDA Forest Service Okanogan National Forest map.

Finding the trailhead: From U.S. Highway 97 at the north end of the town of Tonasket, turn right onto Jonathan Street where a sign points you toward Havillah and the Sitzmark Ski Area. Follow this paved county road through hills and rangeland to the tiny settlement of Havillah, 15.4 miles from Tonasket. Turn right (east) here onto West Lost Lake Road. At the end of the pavement, after 0.8 mile, turn right (south) onto gravel Forest Service Road 33. Drive another 3.3 miles and turn right (south) again, onto Forest Service Road 300, where you'll find a sign for the Bonaparte Trail. For the lower trailhead, follow this dirt road 1.2 miles to a destination-and-mileage sign and park just before the road crosses a small creek. For the upper trailhead, drive beyond the creek crossing 1 mile farther up FR 300 to a trailhead sign and small turnout on the right (west) side of the road.

If you're driving from the east, follow Washington Route 20 west for 20 miles from Republic and turn right (north) where a sign indicates the Bonaparte Recreation Area. Follow this paved road (Forest Service Road 32) for 8.25 miles and turn left onto FR 33, signed for Lost Lake. Pavement ends at a four-way junction after another 5.2 miles. Stay on FR 33 for another 6.2 miles and turn left (south) onto FR 300, following the directions above for the lower and upper trailheads. *DeLorme Washington Atlas & Gazetteer* page 115, B7.

The Hike

Isolated Mount Bonaparte, one of the westernmost peaks of the Rocky Mountains in the United States, commands a far-reaching, panoramic view of northeastern and north-central Washington, from Idaho's Selkirk Crest in the east to peaks of the eastern North Cascades to distant ranges in southern British Columbia.

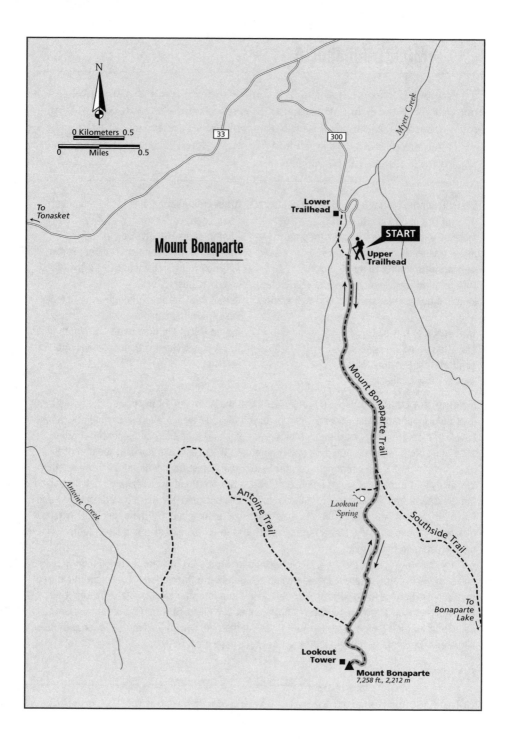

Mount Bonaparte

N

0 Kilometers 0.5
0 Miles 0.5

To Tonasket

Myers Creek

33

300

Lower
Trailhead

START

Upper
Trailhead

Mount Bonaparte Trail

Antoine Creek

Antoine Trail

*Lookout
Spring*

Southside Trail

To
Bonaparte
Lake

Lookout
Tower

Mount Bonaparte
7,258 ft., 2,212 m

The unobstructed views at the broad, rocky summit make Mount Bonaparte an ideal site from which to detect fires. The USDA Forest Service recognized this fact years ago, choosing the peak as the site for a fire lookout, still in operation today despite the increasing use of aerial fire patrols and lightning detection systems. The original fire lookout house (built circa 1914), minus its crow's-nest viewing platform, still stands on the summit next to a newer tower, built in 1961. Both make for a rewarding history lesson at the end of your hike.

Two trailheads provide access to Mount Bonaparte. The lower trailhead, beginning 1 mile down the road from the upper trailhead, will lead you through 1.3 miles of unremarkable young forest before emerging on the road at the upper trailhead. Unless you're looking for a little extra mileage, start your hike at the upper trailhead. Carry water, and don't be surprised to encounter motorcycles on this trail.

From the upper trailhead, the trail begins an immediate climb and enters a young forest of lodgepole pine, Douglas fir, and western larch, evidence of recent logging in the area. Pause here to enjoy an over-the-shoulder look at hilly rangeland and distant peaks across the border in Canada. As you hike, you may notice an ashlike substance at times along the trail cut. Some geologists believe it's a result of Glacier Peak's most recent major eruption, approximately 12,000 years ago, which may have blanketed a vast region of the Pacific Northwest with pumiceous ash.

Bear right at the junction with the Southside Trail, quickly passing another trail forking right to Lookout Spring, the only water source along the trail (don't expect to find water here after mid-September). After the spring you'll climb steadily upward through lodgepole-dominated forest, occasionally spotting glass insulators, remnants of the telephone line that served the lookout until the 1960s. You may also notice an older, fainter trail crossing and recrossing the newer trail, which climbs more gradually.

You'll climb 1.5 miles more before reaching the westbound Antoine Trail, seldom used because it begins on private land. By now you may notice that the forest has changed, showing signs of the short growing season on this cold, shady north slope. Engelmann spruce, subalpine fir, and white-bark pine—trees characteristic of timberline environments—begin to edge out lower-elevation forests. Understory plants here consist of grouse whortleberry, mountain azalea, and red heather.

Continue another 0.5 mile through increasingly open forests to the broad, boulder-strewn summit. The small cabin below today's fire tower is the first lookout, built of hand-hewn timbers. In addition to the two lookouts on the summit, notice the twisted, stunted "forest" that manages to survive in the extremes of cold, wind, and snow here. Primarily subalpine fir and white-bark pine, these types of trees are known to botanists as krummholz, after the German word for "crooked wood."

The far-ranging views include summits of the eastern North Cascades, from the Sawtooth Ridge east of Lake Chelan in the southwest to Chopaka Mountain and the Canadian Cascades in the northwest. The latter peaks rise abruptly westward from the depths of the arid Okanogan Valley. You'll be able to see Osoyoos Lake in the northwest, straddling the border between Washington and British Columbia. To the east are ranges of the Rockies, from the nearby Kettle Range to the distant Selkirk Crest in Idaho.

For even better views, climb the fire lookout tower, being respectful of the volunteers who still staff the lookout to spot fires during the summer fire season. Since many days may lapse between visits from hikers on this lonely summit, you might find the on-duty volunteer eager to chat and give you a tour of the lookout.

If you're looking to camp on the summit, a few small campsites have been cleared below the lookout tower; one even has a picnic table and fire pit. A cistern has been constructed to catch rainwater, but this is the sole source of water for the lookout on duty, so it's a good idea to bring your own.

Once you've had your fill of the views, retrace your steps to the trailhead.

Key Points

0.0 Start at the upper trailhead for Mount Bonaparte Trail 306.

1.1 Reach a junction with Southside Trail 308, which leads left (east) to Bonaparte Lake. Continue straight ahead on the main trail.

1.2 Reach a signed trail to Lookout Spring branching right (west) off the main trail. This is the only source of water along the trail.

2.6 Reach a junction for the Antoine Trail, which leads right (west). Continue straight ahead on the main trail.

3.2 Reach the fire lookout tower on the summit.

6.4 Arrive back at the upper trailhead parking lot.

Hike Information

Local information
Tonasket Visitor Information Center,
(509) 486-4429, www.tonasket.org.
Okanogan Highlands Alliance, Tonasket, WA,
(509) 485-3361.

Local events/attractions
The Tonasket Bluegrass Festival comes to town in late June; find out more on the town's Web site.

Accommodations
Junction Motel, (509) 486-4500.
Spectacle Lake Resort, (509) 223-3433.

Restaurants
Okanogan River Co-op, (509) 486-4188.

38 Sherman Peak

From the highest pass in the state accessible by paved road, climb just under 3.5 miles to this rocky, prominent Kettle Crest peak in the Colville National Forest. Along the way you'll pass through the eerie charred remains of forest burned by the 1988 White Mountain fire and witness the fascinating process of postfire forest recovery.

Start: At the signed Kettle Crest Trail 13 Trailhead on the south side of Washington Route 20, 0.1 mile east of Sherman Pass.
Length: 6.9-mile loop trail.
Approximate hiking time: 3½ hours.
Difficulty rating: Moderate, due to modest length and elevation gain. (**Note:** The final 0.2 mile to the summit is a moderate rock scramble.)
Trail surface: Dirt trail with an off-trail climb over boulders and scree to reach the summit.
Elevation gain: 1,710 feet.

Land status: National forest.
Nearest town: Republic, WA.
Other trail users: Equestrians, mountain bikers.
Canine compatibility: Dog friendly.
Trail contacts: Colville National Forest, Republic Ranger District, (509) 775-3305, www.fs.fed.us/r6/colville.
Schedule: Late June through early October.
Fees/permits: None required.
Maps: USGS Sherman Peak 15-minute quad; USDA Forest Service Colville National Forest map.

Finding the trailhead: Follow WA 20 to Sherman Pass, 17 miles east of the town of Republic or 24.75 miles west of the town of Kettle Falls. Park at the trailhead on the north side of the road and walk 0.1 mile west along WA 20—you'll find the signed trailhead on the south side of the road. *DeLorme Washington Atlas & Gazetteer* page 117, D5.

The Hike

South of Sherman Pass the Kettle Crest rises abruptly to a series of rugged and rocky summits—Sherman and Snow Peaks, Bald and White Mountains—that contrast markedly with the gentle, rolling uplands to the north. Here the granite and gneiss bedrock core of the Kettle Dome is fully exposed, and the Kettle Crest South Trail, although well designed and constructed, is more demanding than the North Trail, as it climbs rocky slopes up and around these rugged peaks.

Although the steep and rocky flanks of Sherman Peak reach skyward less than 1 mile south of Sherman Pass, the Kettle Crest South and Sherman Peak Loop Trails offer easier access to the peak for most hikers. The final 0.2 mile to the summit, an off-trail route culminating in a rock-hop up Sherman Peak's summit ridge, should be attempted only by more experienced hikers.

In August 1988 several lightning strikes near the south end of the Kettle Crest ignited the 20,000-acre-plus White Mountain fire. The destructive blaze consumed much of the pine and fir forests of the southern Kettle Crest but, fortunately, was stopped just north of WA 20, sparing the northern Kettle Crest.

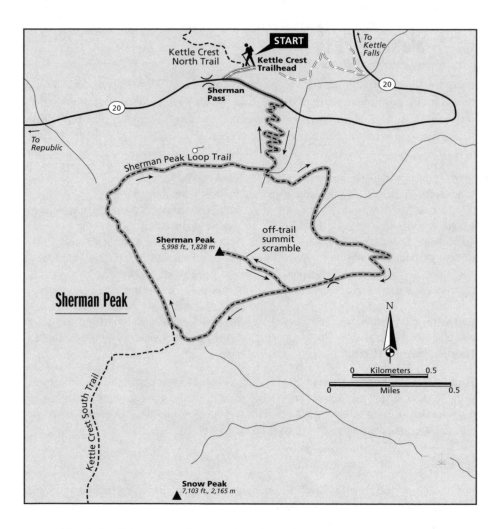

Much of this hike passes through the charred remains of these forests, and the whistling of their spooky, silvery remains in the wind may send a chill up your spine. In fact, the brittle, dead snags can easily blow over, posing a hazard to unsuspecting hikers on windy days. But amid the destruction you'll also notice nature's quick response to the fire, which was once a periodic, natural event before the advent of fire suppression. The open forest understory now hosts a lush carpet of grasses, pink fireweed, and small shrubs and tree saplings. This postfire ecosystem has attracted an increasing number of mule deer into the area, which you may be lucky to spot on your hike.

From the parking area, walk east up the road where you'll find the Kettle Crest South Trail on the south side of the highway. The trail immediately begins climbing steadily among granite boulders under a shady canopy of lodgepole pine, western larch, Douglas fir, and subalpine fir.

Climbing at a moderate grade with occasional switchbacks beneath the looming north slopes of Sherman Peak, you'll reach a junction at about 0.8 mile from the highway, just before the main trail bridges a small, spring-fed creek—the only water available en route. Here you're presented with two options to loop around the base of Sherman Peak. The right fork, the Sherman Peak Loop Trail, winds 1.9 miles around the north and west slopes of Sherman Peak, eventually connecting back up with the Kettle Crest Trail in a saddle between Sherman Peak and Snow Peak. By continuing straight ahead on the Kettle Crest South Trail, you'll traverse the east and south slopes of Sherman Peak before reaching the same junction. For now, continue straight ahead on the Kettle Crest South Trail.

▶ **Fires naturally occur at intervals of 200 to 300 years in lodgepole pine forests. These are often high-intensity fires that kill trees, and while they may seem to bring devastation to the landscape, they're an integral part in the cycle of forest renewal. Soon after a fire grasses, shrubs, and eventually small tree seedlings begin to regrow in the area, forebears of the next generation of forest.**

After another 0.2 mile you'll curve around the shoulder of a low ridge and enter the bleak landscape of charred and bleached snags, then contour into a small cirque basin. Curving around the basin, the trail switchbacks four times, eventually topping out at a 6,300-foot saddle, about 0.5 mile east of Sherman Peak and 2 miles from the trailhead. Trailside snags frame your first view of rugged Snow Peak, Barnaby Buttes, and White Mountain to the south.

Hike another 0.3 mile from the saddle. For those with the energy and skill to scramble up Sherman Peak's rocky summit, leave the trail here, making sure to note where you've left the trail. Turn right off the trail and climb west up the increasingly steep ridge among open, grassy slopes. You'll soon reach the base of the summit, where the ridge is composed of loose, rubbly gneiss. If you're not comfortable scrambling over boulders and loose scree, you might want to stop here and be content with the view.

For others, start your final short scramble to the rocky, cairn-dotted summit, where you'll find a commanding 360-degree panorama. Sherman Peak's central location in northern Washington between the Cascades and the Idaho line offers interesting perspectives of mountains that most Washington hikers have never enjoyed. On the western horizon, beyond the rolling mountains of the Okanogan Highlands, lies the abrupt eastern escarpment of the North Cascades; the jagged peaks of the Sawtooth Range rise in the southwest. Eastward, beyond the Columbia River, the Selkirk Mountains march off toward the horizon, 75 miles distant in

The meadow-strewn upper slopes of Sherman Peak.

the Idaho panhandle. And northward, beyond the rolling highlands of the Kettle Crest, ranks of high ranges stretch into British Columbia's interior.

If you want to complete the loop, retrace your steps to the trail and continue your hike west on the trail to the saddle between Sherman Peak and Snow Peak, where you'll find the intersection with the Sherman Peak Loop Trail. Turn right (north) here, descending along the west and north slopes of Sherman Peak. You'll drop back into the green unburned forest and reach the junction with the Kettle Crest South Trail where you started your loop. From here, turn left (north) and descend the Kettle Crest South Trail to WA 20, retracing your steps to the trailhead.

Key Points

0.0 Start at Kettle Crest Trail 13 on the south side of WA 20.

0.8 Reach a junction for Sherman Peak Loop Trail 72 to the right (west); continue straight on Kettle Crest Trail 13 over a bridge.

1.1 Emerge from green forest into burned remains of forest.

2.0 After climbing switchbacks, reach a saddle, with the rocky summit of Sherman Peak to the right (west).

2.3 To scramble up Sherman Peak, turn right (northwest) and leave the trail, climbing across open slopes (**Note:** There's no trail here, so mark your route for the return to the trail.)

2.8 Reach the summit of Sherman Peak after a rocky scramble.

3.3 Reach the trail again after descending from the summit.

4.2 Arrive at the saddle between Sherman Peak and Snow Peak. Turn right (north) onto Sherman Peak Loop Trail 72 to complete the loop around Sherman Peak back to the trailhead.

6.1 Reach the intersection with the Kettle Crest Trail 13 and the end of your loop. Turn left (north), descending toward WA 20 and the trailhead.

6.9 Arrive back at the trailhead.

Hike Information

Local information
Republic Visitor Center, (509) 775-3387.
Kettle Range Conservation Group, Republic, WA, (509) 775-2017.

Local events/attractions
The Ferry County Fair comes to Republic on Labor Day weekend; find out more from the town's visitor center.

Accommodations
Prospector Inn, Republic, WA, (509) 775-3361.
Curlew Lake State Park, east of Republic.

Restaurants
Ferry County Co-op, Republic, WA, (509) 775-3754.

39 Northrup Canyon

Follow this 5.6-mile out-and-back day hike through a basalt-rimmed canyon in the Grand Coulee country of east-central Washington. Along the way you'll pass through lush streamside forest dense with wildlife and end at a small, trout-filled lake.

Start: At the Northrup Canyon Trailhead and locked gate.
Length: 5.6 miles out-and-back.
Approximate hiking time: 2½ hours.
Difficulty rating: Easy, due to minimal elevation gain.
Trail surface: Dirt road and trail.
Elevation gain: 580 feet.
Land status: State park.
Nearest town: Grand Coulee, WA.
Other trail users: Equestrians, mountain bikes.

Canine compatibility: Leashed dogs are permitted.
Trail contacts: Steamboat Rock State Park, (509) 633-1304, www.parks.wa.gov.
Schedule: Best hiked March through November. While the trail is accessible twenty-four hours a day, developed facilities in Steamboat Rock State Park are open daily from 6:30 A.M. to sunset.
Fees/permits: None required.
Maps: USGS Steamboat Rock Southeast and Electric City 7.5-minute quads.

Finding the trailhead: Follow Washington Route 155 south from Electric City for 6.5 miles or north from U.S. Highway 2 near Coulee City for 16.5 miles to the eastbound Northrup Road, opposite the turnoff for the Steamboat Rock State Park, Northrup Point Boat Launch 1. Follow this gravel road generally eastward, bearing right at three unsigned junctions. You'll reach the locked gate, parking lot, and trailhead after 0.7 mile. *DeLorme Washington Atlas & Gazetteer* page 85, B8.

The Hike

Northrup Canyon lies among the vast reaches of Washington's Columbia Basin—the broad, arid region between the Rockies and the Cascades to the west. It's the side of Washington that catches many visitors by surprise—a region dominated by a plateau of basalt intermittently dissected by deep, narrow river canyons and many dry stream channels, better known as coulees.

As you travel through this region, you may stop to ponder the forces that created such an unusual landscape. Beginning in the Miocene epoch nearly fifteen million years ago, enormous quantities of molten basalt sprang from fissures in the earth's crust throughout eastern Washington and surrounding areas, burying everything in its path, including rivers, lakes, and lush forests. Flow upon flow of these lava floods piled up, creating layers of basalt reaching thicknesses of hundreds of feet.

With the arrival of the ice age, vast sheets of ice pushed southward from Canada, flowing through what is now the Okanogan Valley. Their advance temporarily

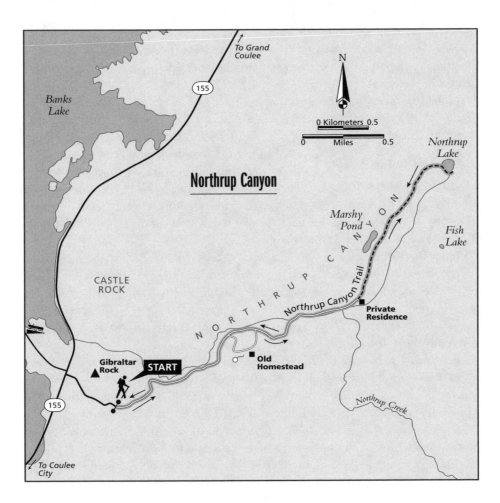

Northrup Canyon

dammed the Columbia River and diverted it southward, where it began eroding a channel into the basalt-covered landscape. About 15,000 years ago another glacier, this one flowing southward from British Columbia into northern Idaho, dammed the Clark Fork River near present-day Sandpoint, Idaho, creating glacial Lake Missoula, a vast impoundment that backed up water far into western Montana.

Periodically the ice dam burst, hurling catastrophic floodwaters across the basalt-covered Columbia Basin and scouring the landscape of eastern Washington into a vast system of channels, or coulees. The largest of all these channels is the Grand Coulee, nearly 50 miles long, 4 miles wide, and 1,000 feet deep. After the Okanogan lobe of the ice sheet receded, the Columbia resumed its original course, transforming the Grand Coulee into a riverless scar across the basin.

Today the north end of Grand Coulee lies submerged under the waters of Banks Lake, just south of the concrete masonry megalith of Grand Coulee Dam. The waters of Franklin D. Roosevelt Lake, impounded by the dam, are pumped into Banks Lake and distributed far to the south and east to farmlands, this extensive plumbing system transforming the area into one of the most productive agricultural regions of the Pacific Northwest.

Northrup Canyon, a basalt-rimmed tributary canyon of the Grand Coulee through which this unique day hike will lead you, is like a Grand Coulee in miniature, with a trout-filled lake resting at its head. It's also home to a diverse plant population, and considering the surrounding desiccated landscape, you may be surprised to find lush vegetation including birch, Douglas fir, and ponderosa pine carpeting portions of the canyon floor. The diverse streamside habitat here also makes it one of the more popular birding locations in the Grand Coulee region.

▶ **The Grand Coulee Dam is North America's largest masonry structure.**

From the locked gate in the shadow of Gibraltar Rock, follow the sagebrush-lined dirt road eastward. You'll soon reach the canyon bottom, where mosquitoes can be troublesome during early summer. After hiking briefly through lush streamside growth, you'll reach open ground where you'll have good views up the canyon. Precipitous basalt cliffs, dotted by ponderosa pines and Douglas firs, rise abruptly north and south above the canyon floor.

Less than 1 mile from the trailhead, you'll pass two southbound tracks that lead to the site of an old homestead. Shortly, the road circumnavigates a broad meadow, passing an area of exposed granite at its eastern edge. This rock is presumed to be part of the prebasalt granite landscape reexposed by the Spokane floods.

Shortly beyond is a jumble of columnar basalt along the streambed. When molten basalt cools at the surface, it often fractures into these interesting columns. Well-known examples include the Devil's Tower in Wyoming and the Devil's Postpile in California.

The road skirts another large meadow and reaches a private residence. At this point the canyon splits; the right fork cuts deep into the basalt toward the southeast (Northrup Creek), while the left fork continues its northeast course (Northrup Canyon). Beyond the house, under a power line, the trail, faint in places, leads past a chicken house and up the canyon through sagebrush, Douglas fir, and ponderosa pine. You're in rattlesnake country here, so walk with caution.

Soon the route becomes easy to follow as it climbs moderately, winding among granite boulders and sparse forest. The trail soon passes a marshy pond. As it climbs above a second pond, it crosses yet another meeting place of older granite and the younger basalt, with the latter dominating the trailside briefly ahead. Wildflowers, grasses, and scattered trees help soften the appearance of the otherwise hard, dry landscape here.

Shortly beyond the two ponds, the trail climbs to a sparsely forested, granitic knoll. From here you'll get a nice glimpse into the inviting northern reaches of the canyon. Then the trail briefly negotiates the ridgeline separating the two forks of the canyon, passes a seasonal pond, and reaches Northrup Lake.

This two-acre-plus lake supports a healthy trout population that should keep anglers busy. It's encircled by cliffs of basalt, shaded by ponderosa pines and Douglas firs, and bordered by lush riparian vegetation.

After enjoying this unique hiking area for the day, retrace the route to the trailhead.

Key Points

0.0 Start your hike along the road at the gated trailhead.

0.8 Pass two southbound tracks that lead to the site of an old homestead, continuing straight ahead.

1.5 Skirt a large meadow and reach a private residence and trail junction. Stay left for Northrup Canyon.

2.0 Pass a marshy pond.

2.8 Arrive at 2,130-foot-high Northrup Lake.

5.6 Arrive back at the trailhead and parking area.

Hike Information

Local information

Grand Coulee Dam Area Chamber of Commerce, (509) 633-3074, www.grandcoulee dam.org.
A viewpoint for wintering bald eagles is located just east of the trailhead parking lot.

Accommodations

Gold House Inn B&B, Grand Coulee, WA, (509) 633-3276.
Steamboat Rock State Park, (509) 633-1304.

40 Abercrombie Mountain

Climb 3.5 miles to one of Washington's most remote peaks with lofty views from a rocky, exposed ridge, the former site of a fire lookout. This windswept vantage point near the Canadian border doesn't see too many visitors, so you're likely to find lonely trail here and enjoy one of the highest summits east of the Cascades by yourself.

Start: From North Fork Silver Creek Trail 117 at the end of Forest Service Road 300.
Length: 7 miles out-and-back.
Approximate hiking time: 4 hours.
Difficulty rating: Moderate, due to moderate length and elevation gain.
Trail surface: Overgrown logging road and dirt trail.
Elevation gain: 2,308 feet.
Land status: National forest.
Nearest town: Colville, WA.

Other trail users: Equestrians, mountain bikes.
Canine compatibility: Dog friendly.
Trail contacts: Colville National Forest, Colville Ranger District, (509) 684–4557, www.fs.fed.us/r6/colville.
Schedule: July through early October.
Fees/permits: None required.
Maps: USGS Abercrombie Mtn. 7.5-minute quad; USDA Forest Service Colville National Forest map.

Finding the trailhead: Follow Washington Route 25 northeast along the Columbia River for 33 miles from the town of Kettle Falls to the town of Northport. Turn right (east) onto Fourth Street where a sign points to Deep Lake. Follow this paved county road 11.3 miles to a junction, and bear left (north) onto Deep Lake Boundary Road toward Deep Lake. (The right fork leads 25 miles south to Washington Route 20, 1.5 miles east of Colville.) You'll reach the crossroads of Leadpoint after another 7.4 miles. Turn right (southeast) onto the dirt-surfaced Silver Creek Road. Bear left after 0.6 mile, following the narrow, poor dirt road to the Colville National Forest boundary, where the road improves. At 1.9 miles from Leadpoint, turn left (north) at a sign for Abercrombie Mountain. This road, which becomes narrow and rutted, leads 10 miles to its end at the trailhead. *DeLorme Washington Atlas & Gazetteer* page 118, A4.

The Hike

A series of major north–south ridges extend eastward from the Columbia River in northeastern Washington, marching into the panhandle of Idaho. These are known as the Selkirk Mountains, the highest peaks east of the Cascades. At 7,308 feet, Abercrombie Mountain is the second highest peak in the Washington Selkirks, and it offers a panoramic view of mountain ranges both near and far.

The hike begins on an old, closed logging road, climbing through young forested northwest slopes, crossing several rivulets along the way. You'll want to carry plenty of drinking water for this mostly dry hike or fill up here at the only water along the trail. Above you looms the rounded summit of Abercrombie Mountain, while to the northwest you may also get glimpses here of distant summits of British Columbia's Christina Range.

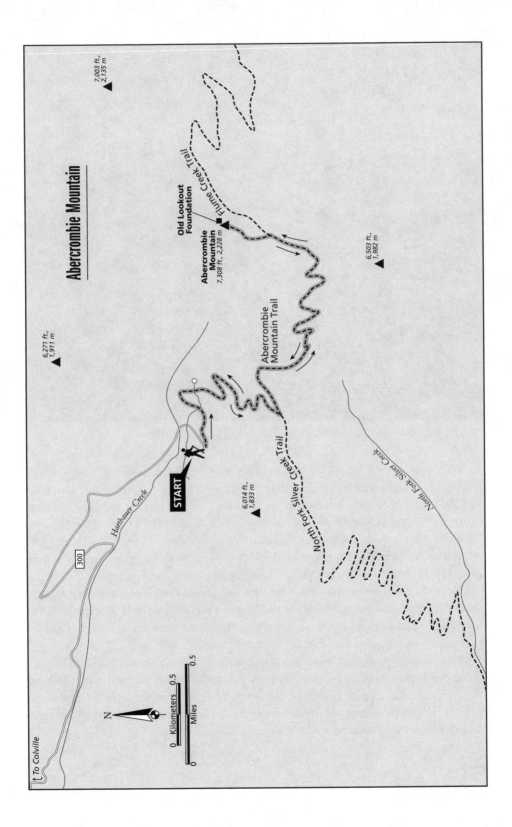

Abercrombie Mountain

To Colville

300

Harbauer Creek

START

6,271 ft.,
1,911 m

6,014 ft.,
1,833 m

North Fork Silver Creek Trail

Abercrombie Mountain Trail

Abercrombie
Mountain
7,308 ft., 2,228 m

Old Lookout
Foundation

Flume Creek Trail

7,003 ft.,
2,135 m

6,503 ft.,
1,982 m

North Fork Silver Creek

N

0 Kilometers 0.5

0 Miles 0.5

A cairn rises from the rocky jumble of Abercrombie Mountain.

After a moderate ascent, the old logging road ends and reverts to trail, quickly leading to a saddle and trail junction at 5,750 feet. The right-forking trail descends steadily to the North Fork Silver Creek Trailhead. You'll turn left and hike through subalpine fir and lodgepole pine to another saddle 0.25 mile to the northeast.

Here the trail jogs south and climbs moderately across burned-over southwest slopes that are slowly being reforested by lodgepole pine, along with mounds of bear grass, lupine, whortleberry, huckleberry, pearly everlasting, and yarrow.

Near the open, grassy summit ridge, the trail passes through an area of weather-sculpted, twisted snags, remnants of the stunted timberline forest that once stood here. Among these snags are young subalpine firs, along with white-bark and lodgepole pines—the next generation of timberline forest.

Avoid a faint trail that heads northeast, and instead climb for 0.25 mile north along the increasingly open ridge marked by cairns. Here the faint trail climbing from Flume Creek joins your trail on the right (east). You'll swing left and leave behind the last persistent, weather-twisted trees, climbing past a makeshift weather shelter to the cairn-marked, rocky summit.

Now it's time to take in the panorama from your lofty viewpoint. The swath of cleared forest marking the international boundary between the United States and Canada is plainly visible, stretching westward. Forming the western horizon is the Kettle River Range and, over the border to the northwest, the Christina Range.

A sliver of the Columbia River is visible below to the northwest. Beyond lie the towns of Grand Forks and Rossland, British Columbia, as well as a Canadian power plant. Distant, rugged peaks of the Selkirks are visible to the horizon in the north and northeast across the border.

To the east is the forested valley of the Pend Oreille River and beyond, the Salmo-Priest Wilderness. On the eastern horizon is a range of impressive granite crags—Idaho's Selkirk Crest.

When you've gotten your fill of this tremendous, geographically diverse view, retrace your steps to the trailhead.

Key Points

0.0 Start at the North Fork Silver Creek Trail 117.

0.4–1.0 Cross a series of small springs, the only water source along the trail.

1.3 The old logging road reverts to trail.

1.4 Reach a junction and turn left (northeast) onto the Abercrombie Mountain Trail. The North Fork Silver Creek Trail continues to the right.

3.0 Reach the broad, grassy summit ridge.

3.2 Reach the junction with the faint Flume Creek Trail climbing from the northeast. Continue straight ahead toward the summit.

3.5 Reach the summit rock cairns and old lookout foundation.

7.0 Arrive back at the trailhead and parking area.

Hike Information

Local information
Colville Chamber of Commerce Visitor Information Center, (509) 684-5973, www.colville.com.

Local events/attractions
The Northeast Washington Fair is held in Colville in early August; check the town's Web site for more information.

Accommodations
Bennie's Colville Inn, Colville, WA, (509) 684-2517.

Restaurants
North Country Co-op, Colville, WA, (509) 684-6132.

Angler's Grill, Colville, WA, (509) 685-1308.

41 South Salmo River

This 6.2-mile out-and-back backpack will take you to Washington's remote South Salmo River in the heart of the Salmo-Priest Wilderness. You'll enjoy good fishing, the isolation of a deep canyon, and the outside chance of spotting one of the few remaining woodland caribou in the United States that roam this wild corner of the state.

Start: At the Salmo Pass Trailhead off Forest Service Road 2220.
Length: 6.2 miles out-and-back.
Approximate hiking time: 3½ hours.
Difficulty rating: Moderate, due to moderate elevation loss and gain on the return trip.
Trail surface: Dirt trail.
Elevation gain: 1,835 feet on the return trip.
Land status: Federal wilderness area.
Nearest town: Metaline Falls, WA.
Other trail users: Equestrians.

Canine compatibility: Leashed dogs are permitted.
Trail contacts: Colville National Forest, Sullivan Lake Ranger District, (509) 446–2691, www.fs.fed.us/r6/colville.
Schedule: July through early October.
Fees/permits: None required.
Maps: USGS Salmo Mtn. (Washington–Idaho–British Columbia) 7.5-minute quad; USDA Forest Service Colville National Forest map.

Finding the trailhead: From Washington Route 31 just south of Ione, turn east onto paved Pend Oreille County Road 9345 where a sign points to Sullivan Lake. Drive past the deep, 3.5-mile-long lake to a junction with eastbound Forest Service Road 22, 13.2 miles from the highway. (This junction can also be reached by driving 6.5 miles north then east from Metaline Falls and following Sullivan Lake signs.) Turn right (east) onto FR 22 where a sign points to Salmo Mountain and Priest Lake. This good gravel road follows the course of Sullivan Creek and reaches a junction with northbound FR 2220 just after a stream crossing at 6.1 miles. Bear left at this four-way junction and follow FR 2220, ignoring numerous signed spur roads, to a ridgetop junction with left-forking Forest Service Road 270, which leads to a tremendous view atop Salmo Mountain, 18.7 miles from the county road. Bear right here and proceed 0.3 mile to the road's end at the Salmo Pass Trailhead. *DeLorme Washington Atlas & Gazetteer* page 119, A8.

The Hike

In many mountainous areas, canyons harbor climatic conditions very different from those of surrounding slopes. Such is the case in the canyon of the South Salmo River, where a lush, inland rain forest is nurtured by abundant precipitation and a modicum of sunlight. This is one of only a few such rain forests in the northern Rocky Mountains.

Another unique feature of this trip into the Salmo–Priest Wilderness is that you'll be entering the domain of grizzly bears, woodland caribou, and a host of other animals that symbolize the true wildness of this area, arguably the wildest

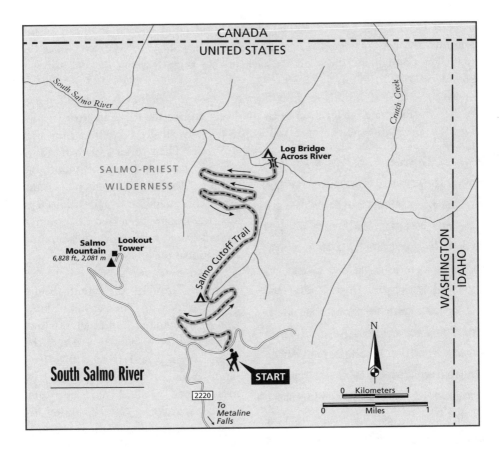

country left in Washington. The abundant goatsbeard lichens clinging to stately old-growth trees on the shadier slopes are the preferred diet of the few woodland caribou that roam here.

The Salmo-Priest Wilderness, protected by Congress in 1984, encompasses more than 50,000 acres, including 41,335 acres of prime wildlife habitat in Washington. North of the border in British Columbia, logging, power lines, and roads threaten the region, creeping right up to the international border. In Idaho more roadless area has been proposed for wilderness status, including the Wild and Scenic Upper Priest River. But for now, logging is a constant threat there as well.

This hike begins in subalpine forest and heads constantly downhill to a temperate rain forest on the South Salmo—a forest reminiscent of those found in soggier parts of the state. That the climate along the South Salmo is so similar to that of the western Cascades is a remarkable fact when you consider that the Salmo-Priest Wilderness lies almost 250 miles from the ocean.

From the trailhead, you'll begin descending moderately through a north-slope forest of Engelmann spruce and subalpine fir, where you may find patches of snow well into early July. The well-graded trail crosses a small creek twice during the initial 0.75

mile. At times you'll get tree-framed glimpses northward beyond the heart of the Salmo to a Canadian ridge that soars nearly 3,000 feet above the canyon. Notice the swath cut through the forest on the face of that ridge marking the international boundary.

As the trail descends below 5,500 feet, the western hemlock (less common east of the Cascades) and western red cedar gradually replace the subalpine forests, with a few scattered white pines as well. You'll cross the same small creek a third time after 1.5 miles. Then you'll cross high above the west bank of the creek and into the Salmo Mountain Research Natural Area. This is land on which various natural features are preserved in an undisturbed state solely for research and educational purposes.

▶ **Woodland caribou are considered the most endangered large mammal in the lower forty-eight states. These noble animals were historically distributed throughout many northern states from Maine to Washington, but in the lower forty-eight they are now only found in the Selkirk Mountains of Idaho and Washington. The U.S. Fish and Wildlife Service is currently implementing a reintroduction program, and plans are under way to transplant sixty caribou to northeast Washington to bolster the herd. They like old-growth stands of cedar and hemlock, subalpine fir, and Engelmann spruce that support arboreal lichens, a mainstay of their diet. Biologists estimate that there are less than one hundred caribou in the region now.**

From here, you'll proceed steadily downward toward the South Salmo River under an increasingly shady canopy of hemlock and cedar, reaching a foot log, your only way across the river, at an elevation of 4,075 feet. Good campsites lie nearby, shaded by moss-draped western red cedar and western hemlock. One campsite lies along the north shore of the river, a second 400 feet back up the trail toward the trailhead. Understory plants are typical of a moist forest environment; they include ferns, bunchberry dogwood, and the elegant calypso orchid, which blooms in late spring.

Anglers can proceed upstream or downstream in search of cutthroat trout, abundant along the South Salmo.

This is grizzly bear country, too, so make sure you do all of your cooking away from your tent, and hang all food and garbage at least 10 feet high.

If you want to extend your trip, you can make a rewarding 18-mile loop by following the trail upstream past several campsites. You'll reenter subalpine forest before passing a spring and climbing to the dry divide separating the South Salmo from the Priest River. Snowy Top, rising to 7,572 feet, is a popular destination lying just north of the trail along the divide. Boundary Lake, another potential destination if you're willing to bushwhack for a mile across rugged terrain, straddles the border between Idaho and British Columbia just a short distance to the northwest.

The extended loop returns to the trailhead via a protracted but view-filled ridge walk. Keep in mind that water is nonexistent along the ridge, so you'll either need to pack a supply, go before all the snow melts in early July, or simply hike through to the South Salmo or Boundary Lake, the only reliable water sources en route.

For the shorter trip, simply retrace your steps to the trailhead.

Key Points

0.0 Start from the trailhead on the north side of Salmo Pass.

0.8 Cross a small creek twice during the initial 0.8 mile.

1.5 You'll cross the same small creek a third time, passing a small campsite on the opposite bank.

3.1 Reach the log bridge across the South Salmo River. Good campsites lie nearby.

6.2 Arrive back at the trailhead.

Hike Information

Local information
Visitor information for Ione and Metaline Falls, (509) 446-4108.

Accommodations
Washington Hotel, Metaline Falls, WA, (509) 446-4415.

Sullivan Lake and Noisy Creek campgrounds on Sullivan Lake, (509) 446-2691.

42 Grassy Top

This 7.6-mile out-and-back day hike gently wanders along a ridge through subalpine forests to a grassy summit in the Selkirk Mountains. Along the way views unfold into the rugged Idaho interior. Starting at a high elevation and having minimal elevation gain, this easy hike makes a good introduction to hiking for beginners and children.

Start: From Trail 503 on the south side of Forest Service Road 22 just below Pass Creek Pass.

Length: 7.6 miles out-and-back.

Approximate hiking time: 4 hours.

Difficulty rating: Easy, due to minimal elevation gain.

Trail surface: Dirt trail.

Elevation gain: 920 feet.

Land status: National forest.

Nearest town: Ione, WA.

Other trail users: Equestrians, mountain bikes.

Canine compatibility: Dog friendly.

Trail contacts: Colville National Forest, Sullivan Lake Ranger District, (509) 446–2691, www.fs.fed.us/r6/colville.

Schedule: Late June through early October.

Fees/permits: None required.

Maps: USGS Pass Creek 7.5-minute quad; USDA Forest Service Colville National Forest map.

Finding the trailhead: From Washington Route 31 just south of Ione, turn east onto paved Pend Oreille County Road 9345 where a sign points to Sullivan Lake. Drive past the deep, 3.5-mile-long lake to a junction with eastbound FR 22, 13.2 miles from the highway. (This junction can also be reached by driving 6.5 miles north then east from Metaline Falls and following Sullivan Lake signs.) Turn right (east) onto FR 22; this good gravel road follows the course of Sullivan Creek, crosses the creek, and reaches a junction with northbound Forest Service Road 2220 after 6.1 miles. Just after the crossing, turn right (southeast), following FR 22 and a sign pointing to Salmo Mountain and Priest Lake. Follow this narrow, sometimes steep, and winding dirt road for another 7.8 miles to Pass Creek Pass and park here. The signed Grassy Top Trail begins 0.1 mile back down the road, west of the pass, on the south side of the road. *DeLorme Washington Atlas & Gazetteer* page 119, B8.

The Hike

The easy amble from Pass Creek Pass to Grassy Top will lead you through old-growth, subalpine forests to—you guessed it—a grassy mountaintop where panoramas of northeastern Washington, northern Idaho, and southern British Columbia unfold.

You'll find the trailhead just west of Pass Creek Pass, where it quickly descends to a register box and begins a moderate climb to the ridgetop. Along the way the trail traverses north and then west on slopes blanketed by a mixed forest of Engelmann spruce, subalpine fir, lodgepole and white pine, western larch, and Douglas fir.

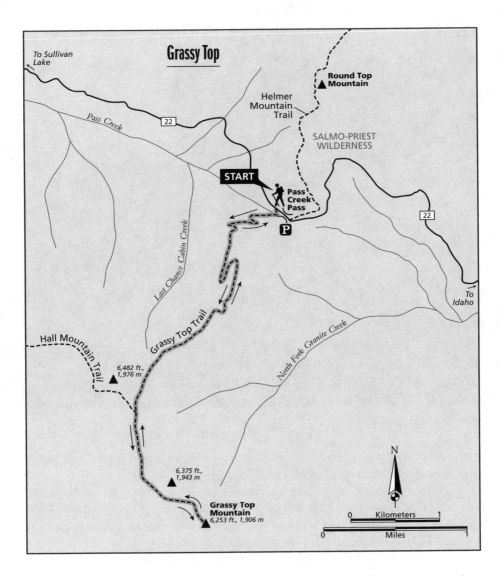

Grassy Top

To Sullivan
Lake

Round Top
Mountain

Helmer
Mountain
Trail

Pass Creek

22

SALMO-PRIEST
WILDERNESS

START

Pass
Creek
Pass

P

22

To
Idaho

Last Chance Cabin Creek

North Fork Granite Creek

Hall Mountain Trail

Grassy Top Trail

6,482 ft.,
1,976 m

6,375 ft.,
1,943 m

Grassy Top
Mountain
6,253 ft., 1,906 m

N

0   Kilometers   1

0   Miles   1

You'll get much of your elevation gain behind you in this first mile, reaching the main ridgetop divide after hiking in subalpine forest. For the next mile you'll alternate between east and west slopes before reaching a junction with the Hall Mountain Trail. Hall Mountain, 5 miles to the west, is home to a band of bighorn sheep.

Along the way you'll get glimpses of the views to come from small pocket meadows on the ridgetop. As you look to the west, you can see that Washington's Selkirk Mountains consist of two major divides rising east and west of the Pend Oreille River Valley. Here the eastern divide along the Idaho border contains wild country,

On the trail to Grassy Top.

home to moose, grizzly bear, and a small band of woodland caribou that ranges southward from the mountains of southeastern British Columbia.

Old-growth forests are a chief component of the woodland caribou's habitat. North of Pass Creek Pass, these forests are thankfully protected by the 41,335-acre Salmo-Priest Wilderness, but south of the pass you'll be able to look out over the logging roads and clear-cuts that threaten this crucial habitat.

Beyond the Hall Mountain junction, the trail continues south along west-facing slopes. Soon it breaks out of forest onto grassy slopes and passes scattered timberline trees. Some trailside pines have been stripped of bark by porcupines in search of the nutritious cambium layer between the bark and the sapwood. Porcupines seem to prefer pines, since the bark of nearby subalpine firs remains intact.

Broad views both south and west will accompany you along these open slopes. You'll be able to see the Kettle River Range to the west and isolated Abercrombie Mountain to the northwest. After an easy mile from the previous junction, the trail reaches a saddle at 6,200 feet. An unsigned, unmaintained trail here forks left, climbing a short distance northward along the crest to Peak 6375, where views surpassing those from Grassy Top can be enjoyed.

But to reach the pleasant, flat, inviting summit of Grassy Top, stay on the main trail and climb easily to the 6,253-foot mountain. To the west the forest of subalpine fir obscures your view, but to the east the view is glorious. In that direction you'll see the Priest River Valley and the rugged Selkirk Crest of Idaho. To the north you can gaze along the Shedroof Divide to Snowy Top and beyond to distant Canadian peaks.

Once you've had your fill of the views and taken your obligatory nap in the sun, retrace your steps to the trailhead.

Key Points

0.0 Start at a sign for Grassy Top Trail 503 on the south side of FR 22, 0.1 mile west of Pass Creek Pass.

0.4 Pass a small, intermittent spring, the only source of water along the otherwise dry trail.

1.8 Reach a hillside meadow with views to the west toward Idaho.

2.0 Reach a junction where the Hall Mountain Trail turns right (west); continue straight ahead on the Grassy Top Trail.

3.6 Reach the saddle for Grassy Top and Peak 6375 and turn right (south) to reach the summit. The left fork leads to views on Peak 6375.

3.8 Reach the summit of Grassy Top.

7.6 Arrive back at the trailhead.

Hike Information

Local information
Visitor information for Ione and Metaline Falls, (509) 446-4108.

Accommodations
Outpost Resort, Ione, WA, (509) 445-1317.

Sullivan Lake and Noisy Creek National Forest campgrounds on Sullivan Lake.

43 Mount Kit Carson

This 4.1-mile semi-loop day hike will lead you to a rocky summit on the western fringes of the Rocky Mountains only an hour's drive from Spokane in Mount Spokane State Park.

Start: An unmarked trail at the Smith Gap Trailhead.
Length: 4.1 miles on a semi-loop trail.
Approximate hiking time: 2½ hours.
Difficulty rating: Moderate, due to short length but steep terrain.
Trail surface: Wide forest trail.
Elevation gain: 1,171 feet.
Land status: State park.
Nearest town: Spokane, WA.
Other trail users: Equestrians, mountain bikes.
Canine compatibility: Leashed dogs are permitted.

Trail contacts: Mount Spokane State Park, (509) 456-4169, www.parks.wa.gov.
Schedule: Best hiked from mid-July through mid-October. The park is open daily from 6:30 A.M. to dusk.
Fees/permits: A $5.00 state park day-use fee is charged.
Maps: USGS Mt. Spokane 15-minute quad (trail not shown on quad); Mount Spokane State Park brochure and trails map.

Finding the trailhead: Drive 10 miles north of Spokane on U.S. Highway 2 to eastbound Washington Route 206, indicated by a Mount Spokane State Park sign. Follow this winding, paved road for 16.8 miles to the Mount Kit Carson Loop Road parking area. *DeLorme Washington Atlas & Gazetteer* page 89, A7.

The Hike

Spokane residents are fortunate to live at the foot of the Rocky Mountains, where enormous opportunities to enjoy the outdoors lie nearby. Only an hour's drive from downtown Spokane, Mount Spokane State Park consists of a large dome of granite south of Washington's Selkirk Mountains, offering a variety of short trail walks. While you won't get a wilderness experience here, you can briefly flee the pressures of city life to stroll in the mountains for a few hours or a day.

The short but rigorous hike to Mount Kit Carson offers a good workout and broad views of mountains, fertile valleys, and Washington's second largest city. Keep an eye out for the moose, cougars, bobcats, black bears, turkeys, and white-tailed deer that are quite common in the area.

From the parking area, walk north across the road to the Mount Kit Carson Loop Road entrance. This dirt road leads 1.2 miles past several shady picnic areas to Smith Gap. The obvious trail (unmarked except for a NO VEHICLES ALLOWED sign) begins on the north side of the road past several picnic areas at Smith Gap. From Smith Gap, the wide, unmarked trail climbs quickly past two right-forking trails into

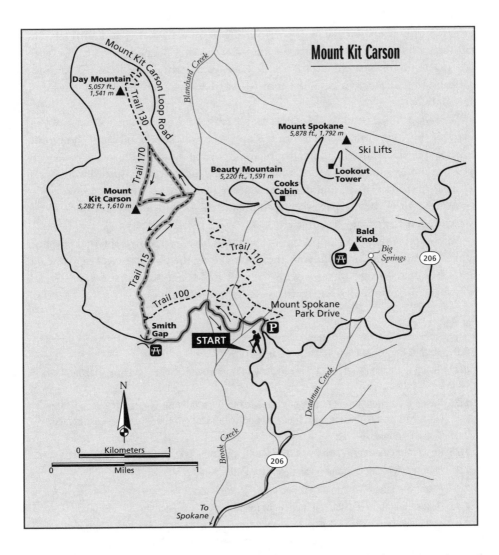

Mount Kit Carson

a forest dominated by lodgepole pine. The dusty trail climbs steeply past a variety of understory plants, including Sitka alder, Douglas maple, mallow ninebark, spirea, Oregon grape, wild rose, huckleberry, bracken fern, ocean spray, thimbleberry, snowberry, and pearly everlasting.

After less than 1 mile of steady climbing, the trail levels off on a grassy spur ridge, a shoulder of Mount Kit Carson. You'll ignore a faint path forking left and traverse east-facing slopes under a canopy of Douglas fir, western larch, and lodgepole pine to a junction. The right fork quickly leads to the Mount Kit Carson Loop Road, but you'll turn left at the junction and then fork right almost immediately, heading northwest under a shady forest canopy dominated by lodgepole pine, with an understory of huckleberry, bear grass, and menziesia.

This nearly level trail reaches a junction after 0.5 mile, where you'll turn left. The trail then climbs moderately through a thick stand of lodgepole pines to the summit ridge and another junction 0.5 mile later. Bear right, quite soon reaching the exfoliating granite crown of 5,282-foot Mount Kit Carson, where your rewarding view unfolds.

Westward lies a patchwork of forest and rangeland, stretching to the timbered ridges of the westernmost reaches of the northern Rockies. Southward the mountains steadily descend into the valley of the Spokane River, with views beyond of Spokane and its suburbs. A continuous mountainscape extends eastward to the crest of the Bitterroot Range, straddling the border between Idaho and Montana. The domelike summit of Mount Spokane dominates the skyline a mere 1.5 miles to the east, cluttered with radio transmitters.

To complete the semi-loop from the summit, hike back down the trail and bear right at the first junction, hiking northeastward along the grassy ridge. Then descend through timber to the junction with the trail to Mount Kit Carson Loop Road. From here, turn right and retrace the steep route to Smith Gap.

Key Points

0.0   Start at the Lower Loop Trailhead at Smith Gap.

0.3   Reach a junction with Trail 100 branching off to the right (east). Continue straight ahead on Trail 115.

1.25 Reach a junction. The right fork quickly leads to the Mount Kit Carson Loop Road. Turn left (west) at the junction onto Trail 170 and then fork right (northwest) almost immediately onto Trail 130.

1.75 Reach another junction and turn left (south) onto Trail 170.

2.3   After reaching the summit ridge, bear right to the summit.

2.4   Reach the summit of Mount Kit Carson.

2.5   Descending from the summit, bear right (east) at the first junction.

2.9   At the junction with the trail to Mount Kit Carson Loop Road, bear right (south) and retrace your steps on Trail 115 toward Smith Gap and the trailhead.

4.1   Reach the trailhead and parking area.

Hike Information

Accommodations
Mount Spokane State Park campgrounds, (509) 456-4169.
Bear Creek Lodge, Spokane, WA, (509) 238-9114.

Restaurants
The Onion, Spokane, WA, (509) 624-9965.
Bayou Brewing Company, Spokane, WA, (509) 484-4818.

Honorable Mentions

Northeast Washington

H57 Fir Mountain

Located south of Republic in the Kettle Crest Range, this trail gets right to the point, climbing steadily for 2 miles to the 5,600-foot summit. But it's well worth it—from the top, you'll find all-encompassing views of the surrounding ranch country, as well as the peaks as far as southern British Columbia.

To get there from the town of Republic, drive 8.5 miles west on Washington Route 20 to the Sweat Creek rest stop. Turn left (south) onto Forest Service Road 31 opposite the rest stop and continue 1.5 miles to the trailhead. For more information, contact Okanogan National Forest, Tonasket Ranger District, (509) 486–2186, www.fs.fed.us/r6/oka. *DeLorme Washington Atlas & Gazetteer* page 116, C1.

H58 Barnaby Buttes

This enjoyable but demanding 12-mile out-and-back hike follows the Kettle Crest South Trail north from its southern terminus to remote Barnaby Buttes, a former lookout site. The trail leads through both charred and virgin forests along the edges of the massive 1988 White Mountain fire. The views are panoramic from this former lookout site. Northward the tall, conical peaks of Bald Mountain, as well as Snow and Sherman Peaks, loom in the foreground of the gentle summits of the northern Kettle Crest.

To get there, follow Washington Route 20 to the east end of the South Sherman Road (Forest Service Road 2020) 12.2 miles east of Sherman Pass and 15 miles west of Kettle Falls. The turnoff is located between mileposts 331 and 332. Follow this good gravel road, with a washboard surface in places, west up South Sherman Creek for 6.6 miles, then turn left onto Barnaby Creek Road 2014. Follow this good dirt road 4.1 miles and turn right at the junction with Forest Service Road 250, which is signed for White Mountain and the Kettle Crest Trail. This narrow dirt road, with occasional turnouts, climbs steadily through forest and past clear-cuts to a four-way junction on Onion Ridge after another 4.4 miles. Turn right into the spacious parking area at the White Mountain Trailhead. For more information, contact Colville National Forest, Republic Ranger District, (509) 775–7400, www.fs.fed.us/r6/colville. *DeLorme Washington Atlas & Gazetteer* page 117, D5.

H59 Albain Hill Road to Copper Butte

In 1892 the state of Washington passed legislation authorizing the construction of the state's first official state highway, linking Marblemount and Pacific coast ports with Marcus and the busy riverboat traffic on the Columbia River. The most difficult task of the project required carving the road over the lofty divide of the Kettle Crest. When completed, this segment of the road remained impassable to freight wagons; with the heavy snows of winter, passage over the range even on horseback was often impossible. By 1898, when a better route was established over Sherman Pass to the south, the Old State (or Stage) Trail was abandoned. Today only 7 miles of this historic route remains, and this day hike traces 1.7 miles of the road on the westbound grade to the Kettle Crest. The remainder of the hike, to a former lookout site on Copper Butte, follows one of the steepest sections of the Kettle Crest Trail. But panoramic views are the reward for your efforts.

To get there, follow Washington Route 20 west from Kettle Falls for 21.5 miles to northbound Albain Hill Road (Forest Service Road 2030). Eastbound drivers will find this turnoff 4.1 miles east of Sherman Pass where the highway executes a horseshoe bend from north to southeast. Follow that gravel road northward 3.8 miles to the junction with eastbound Forest Service Road 9565 (Deadman Creek Road) and continue straight ahead (north) on FR 2030, a narrow undulating mountain road. After driving another 3.6 miles, turn left where a sign indicates the Old Stage Road Trail, and follow this spur for 250 yards to the trailhead parking area. For more information, contact Colville National Forest, Republic Ranger District, (509) 775–7400, www.fs.fed.us/r6/colville. *DeLorme Washington Atlas & Gazetteer* page 117, C5.

H60 Kettle Crest North Trail

By Cascade standards the peaks of the Kettle Crest aren't high mountains; the highest summits barely exceed 7,000 feet. But north of Sherman Pass, the area contains excellent hiking country with a character entirely different from that of other wildlands in the state. Feelings of remoteness and isolation accompany hikers into these mountains, a delightful change for those weary with the crowded trails and campsites so common in better-known areas. This rewarding hike traverses the initial 7.5 miles of the Kettle Crest North Trail, featuring subalpine forests and parkland, broad views, and lonely trails.

To get there, follow Washington Route 20 to Sherman Pass, 17 miles east of Republic or 24.75 miles west of Kettle Falls. Turn north onto Forest Service Road 495, signed for Kettle Crest Trail, and you'll reach the trailhead parking area within 0.1 mile. For more information, contact Colville National Forest, Republic Ranger District, (509) 775–7400, www.fs.fed.us/r6/colville. *DeLorme Washington Atlas & Gazetteer* page 117, D5.

H61 Hoodoo Canyon

Hoodoo Canyon—deep, narrow, and glacier carved—lies within the heart of the Kettle Crest. The trails of this range are seldom used, but most lead into extraordinary country. Diverse flora and views into spectacular Hoodoo Canyon are the major attractions of this moderate day hike. Views are good into the narrow chasm of Hoodoo Canyon, where precipitous granite cliffs rise abruptly from the valley floor. The rugged, glacier-smoothed granite east wall of 5,313-foot Coyote Mountain soars 2,000 feet above the canyon bottom to the west. Recent logging may be the only fly in the ointment of this trail, and you'll have to pass through portions of logged area along the way. Your trail traverses to the brink of the canyon, where four short switchbacks lead to aptly named Emerald Lake 2.8 miles from the trailhead. The shoreline is rocky and irregular, and cliffs soar skyward from the water's edge.

To get there, follow Washington Route 20 west from Kettle Falls for 21.5 miles to the northbound Albain Hill Road (Forest Service Road 2030). Eastbound drivers will find this turnoff 4.1 miles east of Sherman Pass where the highway executes a horseshoe bend from north to southeast. Follow that gravel road northward 3.8 miles to the junction with eastbound Forest Service Road 9565 (Deadman Creek Road). Then turn right. You'll reach a large clearing on the south side of the road where a sign indicates the Hoodoo Canyon Trail after 8.8 miles from the previous junction. For more information, contact Colville National Forest, Kettle Falls (Three Rivers) Ranger District, (509) 738–6111, www.fs.fed.us/r6/colville. *DeLorme Washington Atlas & Gazetteer* page 117, C6.

H62 South Fork Silver Creek

This pleasant 7-mile round-trip hike follows the cool, clear waters of South Fork Silver Creek before a short climb to a ridgetop view of surrounding peaks. From this high point, you'll get views of the rocky summit of nearby Abercrombie Mountain above you, and of river valleys below.

To get there, drive north from Colville on the Colville-Aladdin-Northport Road to the Deep Lake Boundary Road and turn right. Drive north on the Deep Creek Road for 7 miles and turn right (east) onto the Silver Creek Road, driving 1.5 miles to a junction with Forest Service Road 70. Drive this road 1.5 more miles to its end and the trailhead. For more information, contact Colville National Forest, Colville Ranger District, (509) 684–4557, www.fs.fed.us/r6/colville. *DeLorme Washington Atlas & Gazetteer* page 118, A4.

H63 Hellmer Mountain

The eastern crest of the Selkirk Mountains in northeastern Washington forms a lofty divide from the town of Newport north to the Canadian border. The northernmost

21-mile segment of this crest—the Shedroof Divide—is protected within the boundaries of the Salmo-Priest Wilderness and an adjacent roadless area in Idaho. Seldom tread by hikers, the Shedroof Divide Trail north of Pass Creek Pass is more often traveled by mule deer, elk, and, occasionally, by grizzly bears and woodland caribou. This 10.4-mile out-and-back hike will take you past views stretching eastward to the glacier-carved granite peaks of the Selkirk Crest in Idaho and northward to the mountainous wonderland of southeastern British Columbia. The true summit of Hellmer Mountain, little more than a bump on this otherwise high-traversing hike, is difficult to spot—a better option is to wander the ridge as far as you'd like and simply retrace your steps when you've had your fill.

To get there from Washington Route 31 just south of Ione, turn east onto paved Pend Oreille County Road 9345 where a sign points to Sullivan Lake. Drive past the deep, 3.5-mile-long lake to a junction with eastbound Forest Service Road 22, 13.2 miles from the highway. (This junction can also be reached by driving 6.5 miles north then east from Metaline Falls and following Sullivan Lake signs.) Turn right (east) onto FR 22; this good gravel road follows the course of Sullivan Creek, crosses the creek, and reaches a junction with northbound Forest Service Road 2220 after 6.1 miles. Just after the crossing, turn right (southeast), following FR 22 and a sign pointing to Salmo Mountain and Priest Lake. Follow this narrow, sometimes steep, and winding dirt road for another 7.8 miles to Pass Creek Pass. From the pass, continue eastward for 0.2 mile. A TRAIL sign indicates the beginning of the trail on the left, or north, side of the road. For more information, contact Colville National Forest, Sullivan Lake Ranger District, (509) 446–2691, www.fs.fed.us/r6/colville. *DeLorme Washington Atlas & Gazetteer* page 119, B8.

H64 Hall Mountain

Hall Mountain in Washington's Selkirk Range makes for a good short peak-bagging outing to a viewpoint high over Sullivan Lake. This 5-mile out-and-back trip climbs through pine forests to wide-ranging views. Around the summit, if you're lucky, you'll be accompanied by bighorn sheep, introduced to the peak by state wildlife managers.

To get there, drive east on Sullivan Lake Road from Metaline Falls to the junction with Forest Service Road 22. Take FR 22 east for 4 miles and turn right onto Forest Service Road 500. Drive 8 miles to the end of the road and the trailhead. (**Note:** The road is closed from mid-August to June 30 to protect the sheep's mating and birthing season.) For more information, contact Colville National Forest, Sullivan Lake Ranger District, (509) 446–2691, www.fs.fed.us/r6/colville. *DeLorme Washington Atlas & Gazetteer* page 119, B7.

H65 Shedroof Mountain

This pleasant day hike passes through an old-growth subalpine forest on its way to a panoramic viewpoint on the slopes of Shedroof Mountain in the Salmo-Priest Wilderness. It's unlikely you'll see a grizzly or caribou on your hike, but you're in their domain here. Like Hellmer Mountain, the summit of Shedroof itself offers limited views and is only accessible by an abandoned trail. This trail can be combined with the trail down to the South Salmo River (see Hike 41) to form a rewarding 18-mile loop backpack, perhaps the most popular hike in the wilderness.

From Washington Route 31 just south of Ione, turn east onto paved Pend Oreille County Road 9345 where a sign points to Sullivan Lake. Drive past the deep, 3.5-mile-long lake to a junction with eastbound Forest Service Road 22, 13.2 miles from the highway. (This junction can also be reached by driving 6.5 miles north then east from Metaline Falls and following Sullivan Lake signs.) Turn east onto FR 22 where a sign points to Salmo Mountain and Priest Lake. This good gravel road follows the course of Sullivan Creek and reaches a junction with northbound Forest Service Road 2220 after crossing a bridge at 6.1 miles. Southbound FR 22 forks right here, leading to Pass Creek Pass and Nordman, Idaho. Bear left at this four-way junction and follow FR 2220, ignoring numerous signed spur roads, to a ridgetop junction with left-forking Forest Service Road 270, which leads to a tremendous view atop Salmo Mountain, 18.25 miles from the county road. Bear right here and proceed 0.3 mile to the road's end at the Salmo Pass Trailhead. For more information, contact Colville National Forest, Sullivan Lake Ranger District, (509) 446–2691, www.fs.fed.us/r6/colville. *DeLorme Washington Atlas & Gazetteer* page 119, A8.

H66 Thunder Creek

This pleasant 5.8-mile out-and-back hike takes you through a dense, cool canopy of forest to a stream on a valley floor. Much like the South Salmo River hike (see Hike 41), the lush forests that line the stream valley here may remind you of those on the west side of the Cascades.

From the town of Metaline Falls, drive east on Sullivan Lake Road past Sullivan Lake to the junction with Forest Service Road 22. Take this road east for 6.1 miles across a bridge to a junction. From here, you'll continue straight ahead where the road changes to Forest Service Road 2220, and turn right onto the Thunder Creek Road (Forest Service Road 345). Park here; the trail begins at the road junction. For more information, contact Colville National Forest, Sullivan Lake Ranger District, (509) 446–2691, www.fs.fed.us/r6/colville. *DeLorme Washington Atlas & Gazetteer* page 119, B8.

H67 Bead Lake

Hike to a tree-ringed lake with shorelines dotted with meadows with wildflowers. The trail follows the east shore of the lake, where you may spot deer and moose grazing along the lakeshore. While the entire trail to the end of the lake is 12 miles out-and-back, you can shorten the hike and wander along the lake's shoreline as far as you wish.

From the town of Newport, drive east on U.S. Highway 2 across the Pend Oreille River into Idaho. Turn north onto the LeClerc Creek Road, cross back into Washington, and drive 3.8 miles to a junction with the Bead Lake Road. Turn right onto Pend Oreille County Road 3029 for approximately 6 miles. Turn right onto Forest Service Road 3215 and follow signs for the Bead Lake Trail for 0.5 mile to the trailhead. For more information, contact Colville National Forest, Newport Ranger District, (509) 447–3129, www.fs.fed.us/r6/colville. *DeLorme Washington Atlas & Gazetteer* page 105, B8.

Southeast Washington

The vast Columbia Basin of southeast Washington lies in sharp contrast to the damp, forested region of Washington west of the Cascades. East of the mountains, a tumultuous legacy of flooding and volcanic eruptions has left behind a complex topography of coulees, buttes, mesas, dry waterfalls, and hanging valleys worthy of exploration. The Cascade Mountains wring moisture from storms sweeping inland off the Pacific Ocean, leaving the state's eastern side as an arid landscape of fragrant sage-covered hills, rolling wheat fields, and mountain slopes more closely resembling those of the Rocky Mountains farther to the east.

Just east of the Cascades, basalt flows have been faulted and folded into a series of large, east–west trending synclines and anticlines called the Yakima Fold Belt. The windswept, open slopes and canyons of the 50,000-acre South Murray segment of the L. T. Murray/Wenas Wildlife Area extend in a band approximately 4 to 8 miles wide from south of the town of Ellensburg to just north of the town of Selah. The area supports a large elk herd, along with mule deer and bear. L. T. Murray's trails have their greatest appeal in spring, when trails in the Cascades still lie buried under a blanket of snow. From April to June, the hills above Yakima Canyon burst to life with a profusion of wildflowers, and you're likely to find sun and blue skies here even if it's gloomy and wet on the west side of the mountains.

Farther east, among the sprawling wheat fields northeast of the city of Pasco, the Juniper Dunes Wilderness preserves the northernmost stands of western junipers, some of which are more than 150 years old. In this intriguing landscape you can wander through windswept sand dunes up to 130 feet high and 1,000 wide, along with the many shrubs and flowers that bloom here in spring.

Tucked into the far southeast corner of the state lies the Umatilla National Forest and the remote Blue Mountains, where streams have incised deep canyons through overlying basalt and mountains have been uplifted more than 6,000 feet above sea level. Explorers Lewis and Clark passed this way in 1805, and Marcus and

Narcissa Whitman crossed the forest in 1836 to establish a mission near Walla Walla, Washington, now a designated National Historic Landmark.

While elk hunting and fishing have historically been the main forms of recreation in the Blue Mountains, the area is increasingly attracting hikers and backpackers drawn to the solitude that can be found on its remote backcountry trails. The 177,000-acre Wenaha-Tucannon Wilderness, lying at the heart of Washington's part of the forest, offers more than 200 miles of trails that wind through lodgepole pine and subalpine fir forests, shady canyons along mountain streams, and over open, grassy ridges carpeted with wildflowers. Elevations range from 2,000 feet on the Wild and Scenic Wenaha River to more than 6,400 feet at the summit of Oregon Butte, the region's highest peak. On your hike you're likely to encounter some of the many wildlife species found here, including Rocky Mountain elk, bighorn sheep, white-tailed and mule deer, black bears, cougars, coyotes, and pine martens. Both the Tucannon and Wenaha Rivers provide spawning habitat for steelhead and chinook salmon, a federally protected species, and there's good fishing for trout for those interested in dipping a line in the water.

44 Yakima Canyon Rim (Skyline)

This 9.2-mile round-trip day hike or overnighter follows a portion of the Yakima Canyon Rim Scenic Trail over open, sage-covered hills above the spectacular 2,000-foot-deep canyon of the Yakima River. Views are expansive in all directions, sun is plentiful, and you'll find a profusion of wildflowers carpeting the hillsides in spring.

Start: Yakima Canyon Rim Scenic Trailhead (Skyline).
Length: 9.2 miles out-and-back.
Approximate hiking time: 4½ hours.
Difficulty rating: Moderate, due to length and moderate elevation gain.
Trail surface: Dirt surface, occasionally climbing over basalt outcrops.
Elevation gain: 2,245 feet.
Land status: State wildlife area.
Nearest town: Selah, WA.

Other trail users: Equestrians.
Canine compatibility: Dog friendly.
Trail contacts: Washington Department of Fish and Wildlife, Ellensburg, WA, (509) 925-6746, www.wa.gov/wdfw/lands/r3wenas.htm.
Schedule: April to November.
Fees/permits: None required.
Maps: USGS Badger Pocket 15-minute and Pomona 7.5-minute quads.

Finding the trailhead: From Interstate 82 just north of Selah, take the Firing Center exit (Exit 26). Proceed west on the Canyon Road for 0.7 mile, then turn left onto the Harrison Road. After 2 miles turn right onto the North Wenas Road; where that road curves sharply to the left after 2.8 miles, continue straight ahead onto the Gibson Road. Turn right (east) within 0.25 mile onto the gravel-surfaced Buffalo Road, winding past scattered farms and driving through semi-arid grasslands. At 2.1 miles bear left, crossing through a fence and over a cattle guard. Park in the rough, overgrown parking area on the right (north) side of the road, 2.75 miles from the turnoff. *DeLorme Washington Atlas & Gazetteer* page 51, C5.

The Hike

The Columbia Basin, a basalt-shrouded landscape between the Rocky Mountains and the Cascade Range, is not simply a large, featureless depression as the name might suggest. Along the western margin of the basin lies a region of great ridges (anticlines) separated by deep troughs (synclines). The Horse Heaven Hills, Saddle Mountains, Yakima Ridge, and Frenchman Hills, among others, dominate the landscape here, reaching heights of 4,500 feet. Far below, the Columbia and Yakima Rivers have cut down through the uplifting land, creating impressive canyons.

This grassland hike along the windswept, basalt-capped ridge that towers above Yakima Canyon follows the initial 4.6 miles of the 18-mile-long Yakima Canyon Rim Scenic Trail, constructed by Washington's Department of Game (now called the Washington Department of Fish and Wildlife) in 1977. Water is scarce along the trail; Twin Springs, little more than a few stagnant pools, is the only available source of

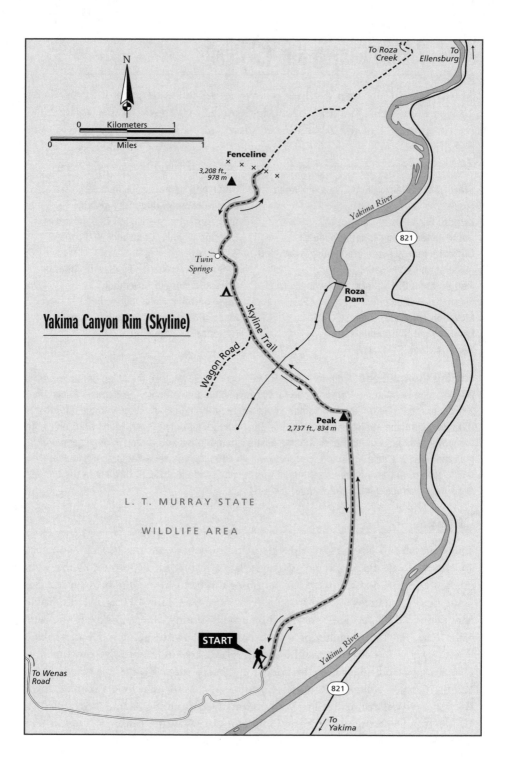

Yakima Canyon Rim (Skyline)

N

Kilometers 0 — 1
Miles 0 — 1

To Roza Creek
To Ellensburg

Fenceline
3,208 ft., 978 m

Yakima River

821

Twin Springs

Roza Dam

Skyline Trail

Wagon Road

Peak
2,737 ft., 834 m

L. T. MURRAY STATE

WILDLIFE AREA

START

To Wenas Road

Yakima River

821

To Yakima

Looking down on the Yakima River from the trail.

water. If you plan to hike the entire 18-mile route, a car shuttle is necessary, and you should keep the trail's limited water sources in mind. And if you're camping, carry a stove, as there is no wood to be found along the route. Campfires are prohibited from April 15 to October 15 due to fire danger.

April and May are the best times for this hike, when temperatures are still cool enough to be comfortable and the show of wildflowers is at its peak. You'll see dozens of flowers, including the ubiquitous yarrow, desert parsley, wild mustard, tar-weed (or fiddleneck), Indian paintbrush, buckwheat, phacelia, golden-aster, woolly sunflower, and single-flowered false sunflower. You may also spot the bighorn sheep and elk that roam the area, along with golden eagles or falcons gracefully gliding on the updrafts above the canyon floor. And while you'll be in view of farmland, houses, and the Roza Dam along the Yakima River below, the solitude you're likely to find on this hike will make up for the lack of surrounding wildness.

From the parking area, briefly follow the road north downhill to the trailhead. There's little in the way of signage at the trailhead, which is to your left, but there is a good tread to follow. After climbing slightly to moderately east to the canyon rim, you'll begin ascending the rim northward, heading for numerous false summits along the ridgeline. The trail is nearly impossible to lose, and HORSE TRAIL signs on tall wooden posts are placed at intervals to keep you on course.

During the 2-mile ascent to the first peak, you're almost immediately rewarded with views south toward the snowy mass of Mount Adams and over the Yakima River Valley. As you climb higher, views of the Cascades to the west come into view, including the looming summit of Mount Rainier. Temperatures here can soar well into the nineties during the summer, so plan on starting early and bringing plenty of sunscreen.

The rimrock trail finally reaches the first true summit along the initial segment of the hike, Peak 2737, at an abandoned fenceline. It then veers away from the canyon rim and drops 237 feet to a saddle overlooking Roza Dam on the Yakima River, passing briefly under a power line. Beyond the power line you'll negotiate a short uphill stretch before steeply dropping to Twin Springs. Along this stretch in springtime, you may notice the beautiful, ground-hugging pink flowers of a species of *Lewisia,* closely related to the famous bitterroot, once an important food source for Native Americans of the region.

The cool shade of Twin Springs is a welcome change of pace, an oasis in this dry, open country. While the springs may be little more than small muddy pools, especially in summer, numerous shrubs compete for moisture and provide shade at this lush site, including serviceberry, chokecherry, and a few 5-foot-tall specimens of tall mahonia, a species of Oregon grape. Poison ivy is also common.

If you're planning to camp, there is a level spot here, but it's best to leave the water source undisturbed in consideration of local wildlife. Instead camp on the ridge just before descending to the springs, enjoying the views and the promise of a glorious sunrise.

Beyond Twin Springs the trail climbs steeply back to the canyon rim, soon traversing the east slopes of Peak 3208, 2,000 feet above the floor of the canyon. At a fenceline where the trail begins its plunge into Roza Creek's broad canyon, leave the trail and climb uphill to the summit of Peak 3208, where you'll find a fire ring and a sweeping, 360-degree view including Mount Adams, Mount Rainier, and the impressive, jagged peaks of the Stuart Range. From the peak, retrace your route to the trailhead.

Key Points

0.0 Start approximately 100 yards down the hill (northwest) from the parking area. Wooden posts on your left mark the beginning of the trail.

0.5 Arrive at your first overlook of the Yakima River.

1.0 Arrive at a small plateau with views south toward the Yakima Valley.

2.3 Arrive at the summit of the first high point, Peak 2737.

2.7 Cross under a set of power lines.

3.0 Arrive in a saddle at an intersection with an old wagon road and an overlook of Roza Dam. Continue straight ahead.

3.4 Pass a campsite just off the trail before descending to Twin Springs.

3.5 Arrive at Twin Springs.

4.4 Arrive at a fenceline where the trail begins descending toward Roza Creek. Leave the trail, turning left (west) up the hill to scramble to a broad viewpoint at the top of Peak 3208.

4.6 Arrive at the high point with a large fire ring and the turnaround point.

9.2 Retrace your steps, arriving back at the trailhead.

Hike Information

Local information

Yakima Valley Visitors and Convention Bureau, (509) 575-3010.

Northwest Arid Lands: An Introduction to the Columbia Basin Shrub-Steppe by Georganne P. O'Connor and Karen Wieda.

Local events/attractions

Selah's Community Days, third weekend of May, www.selahdays.org.

Central Washington State Fair, September, www.fairfun.com.

Accommodations

Birchfield Manor Bed and Breakfast, Yakima, WA, (509) 452-1960.

Yakima Sportsman State Park campground, (888) 226-7688.

Restaurants

Grant's Brewery Pub, Yakima, WA, (509) 575-2922.

The Greystone Restaurant, Yakima, WA, (509) 248-9801.

45 Ginkgo Petrified Forest

Follow an easy 1.5-mile loop through a desert region of central Washington, and see one of the largest collections of ancient forest fossil remnants in the country.

Start: From the trailhead parking lot and ranger's residence off the Vantage Highway.
Length: 1.5-mile loop.
Approximate hiking time: 45 minutes.
Difficulty rating: Easy, due to wide, gentle trail and short distance.
Trail surface: Paved and gravel surface.
Elevation gain: 330 feet.
Land status: State park.
Nearest town: Vantage, WA.
Other trail users: None.
Canine compatibility: Leashed dogs are permitted.

Trail contacts: Washington State Parks, Ginkgo Petrified Forest State Park, (509) 856-2700, www.parks.wa.gov.
Schedule: Open 8:00 A.M. to dusk, October 1 to March 31. Open 6:30 A.M. to dusk, April 1 to September 30.
Fees/permits: Suggested donation of $1.00 at the visitor center.
Maps: USGS Ginkgo 7.5-minute quad; Washington State Parks Trees of Stone Trail Guide.

Finding the trailhead: From Interstate 90 on the west side of the Columbia River, about 26 miles east of Ellensburg and 42 miles west of Moses Lake, take the Vantage exit and proceed north. After passing the interpretive center (stop in to see exhibits and pick up a trail map), the road bends west. Follow signs pointing to TRAILS. You'll reach the trailhead parking area on the right (north) side of the road 2.75 miles from I-90. *DeLorme Washington Atlas & Gazetteer* page 51, A8.

The Hike

This short hike through Ginkgo Petrified Forest State Park, in addition to being a fine leg stretcher for travelers along I-90, provides many insights into the past natural history of the region and one of the largest natural collections of petrified wood in the country. If you come here during summer, be sure to bring water for this hot, dry hike.

From the trailhead, follow the paved path to the east, passing the display showing a map of the trail system constructed by the Civilian Conservation Corps during the 1930s. You'll start out on the hiking trail and loop back via any one of the interpretive trails.

Standing on the bone-dry hillsides above the Columbia River, it may be hard to believe that a lush forest once covered this arid landscape, but during the Miocene epoch (twenty-six million to twelve million years ago) the landscape of this area of central Washington was the complete opposite of what you'll find today. Lacking a

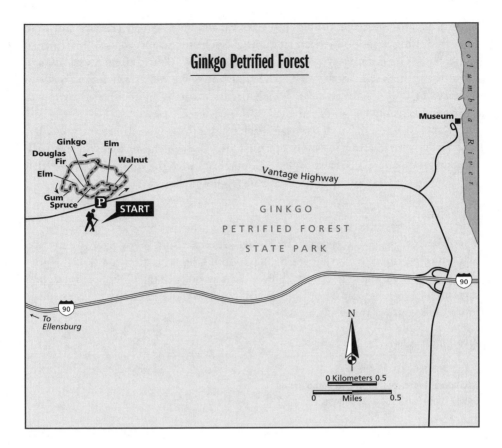

Ginkgo Petrified Forest

Cascade Range to intercept incoming Pacific Ocean moisture, the Vantage area's damp climate supported thick forests, along with lakes, swamps, and streams.

Periodically basalt erupted from numerous fissures in the earth's crust throughout the present-day Columbia Basin, spreading over the region and burying everything in its path. The cliffs along the Columbia River near Vantage are composed of this basalt, with each layer representing a successive lava flow. The petrified logs you'll see today at the Ginkgo Forest were entombed by these outpourings of basalt, yet were miraculously protected from incineration by the abundant water that rapidly cooled the lava.

You'll soon leave the paved path, climbing eastward along a low ridge. The alkaline ground is sparsely covered with sagebrush, greasewood, and bunchgrass. Keep an eye out for rattlesnakes; gopher snakes are also common. As you gain elevation, the Columbia River comes into view.

As you pass the various remnants of petrified trees, you may find it intriguing that over fifty species of trees representing more than thirty genera have been identified in the Ginkgo Petrified Forest. Logs from the higher hills, including remnants of spruce and Douglas fir, drifted into Lake Vantage from cooler climates and were preserved along with locally occurring species such as elm, ginkgo, sycamore, maple, and hickory. Ginkgo trees were widespread worldwide 100 to 200 million years ago, when the planet's climate was much different. Today the only surviving member of this class of tree is *Ginkgo biloba,* which occurs naturally in an isolated region in China and is planted as an ornamental in this country.

Just before the trail bends westward back toward the trailhead, take the upper left fork if you want to see many more petrified logs. But whichever trail you take back to your car, you'll surely have gained an appreciation of the dramatic changes that have altered the environment over the past few million years.

Key Points

The Trees of Stone Interpretive Trail offers several short loops past twenty-two exhibits of petrified trees. A longer, 3-mile loop hiking trail offers additional opportunities to wander the sage-covered hills and catch views of the Columbia River and surrounding area. Pick up a copy of the trail guide at the interpretive center or refer to the trail guide at the trailhead.

Hike Information

Accommodations
Wanapum Recreation Area and campground,
(888) 226–7688 for reservations.

46 Juniper Dunes

This easy round-trip springtime day hike will lead you through one of eastern Washington's most intriguing landscapes and wilderness areas, past stands of juniper and over impressive sand dunes.

Start: From the trailhead at the end of the Joy Road on the Juniper Dunes Ranch.
Length: 1.8 miles out-and-back, with possible longer hikes.
Approximate hiking time: 1 hour.
Difficulty rating: Easy, due to gentle terrain and short length.
Trail surface: Narrow trail, poorly defined in places; a walk through grassland and sage.
Elevation gain: 170 feet.
Land status: Federal wilderness area, accessed across private land.

Nearest town: Pasco, WA.
Other trail users: None.
Canine compatibility: Not dog friendly.
Trail contacts: Bureau of Land Management, Spokane District Office, (509) 536–1200, www.or.blm.gov/Spokane.
Schedule: Access for hiking via the north trailhead is permitted from March through May.
Fees/permits: None required.
Maps: USGS Levey Northeast 7.5-minute quad.

Finding the trailhead: From the Pasco-Kahlotus Road, 22 miles northeast of Pasco or 17.2 miles south of Kahlotus, turn west onto the Snake River Road at a sign for the town of Eltopia. Follow this winding paved road through rolling wheat fields for 3.4 miles, then turn left onto the gravel-surfaced East Blackman Ridge Road. After another 2.4 miles, turn left onto the Joy Road. Follow this dirt and gravel road past the Juniper Dunes Ranch for 2 miles to its dead end at the trailhead. *DeLorme Washington Atlas & Gazetteer* page 40, A2.

Note: The wilderness is also accessible from the southwest, also across private land, by turning west off the Pasco-Kahlotus Road onto the private Peterson Road. You'll want four-wheel drive here, as the last 2 miles of driving are across sand. Call the BLM office for more detailed information on directions, conditions, and landowner access restrictions.

The Hike

Sand dunes aren't unheard of in eastern Washington, as they commonly form along the banks of the Columbia and Snake Rivers. But nowhere else are they as abundant as in the Juniper Dunes, where nearly 10 square miles of sand dunes and groves of western juniper are protected as wilderness under the jurisdiction of the Bureau of Land Management (BLM). This is the only wilderness area in the entire Columbia Basin and a fascinating insight into this remote, arid part of Washington.

The trailhead, the only access point to the wilderness, lies on the property of the Juniper Dunes Ranch, only 100 yards from the wilderness boundary. The owner graciously allows day hiking from March through May only, due to high summer fire danger, and no overnight parking is permitted.

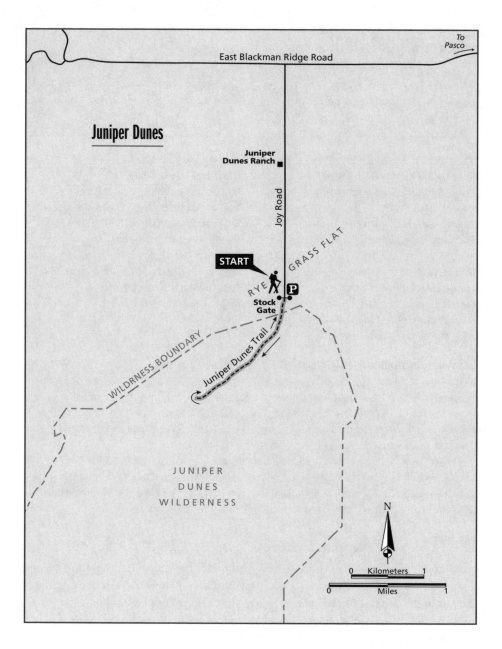

Miles and miles of sand dunes—some carpeted with shrubs, wildflowers, and junipers, and others nearly barren—rise in marked contrast to the uniformity of the surrounding wheat fields. The area is characterized by hundreds of dunes with no prominent ridges or drainages; all drainages end in interdune depressions. There is no particular destination for your hike other than the dunes and the junipers, and you may only walk a mile or so from the trailhead. If you're looking for solitude, you'll likely find it beyond that point.

Respect the property rights of the owner of Juniper Dunes Ranch to ensure future access to the area. Enter the area only if the time and conditions are appropriate, according to the sign at the trailhead. Never build fires, and always be sure the stock gates are closed behind you.

From the trailhead, follow jeep tracks south across Rye Grass Flat, pass through another stock gate, and enter the wilderness area. From here the trail, sometimes disappearing in the sand, leads southwest for about a mile to the first stand of western junipers. In spring you'll enjoy a colorful display of wildflowers, including yarrow, common phacelia, blue penstemon, hawksbeard, winged dock, wallflower, desert parsley, flax, wyethia, and evening primrose. Shrubs include sagebrush, bitterbrush, and rabbitbrush, which has bright yellow flowers in the fall.

Once you reach the first junipers, you can either backtrack to the trailhead or roam deeper into the surreal landscape at will.

Key Points

0.0 Start at the trailhead at the end of the Joy Road. Walk through the stock gate, being sure to lock it behind you.

0.1 Arrive at the second stock gate and cross into the wilderness area.

0.9 Arrive at the first stand of junipers and the turnaround point. From here, you can also continue beyond the trail to explore the dunes, making sure to retrace your steps to the trailhead.

1.8 Arrive back at the parking area.

Hike Information

Local information
Tri-Cities Visitor and Convention Bureau, (509) 735-8486, www.visittri-cities.com. *Northwest Arid Lands: An Introduction to the Columbia Basin Shrub-Steppe* by Georganne P. O'Connor and Karen Wieda.

Local events/attractions
Cinco de Mayo, Pasco, WA.

Accommodations
Vineyard Inn, Pasco, WA, (509) 547-0791.
Charbonneau Park campground, (509) 547-7783.

Restaurants
Rattlesnake Mountain Brewing Company, Richland, WA, (509) 783-5747.
Casa Chapala, Pasco, WA, (509) 586-4224.

47 Tucannon River

Following the Tucannon River, this easy 8.2-mile round-trip day hike or overnighter wanders through cool and shady old-growth forest along one of the largest streams in the Blue Mountains. Stop and dangle your feet in the water on a hot day, or bring your tent and enjoy the solitude and the sounds of the tumbling stream for a night or two.

Start: The Tucannon River Trail off the Tucannon River Road.
Length: 8.2 miles out-and-back.
Approximate hiking time: 4 hours.
Difficulty rating: Easy, due to the gentle terrain.
Elevation gain: 520 feet.
Trail surface: Forest trail.
Land status: National forest.
Nearest town: Pomeroy, WA.
Other trail users: Equestrians.
Canine compatibility: Dog friendly.
Trail contacts: Umatilla National Forest, Pomeroy Ranger District, (509) 843-1891, www.fs.fed.us/r6/uma.

Schedule: May to November.
Fees/permits: Parking at the trailhead requires a $5.00 day pass or $30.00 annual Northwest Forest Pass. You can purchase a pass at www.fs.fed.us/r6/feedemo or by calling (800) 270-7504.
Maps: USGS Panjab Creek and Stentz Spring 7.5-minute quads; USDA Forest Service Wenaha-Tucannon Wilderness map and Umatilla National Forest map.

Finding the trailhead: From U.S. Highway 12, 13.3 miles north of the town of Dayton, turn east onto the Tucannon Road; a sign here indicates Camp Wooten. Follow this paved road through the Tucannon River Valley, ignoring the left fork to Camp Wooten and the Tucannon campground after 28 miles. Continue south up the Tucannon River Road to a junction 31.4 miles from US 12. Following the sign for the Tucannon River Trailhead, turn left onto this sometimes narrow and rough dirt road for 5 miles to its end at the trailhead. *DeLorme Washington Atlas & Gazetteer* page 42, C4.

The Hike

This leisurely walk along the northern boundary of the Wenaha–Tucannon Wilderness will guide you along a cool mountain stream and through an old-growth forest. The shady trail provides a particularly welcome break from the hot, dry days of summer, and the gentle trail and abundant campsites provide a good chance to introduce kids and novices alike to the joys of camping. While fishing for rainbow trout can be good here, you'll want to toss back any salmon you might catch, as the Snake River chinook salmon is now a federally protected species. Because of new salmon

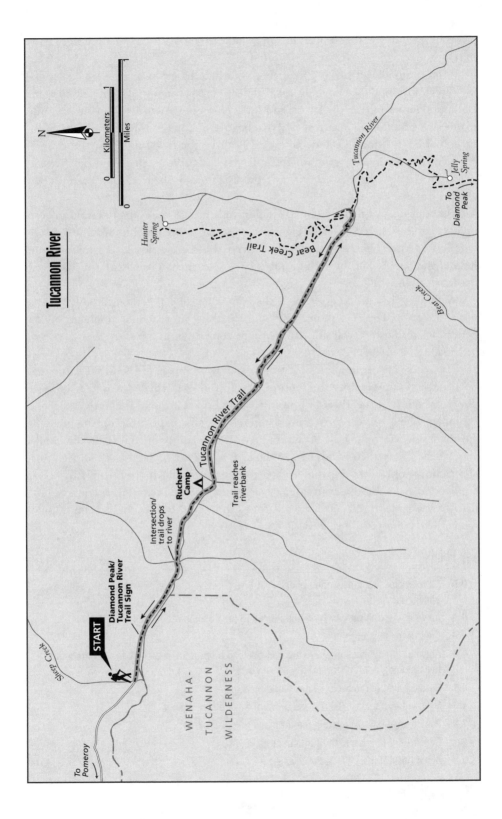

Tucannon River

N

Kilometers

Miles

0   1

0

To Pomeroy

Sheep Creek

START

Diamond Peak/
Tucannon River
Trail Sign

WENAHA-
TUCANNON
WILDERNESS

Intersection/
trail drops
to river

Ruchert
Camp

Tucannon River Trail

Trail reaches
riverbank

Bear Creek Trail

Hunter
Spring

Tucannon River

Bear Creek

To
Diamond
Peak

Jelly
Spring

protection rules, you'll also need to camp and cook at least 75 feet away from running water.

From the trailhead parking lot, begin your hike by crossing a bridge and walking along an old, closed logging road under a forest canopy of grand fir, western larch, ponderosa pine, Douglas fir, and lodgepole pine. After 1 mile you leave the roadbed, continuing on a narrow trail that begins to drop toward the river. The small, shrubby tree growing in the deep shadows cast by the towering forest is the western yew. Distinguished by its rough, scaly, reddish bark, green to red berries, and sharp, flat needles, the western yew is typically found in shady canyon bottoms and along streambanks.

Other plants that thrive along the trail include prince's pine, the beautiful calypso orchid (an endangered species), queen's cup, violet, and false Solomon's seal. More wildflowers you'll likely notice include wild strawberry, clover, yarrow, larkspur, lupine, and spirea. Shrubs include Douglas maple, mallow ninebark, huckleberry, ocean spray, and wild rose.

Within earshot of the river all of the way, you'll find potential campsites along the entire route. The Tucannon River, while nothing more than a mountain stream here in its headwaters, will still tempt you to cool down in the many easily accessible small pools along the way.

The forest opens up enough at times to allow glimpses of the heavily forested, north-facing slopes across the stream. Once you've reached the waters of Bear Creek, which join the Tucannon from the south, you'll find a junction and a few campsites where you can turn around and retrace your steps, camp for the night, or continue on. The right fork of the trail crosses the Tucannon River, briefly climbs above Bear Creek, then winds toward the Diamond Peak high country. The left fork climbs north out of the canyon, leading to Hunter Spring and ultimately to Forest Service Road 40 coming from Pomeroy. For views of the surrounding country, hidden for the past 4 miles, take the left fork for about 0.5 mile to an open hillside, where the landscape comes into view.

Key Points

0.0 Start by crossing the wooden bridge over Sheep Creek at the east end of the trailhead parking lot.

0.4 Arrive at the trail sign for Diamond Peak and the Tucannon River Trail.

0.6 Cross a small stream.

1.0 Arrive at an intersection where the trail starts to drop to the river. Take the right (south) fork, heading downhill toward the river.

1.1 Pass the first of many campsites along the river.

1.6 Descend to the river's banks and arrive at a good resting spot.

2.8 Pass a large campsite along the river.

4.1 Reach Bear Creek and the turnaround point.

8.2 Arrive back at the trailhead and your car.

Hike Information

Local information
Pomeroy Chamber of Commerce, www.click pomeroy.com.

Local events/attractions
The Garfield County Fair comes to Pomeroy in mid-September; find out more on the town's Web site.

Accommodations
Pioneer Motel, Pomeroy, WA, (509) 843-1559.

Several USDA Forest Service campgrounds are also located along the Tucannon Road, (509) 843-1891.

Restaurants
Donna's Drive-In, Pomeroy, WA.

Patit Creek Restaurant, Dayton, WA, (509) 382-2625.

48 Oregon Butte

The Oregon Butte Trail leads you through fragrant ponderosa pine forests and wild-flower-splashed meadows to grand views on the summit of the highest point in Washington's Blue Mountains. The moderate climb offers plenty of solitude, and at the summit you'll find a historic fire lookout, still active today, and far-ranging views stretching into nearby Oregon and Idaho.

Start: From the Misery Mountain Trailhead (3113) off Forest Service Road 4608.
Length: 6 miles out-and-back.
Approximate hiking time: 3½ hours.
Difficulty rating: Moderate, due to modest elevation gain and moderate grade.
Trail surface: Forest trail.
Elevation gain: 1,250 feet.
Land status: Federal wilderness area.
Nearest town: Pomeroy, WA.
Other trail users: Equestrians.
Canine compatibility: Leashed dogs are permitted.

Trail contacts: Umatilla National Forest, Pomeroy Ranger District, (509) 843–1891, www.fs.fed.us/r6/uma.
Schedule: July through mid-October.
Fees/permits: Parking at the trailhead requires a $5.00 day pass or $30.00 annual Northwest Forest Pass. You can purchase a pass at www.fs.fed.us/r6/feedemo or by calling (800) 270-7504.
Maps: USGS Oregon Butte 7.5-minute quad; USDA Forest Service Wenaha-Tucannon Wilderness map and Umatilla National Forest map.

Finding the trailhead: From U.S. Highway 12, 13.3 miles north of the town of Dayton, turn east onto the Tucannon Road; a sign here indicates Camp Wooten. Follow this paved road through the Tucannon River Valley, ignoring the left fork to Camp Wooten and the Tucannon campground after 28 miles. Continue south up the Tucannon River Road 2 miles beyond the end of the pavement to the junction with Forest Service Road 4620, signed for Godman Guard Station. Turn right and follow this steep and sometimes rough dirt road for 4.2 miles to Forest Service Road 46 at Mountain Top Junction. Bear left and follow this good dirt road as it ascends the ridge southward, ignoring several smaller spur roads along the way. After another 12.1 miles, bear left on descending Forest Service Road 4608 at a junction (if you reach the Godman campground, you've gone too far). You'll pass the Godman Guard Station and several signed spur roads as you follow this narrow, winding dirt road for 3.6 miles to a three-way junction. Bear right, following a rough road for another 2.7 miles to the large trailhead parking area. *DeLorme Washington Atlas & Gazetteer* page 42, D3

The Hike

Oregon Butte, the apex of the Blue Mountains, offers a scenic introduction to the remote backcountry of the Wenaha-Tucannon Wilderness. Along the trail you'll pass through forests and meadows en route to sweeping ridgetop views where you can survey the landscape stretching from the hazy wheat fields of the Columbia Plateau in the west to the peaks of Oregon's Eagle Cap Wilderness to the south. If you're

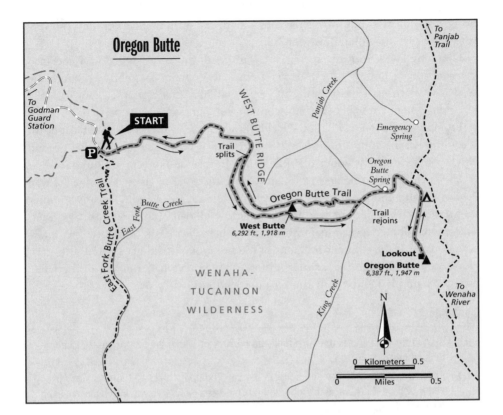

Oregon Butte

looking for more exploration, numerous springs, abundant possible campsites, and a wide choice of cross-country side trips along the high ridges beyond Oregon Butte offer ample incentive for an extended backpack trip. Adventurous hikers can continue following the trail for 13 more miles to the Wenaha River, just over the state line in Oregon.

From the trailhead, the Mount Misery Trail—a wide and well-graded trail—climbs steadily eastward on the shady north slope of the ridge beneath a canopy of Engelmann spruce, subalpine fir, and western larch. Trailside slopes here are covered in a green carpet of arnica and vanilla leaf. Upon reaching West Butte Ridge, the trail moderates after just over 1 mile and reaches a fork. The left fork, 0.9 mile long, contours through spruce-fir forest on the north slope of West Butte, while the right fork, 0.1 mile longer, climbs up and over the butte and offers good views to the west and south.

The two trails rejoin on the saddle just east of West Butte, beyond which you contour easily for 0.3 mile to cold, shady Oregon Butte Spring. This vigorous spring is piped into a long log water trough and is a logical resting place before climbing on to Oregon Butte. Between the spring and the ridge north of Oregon Butte, numerous unsigned trails can be confusing. The path that climbs steeply from the spring is the shortest but most strenuous way to the summit. Stay on the main trail that curves left (north) and heads uphill.

Climbing away from the spring, the trail passes through a wildflower-speckled park and into a pine-fir forest. After curving around one switchback, ignore the steep, well-worn path shortcutting the next switchback, and after another 0.1 mile bear right where a northbound trail continues straight ahead.

From this junction, you'll quickly climb to a saddle in the ridge ahead just north of a campsite, 0.3 mile from the spring. Proceed south past the campsite, beyond which you'll climb just under 0.5 mile to the historic lookout at the summit.

Views are far-ranging and panoramic, reaching as far as the peaks of the Seven Devils in Idaho and the lofty, snow-streaked Wallowas in Oregon. In early summer the meadows beneath your feet are alive with wildflowers, including yarrow, aster, penstemon, lupine, Indian paintbrush, and buckwheat. You may also be lucky enough to meet the summer residents of the fire lookout and get invited in to take a look around and sign the visitor register. When you've had your fill of the fabulous views, simply retrace your route to the trailhead.

Key Points

0.0 Start at the east end of the large trailhead parking lot, where the trail begins its climb through forest.

1.1 Reach a ridgetop meadow and a fork in the trail. The upper trail (right fork) climbs up and over West Butte, while the lower left fork traverses through forest, eventually rejoining the upper trail.

1.4 Views on West Butte (upper trail) open up to the south toward Oregon's Eagle Cap Wilderness and the Wallowa Mountains.

2.0 The upper and lower trails rejoin.

2.3 Arrive at Oregon Butte Spring, the only water source along the trail.

2.5 Arrive at an unsigned trail junction and bear right (east), ignoring the trail heading straight (north).

2.6 Pass a ridgetop campsite in the trees on your left (east).

3.0 Arrive at the fire lookout and your turnaround point.

6.0 Return to your car at the trailhead parking lot.

Hike Information

Local information
Pomeroy Chamber of Commerce, www.click pomeroy.com.

Local events/attractions
The Garfield County Fair comes to Pomeroy in mid-September; find out more on the town's Web site.

Accommodations
Pioneer Motel, Pomeroy, WA, (509) 843-1559.

Godman campground and Godman Guard Station Cabin, (509) 843-1891.

Restaurants
Donna's Drive-In, Pomeroy, WA.

Patit Creek Restaurant, Dayton, WA, (509) 382-2625.

Honorable Mentions

Southeast Washington

H68 Panjab Creek Loop

This 12-mile, weekend backpack semi-loop at the northern tip of the Blue Mountains serves up scenery ranging from windswept ridges to deep, forested canyons in the Wenaha–Tucannon Wilderness.

From U.S. Highway 12, 13.3 miles north of Dayton, turn east onto the Tucannon Road; a sign here indicates Camp Wooten. Follow this paved road through the Tucannon River Valley, ignoring the left fork to Camp Wooten and the Tucannon campground after 28 miles. The pavement ends here, but a good gravel road continues. Avoid a right fork after another 1.75 miles; proceed toward the Panjab campground. In another 2.6 miles the road forks once again. Hikers bound for the Tucannon River Trail will bear left, but you should go straight, almost immediately passing the Rattlesnake Trailhead, the terminus of this hike. After 2.4 miles you reach the Panjab Trailhead on the left (east) side of the road.

If you're approaching from the east, turn south off US 12 onto the paved Tatman Mountain Road (a sign here indicates Camp Wooten) about 4.25 miles west of Pomeroy. After 1.2 miles continue straight ahead on pavement (Linnville Gulch Road), ignoring the Tatman Mountain Road, which forks to the left. Linnville Gulch Road climbs steadily for 5.4 miles; then the pavement ends at the juncture with Blind Grade Road, and it becomes a good dirt road. In 2 miles the road plummets into the canyon of the Tucannon River. There you join the Tucannon River Road, turn left, and follow the above directions to the trailhead. The trailheads are 2.4 miles apart, so you may want to plan a car shuttle. For more information, contact the Umatilla National Forest, Pomeroy Ranger District: (509) 843–1891, www.fs.fed.us/r6/uma. *DeLorme Washington Atlas & Gazetteer* page 42, C3.

H69 Sawtooth Trail

If you're looking for a longer backpack in the Blue Mountains, the Sawtooth Trail leads you through forests and meadows along the scenic Sawtooth Ridge, with views of the Wenaha River Valley below and high points to the west, before dropping to the Wenaha River, the largest river in the wilderness.

From the town of Dayton, head south on Fourth Avenue, which eventually turns into Forest Service Road 64 outside town. Pass the Ski Bluewood Ski Area and turn left onto Forest Service Road 46, 26 miles from Dayton. After 3.5 miles you'll reach Burnt Flat, a broad meadow, and turn south onto a faint dirt road, driving another

0.25 mile to a hilltop. For more information, contact the Umatilla National Forest, Pomeroy Ranger District, (509) 843–1891, www.fs.fed.us/r6/uma. *DeLorme Washington Atlas & Gazetteer* page 42, D2.

H70 West Butte

If you're camping at the Godman campground, the West Butte Trail, which starts across from the ranger station in a large meadow, offers a 16-mile out-and-back tour of several small streams draining into the Wenaha River far below. Campsites are available along the trail on Rainbow Creek.

Hikers approaching from the east should follow directions given for Hike H68, Panjab Creek Loop, to the junction of the Blind Grade and Tucannon River Roads. Continue southward up the Tucannon River Road for another 11.1 miles, 2 miles beyond the end of the pavement, to the junction with Forest Service Road 4620, signed for Godman Guard Station.

Turn right and follow this steep dirt road for 4.2 miles to Forest Service Road 46 at Mountain Top Junction. Bear left here. Follow this good dirt road as it ascends the ridge southward, ignoring several lesser-used spur roads en route. After another 12.1 miles you'll pass a junction with Forest Service Road 4608; proceed straight on FR 46 to the Godman campground and the trailhead.

If you're approaching from Dayton, follow South Fourth Street south for 1 mile from U.S. Highway 12, then turn left (east) onto East Mustard Street (Skyline Drive) and drive 15.2 miles to Mountain Top Junction, where you follow the directions above to reach the trailhead. For more information, contact the Umatilla National Forest, Pomeroy Ranger District, (509) 843–1891, www.fs.fed.us/r6/uma. *DeLorme Washington Atlas & Gazetteer* page 42, D2.

H71 Yakima River Greenway

An oasis in the middle of the arid hills surrounding the Yakima Valley, the Yakima River gives life to the surrounding green fields and the riverside forests teeming with wildlife. This paved trail winds along the river for 14 miles, passing through forest and along the river's banks—you can wander as long as you wish. From Yakima, drive north on Interstate 82, exiting at the Resthaven Road. Turn left (west) at the bottom of the exit ramp onto the Resthaven Road and drive 1.5 miles to the trailhead. For more information, see yakimagreenway.org. *DeLorme: Washington Atlas & Gazetteer* page 50, C4.

Appendix A

Backcountry Rules and Wilderness Regulations

When you hike in the backcountry, you have a responsibility to travel lightly on the land and leave no lasting impression of your wilderness visit. Familiarize yourself with the rules and regulations of each backcountry area before setting out. When in the wilderness, employ techniques to minimize your impact on the land as much as possible.

Many heavily used wilderness areas or wildland zones have special restrictions that may vary from year to year. These restrictions are usually posted at the trailhead. The following list of regulations and suggestions for low-impact traveling are, for the most part, commonsense rules. Study the list before venturing into the backcountry to ensure a safe and enjoyable trip and to minimize your imprint upon the land and the natural community as well as on other visitors.

Mount Rainier, Olympic, and North Cascades National Parks

- Firearms are prohibited in all national parks. However, hunting and trapping are permitted in accordance with Washington State laws in the Ross Lake and Lake Chelan National Recreation Areas, as well as in all national forest areas.
- Dogs and other pets are not permitted on trails, except in the national recreation areas and on the Pacific Crest Trail, where they must be controlled and on a leash at all times. Dogs are permitted in national forest areas unless otherwise posted, but the Forest Service doesn't encourage dogs on trails. They can annoy other hikers and harass wildlife, pollute water sources, and foul campsites. It's best to leave your dog at home.
- Backcountry permits are required for camping in national park or recreation area backcountry, but they aren't required for day hiking in those areas. Permits for Mount Rainier National Park backcountry are required only from June 15 through September 30 each year. The permit system is intended to limit the number of hikers entering trailheads each day, thus preventing overcrowding and allowing visitors the opportunity for solitude and a rewarding wilderness experience. The permit system may seem like a hassle, but it's quite effective in preserving the qualities that visitors seek in the backcountry. Since permits are issued on a first-come, first-served basis, have a flexible itinerary in case the quota for your original destination has been filled for the day.
- Collection of natural features such as rocks, plants, driftwood, and antlers is prohibited.

- Backpackers may camp anywhere in Olympic National Park as long as they employ minimum-impact techniques and camp at least 100 feet from lakes and streams. In North Cascades and Mount Rainier National Parks, hikers must camp at designated trailside campsites or establish their own cross-country camps at least 0.5 mile from maintained trails and 1 mile from designated campsites.

- Fishing is allowed in accordance with Washington State regulations, but hunting is prohibited except in the national recreation areas. Disturbing or molesting wildlife is always prohibited.

- Campfires are restricted to established campsites and may be temporarily prohibited during periods when the danger of forest fire is high. In Olympic National Park all areas above 3,500 feet west of the Elwha and North Fork Quinault Rivers are closed to open fires, and all areas above 4,000 feet east of the Elwha and North Fork Quinault Rivers are closed to open fires.

National Forest and National Park Backcountry

- The three national parks and most wilderness areas in Washington limit to twelve the number of people hiking or camping together. In areas that don't have a group size limit, large groups of hikers should consider splitting up into smaller units and camping and traveling separately, since larger groups invariably have an adverse impact upon campsites and trails.

- Mechanized and motor vehicles, including mountain bikes, are prohibited in all wilderness and national park backcountry. Some roadless areas not officially designated as wilderness may also have motor vehicle restrictions in effect.

- Where terrain permits, camps should be a minimum of 100 feet from lakes, streams, meadows, and trails. Keep in mind that campsites located away from water sources are generally warmer and comparatively insect-free. Carry a supply of water to camp for drinking, cooking, and washing to avoid beating a path to the water source and trampling delicate vegetation. Fragile streamside and lakeshore vegetation may take years to recover after being trampled by too many hikers. If possible, use preexisting sites. If you must camp on a previously unused site, choose a durable spot in the forest on sand or rock slabs. If you clear your spot of any rocks, twigs, or needles, be sure to spread that material back over the site before leaving. Never uproot or damage vegetation, dig trenches, or perform any excavation at any campsite. Leave the site as pristine as you found it. Also, respect the right of other visitors by camping far from occupied campsites (at least 500 feet) and avoiding excessive noise and boisterous conduct that is out of place in the wilderness. Most visitors seek wild places for peace and solitude, so be a good neighbor. Also, camping is not permitted within 200 feet of the Pacific Crest Trail.

- The use of backpack stoves is encouraged in the backcountry. During the summer dry season, in some fragile timberline areas and in areas that are heavily used, campfires may be prohibited. This restriction will be posted at the trailhead.

Campfires leave lasting scars upon the land. If you must build one, keep it small, build it on bare mineral soil, never leave it unattended, and douse the fire with water—never bury it—before leaving camp. Make sure it is cold and completely dead. Never build a fire in subalpine or timberline areas where dead and fallen wood is obviously scarce. Trees in this high-elevation environment have a short growing season and endure the harshest of weather conditions. Twisted, wind-sculpted snags are aesthetically appealing, and no visitor, except perhaps during an emergency, can justify burning the meager amount of fuel available from these silent, enduring sentinels.

- Hikers should refrain from shortcutting switchbacks and walking out of the established trailbed. Doing so can cause an erosion problem that in some cases is difficult to correct. Moreover, the rugged slopes between switchbacks actually require more energy to negotiate and may not save any time at all.

- Storing or caching equipment in the wilderness is prohibited.

- Any destruction, injury, or defacement of natural features is prohibited. Avoid disturbing trees, shrubs, wildflowers, grasses, and so on, which are interrelated segments of the natural community. Do not blaze, carve initials or drive nails into, cut boughs from, or otherwise damage live trees or standing snags. Damaged trees are vulnerable to insects and disease.

- Hikers should refrain from collecting plant or animal life, minerals, or other natural or historic objects. Do not pick wildflowers. They usually wilt quickly, so leave them in their natural setting for others to enjoy. Allow flowering plants to complete their life cycles, thus perpetuating the beauty of the landscape.

- All unburnable refuse should be packed out, including that thoughtlessly left behind by others. Plastics and aluminum foil do not burn and must be packed out with any bottles, cans, and unburnable garbage—never buried. The plastic-coated, airtight foil packages commonly used by backpackers do not actually burn, so be sure to pack them out. Wild animals will quickly dig up buried food scraps. Do not disrupt the natural foraging habits of wildlife by offering food or leaving scraps behind. This also creates animal problems at the site for campers who follow.

- Littering the trail should be avoided. Since even little bits of trash detract from a wilderness experience, put all trash into your pocket or pack while on the trail. Even biodegradable items such as sunflower seed husks or orange peels don't belong in wild country, and they take a very long time to break down into the soil.

- Smoking is discouraged, especially in dry, windy weather. Smoke in a safe location free from any flammable material, and never crush out a cigarette on a log or stump. Be sure all matches and burning tobacco are out dead before leaving the area. Take your butts with you.

- Hunting and fishing are allowed in accordance with state game laws. Target practice in wild areas is discouraged and disrupts the peace and quiet of other visitors. Hunting is prohibited in national parks.
- Water quality should be protected. Camp at least 200 feet from water sources. Some backcountry areas have toilets; if so, use them. If toilets aren't available, bury body wastes in a shallow, 5- to 8-inch-deep hole in the biologically active layer of soil that will quickly decompose it. Carry a small, lightweight garden trowel for this purpose. Locate a spot at least 200 feet from trails, campsites, and existing or potential watercourses so that runoff won't contaminate water supplies. Fish entrails should be burned whenever possible and should never be discarded into water sources. Keep all wash water at least 100 feet from water sources, and don't use soap or detergents in or near water sources or potential watercourses. Even "biodegradable" soaps contain pollutants that can contaminate water. Next time you're in the backcountry, consider using sand or gravel to clean your cookware; it's often much more effective than soaps.
- Pack stock have the right-of-way on backcountry trails. To avoid conflicts with pack stock and packers, stand well off the trail, preferably on the downhill side, and talk to the packer in a normal tone of voice to let the animals know you're there. Some pack animals are easily spooked by sudden noises and movements.
- In the Enchantments area of the Alpine Lakes Wilderness (see Hike H35), there are special regulations in effect: Dogs are prohibited on trails, campfires are prohibited, group size is limited to six people, a two-night camping limit is in effect at campsites, and, from June 1 through September 30, wilderness permits are required for day or overnight use. Three-quarters of these permits can be reserved by mail anytime after March 1 each year. A reservation fee of $1.00 per person per night is required. However, hikers must still drive to the Leavenworth ranger station to obtain their reserved permits. The remaining quarter of the daily quota of overnight permits is available on a first-come, first-served basis. In other backcountry areas throughout the state, sign in at trailhead registers where provided. This information helps the Forest Service meet the needs of hikers in wilderness areas and may help locate lost or injured hikers.
- Any construction altering the natural character of the land, such as rock walls, fire rings or large fireplaces, tables and benches, shelters, bough beds, rock or wood bridges, or trenches, is not permitted. Make an effort to leave little or no trace of your passing.

This long list of rules and regulations may intimidate or seem too restrictive to some hikers. But it's become necessary to preserve the wild character of the land, to minimize the imprint of visitors, and to provide a rewarding outdoor experience for those of us who feel the need to spend time in pristine country that in today's world has become a precious commodity.

Appendix B

Ensuring a Safe Wilderness Experience

No one expects to become sick or injured in the backcountry, but it does happen. Washington's wilderness areas are exactly what the name implies—wild country, where the processes of nature continue as they have from the beginning of time, untamed by the works of humankind.

The following list of potential backcountry hazards is intended to rekindle a sense of awareness of what to expect in Washington's wildlands. Awareness and good judgment are a hiker's best insurance for a safe and enjoyable trip.

- Carry a good first-aid kit, and know how to use its contents.
- Study an area before setting out. Read books, study maps, and obtain as much information as possible from the ranger station nearest your destination. Rangers can tell you about a variety of potential problems, such as bears, high water, lingering snow, bad weather forecasts, and so forth. You frequently pass ranger stations en route to trailheads—an excellent opportunity to gather last-minute information.
- Leave a detailed travel plan with a responsible person before setting out. Let him or her know exactly where you are going, your route of travel, and when you expect to return. Then stick with that plan faithfully. If you fail to return, that person should contact the county sheriff or district ranger in your travel area so that a search can be initiated. If you return later than planned, be sure to notify those agencies so that any search can be discontinued.
- Never enter the backcountry unprepared. Carry a topographic map and a compass, and orient yourself frequently as you proceed, observing and locating peaks or other prominent features. This is particularly important when hiking cross-country (which should, of course, only be attempted by experienced hikers). Some hikers might be surprised at how different country can look from the opposite direction.
- Take along proper equipment. Good, sturdy, comfortable footwear (preferably lug-soled boots), a dependable shelter, warm clothing (wool, fiberpile, and polypropylene are the logical choices for Washington's wet weather, since they maintain much of their insulating value when wet), and plenty of food should be the basic components of every hiker's gear. Equipment should be lightweight, with as little bulk as possible. Consider carrying a tent and other gear that blend in with nature's colors. Numerous books are available to aid beginning hikers in selecting outdoor equipment.

- Do not overextend yourself or members of your group. Choose a hike within the capabilities of all the members of your party, and stick together on the trail, particularly toward nightfall.

- If a storm is imminent or darkness is descending, make camp as soon as possible. Bear in mind that darkness can come quickly to the mountains. Never hike at night.

- Carry an ample supply of drinking water, particularly on hot days. Remember that you can become dehydrated on cool days as well, since cool weather tends to distract you from your thirst. For strenuous activity during hot weather, allow one gallon of water per day per person. Experts believe that hikers should drink whenever they're thirsty and not ration their water supply.

- Avoid hiking alone, particularly while traveling cross-country. If you choose to hike solo, leave a travel plan with someone and stick to it.

- Never take unnecessary chances in the backcountry. Don't be too proud to turn back if high runoff or snow blocks the route or if a member of your party becomes ill or injured. Since the mountains will always be there, take the necessary precautions to ensure that you can return to enjoy them.

- Know the limitations of your body, your experience, your equipment, and the members of your party. Don't exceed those limits.

- If you think you're lost, stop at once, sit down, remain calm, and decide what to do. Study your map and try to locate landmarks that will help orient you. Don't proceed until you're sure of your location and certain you can get back on course. If you left a travel plan with a responsible person, and if you followed that plan, a rescue party will be looking for you soon and should have little trouble locating you. In many backcountry areas, following a creek downstream eventually will lead you to roads and civilization, but in some larger wild areas this may lead you deeper into the backcountry. Be sure of your route to avoid compounding the problem.

- Use the universal distress signal—a series of three shouts, whistles, flashes of light, or the like. If you must build a signal fire, do so only if it can be done safely. Rescuers will be directed to you by the smoke, not the flames. Keep in mind that you may be held financially responsible for expenses incurred during a rescue operation—additional incentive to play it safe in the wilderness.

- Use extreme caution when crossing waterways. Among the more frequently encountered hazards are swift-moving rivers and streams. Some watercourses are bridged, but many are not. Moreover, many bridges wash out on an almost yearly basis during spring runoff or wet winter storms. Don't underestimate the power of fast water; it can and has quickly swept hikers to their deaths. Search up- or downstream for a log crossing or for boulders to hop across, but remember these can be slippery. If you can't find a crossing, you have two choices— either turn back or ford the creek. During spring runoff or if you're confronted with a glacial stream, the water will be at its lowest during the morning hours, since cool overnight temperatures slow the rate of snowmelt.

Have a plan before entering the water. Are there sandbars or waterfalls downstream? Search for a level stretch of water, perhaps where the stream has divided into channels. Enter the water at a spot where you and your gear will wash up onto a sand- or gravel bar in the event you lose your footing.

Cross at a forty-five-degree angle downstream. You can use a stout staff or pole on your upstream side. Since bare legs create less friction with swift water, remove your pants and socks, but put your boots back on for better footing. Unhitch the waist strap on your pack and be prepared to unload it if you slip.

- Acclimate yourself to the elevation if necessary. Washington's mountains aren't excessively high in elevation, but hikers traveling from low-lying areas might need to adjust to the reduced oxygen at higher altitudes, particularly noticeable above 8,000 feet. A rapid change to a higher elevation can result in altitude sickness, characterized by headache, insomnia, loss of appetite, nausea, fatigue, and shortness of breath. Rest, liquids (no caffeine), and high-energy foods, such as dried fruit or candy bars, can help relieve these symptoms. If they persist, however, descend to a lower elevation. Regardless of elevation, take it easy the first few days on the trail.

- Always carry reliable shelter. You might enjoy beautiful, dry weather, but storms can hit at any time. Even in summer, snow is possible, usually above 4,500 feet. East of the Cascades, summer thunderstorms are a threat to hikers. In addition to a reliable tent (which can also shelter you from sometimes intolerable hordes of insects), carry good rain gear and clothing that will maintain its insulating properties when wet. Check extended weather forecasts before setting out, watch the sky, and be alert to changing conditions. Anticipate the possibility of a storm and be prepared.

  Pacific storms can last for two or more days, but thundershowers are typically brief. If you notice the buildup of cumulonimbus clouds and hear thunder, avoid ridges and mountaintops, solitary trees, open areas, rock overhangs, and bodies of water. Seek shelter in a dense grove of small, uniformly sized trees if possible. Stay away from anything that might attract lightning, such as metal tent poles or pack frames. Also, beware of flash floods or rising water. Never camp close to streams or watercourses that you think might rise substantially during heavy rainfall.

- Hole up during inclement weather rather than flee the mountains and risk hypothermia, a potentially deadly lowering of the body's internal temperature. A hiker who is wet, tired, and exposed to the wind is in danger of developing hypothermia. Since it can occur at relatively mild temperatures, many hikers simply cannot believe they are being affected. Observe members of your group. If symptoms such as shivering, fumbling hands, stumbling, slurred speech, and drowsiness are present, immediate treatment is necessary and indeed may save the victim's life.

Remove the victim's wet clothing. Give warm liquids—but not coffee, tea, or anything containing caffeine—to warm him or her internally. Then place him or her in a sleeping bag next to someone or between two other people. Skin-to-skin contact is the most effective way to provide warmth. The Forest Service has abundant information on the causes, symptoms, and treatment of hypothermia; the information is available at most ranger stations.

- Carry an effective insect repellent. Insects are an almost constant source of annoyance during summer in the mountains. Nearly all backcountry areas have varying numbers of mosquitoes in early summer and biting flies in late summer. Natural repellents containing citronella can turn a potentially miserable outing into an enjoyable one.

Wood ticks are common during spring in wooded, brushy, and grassy areas. All ticks are potential carriers of Rocky Mountain spotted fever, Colorado tick fever, and tularemia (rabbit fever), diseases transmitted through the bite of infected ticks.

Cases of Lyme disease have been reported, particularly in moist areas of western Washington. Lyme disease infection usually displays three stages of progression. The first indication often occurs two to three weeks after a bite by an infected tick as an enlarging circle of redness. Later there may be headache, stiff joints, and fatigue. The heart and nervous system can be affected, with paralysis of facial muscles and irregular heartbeat.

When traveling through tick country, a few minor precautions can help ensure a safe outing:

1. Wear clothing that fits snugly around the waist, wrists, and ankles. Layers of clothing are most effective in preventing ticks from reaching the body.

2. Use a strong insect repellent to deter ticks. They don't always bite right away but often crawl around on a potential host for several hours before finding an ideal place to feed on the victim's blood.

3. Examine yourself and your pets frequently while in tick country. If you find a tick, have it removed or remove it as soon as possible. Let a physician remove a tick to avoid infection and the possibility of leaving the tick's head under the skin. If you must remove a tick yourself, protect your hands with gloves, cloth, or a piece of paper. Tweezers are the best tool for the job; use a steady pulling motion, but avoid crushing the tick. The application of tincture of iodine may induce the tick to let go as well as reduce the chances of infection. If the tick's head remains embedded in the skin, a secondary infection may develop. In that event, see a physician to have it removed. After handling a tick, wash your hands and apply antiseptic to the bite.

4. Symptoms of diseases transmitted by ticks usually appear two days to two weeks after a bite. They include severe headaches, nausea, chills, fever, and pain in the lower back and legs. See a physician immediately if you notice these symptoms.

- Purify potentially contaminated water before drinking, brushing your teeth, or otherwise ingesting it. Remember the days when you could drink from mountain streams without a second thought about the purity of those waters? With an increasing number of visitors to Washington's wildlands, the question of water purity is a major concern to hikers. Despite the media attention given to *Giardia lamblia* (a single-celled, microscopic parasite) in recent years, diseases contracted from water sources have been a problem in certain areas from time immemorial. A variety of other germs, in addition to *Giardia*, are present in backcountry surface waters throughout Washington. Most hikers who drink untreated water probably will not contract any symptoms of intestinal illness. But to be safe, hold suspect all backcountry water and take appropriate steps to purify it.

  Rapid boiling for five to ten minutes is a sure way to kill waterborne microorganisms. Since water boils at a lower temperature at high elevations, however, boil it for at least ten minutes to be safe.

  Other purification methods include adding tincture of iodine or a saturated solution of iodine to drinking water. Various purification tablets are available at most backpacking and sporting goods stores. These methods may not be as effective against *Giardia* as boiling, but they are quite effective against a variety of other waterborne organisms. There are also a number of filters on the market that are an effective but expensive means of purifying water. When purchasing a filter, choose one with the smallest pores in its filtration element to ensure removal of the tiniest microorganisms.

  Carrying water from home may be the safest alternative, but it is impractical for extended hikes.

  When you must use water in the backcountry, choose a source upstream from trail crossings and campsites. Better yet, use springwater, which is more likely to be safe, particularly at the spring's source. If you become intestinally ill within three weeks of a backcountry visit, see a physician.

- Take precautions to avoid encounters with bears. Much of Washington's backcountry—from the coast to the mountains—is ideal bear habitat. By and large these animals remain well hidden in the dense forests. Occasionally, though, they are tempted by careless backpackers who bring odorous foods into the backcountry or leave behind food scraps. Check with the ranger station nearest your hiking area about bear problems. In any event, anticipate the possibility of encountering bears on your visit and suspend your food from a tree. This also protects food from marauding rodents.

Grizzly bears range through the northeasternmost corner of Washington and the Pasayten country, but they are rarely seen. Black bears, however, are common throughout much of the state, except for the Columbia Basin.

Parts of North Cascades and Olympic National Parks have their share of bear problems. Since the animals there are protected from hunting, they eventually lose their fear of people and begin viewing hikers as walking smorgasbords.

Suspend your food via the counterbalance method—the safest way to hang food in a tree. Put all food and any other odorous items, such as toothpaste, soap, or garbage, into two evenly weighted stuffsacks and hang them from a sturdy tree limb, ideally 15 feet above the ground (use a long stick) and 10 feet from the trunk. The stuffsacks should hang no more than 5 feet below the tree limb and no less than 10 feet above the ground. Leave packs on the ground with the pockets unzipped to minimize damage by a nosy bear or rodent.

Give bears a wide berth, particularly sow bears with cubs, and if a bear retrieves your food, do not even consider recovering it. Simply learn from your mistake and try to ensure that it will not happen again. Report any bear activity to a nearby ranger station after your hike.

- Also, beware of mountain goats. These typically docile creatures are not direct threats, but they are on a never-ending search for salt. During the hiking season, you represent a potential source.

  Boots, shoulder straps on backpacks, sweaty clothes, and urine all attract mountain goats to high-country campsites. Protect your gear from being eaten by goats, and keep your distance from these potentially dangerous animals.

- Drive with care in the mountains. Driving to trailheads in Washington often involves negotiating narrow one-lane roads, paved or dirt, often heavily traveled by logging trucks. If you are unaccustomed to mountain driving, drive with caution and exercise common sense. Stay on your side of the road, watch for turnouts, and use them if you encounter oncoming traffic. Be prepared to stop your vehicle within less than half the visible distance ahead. One vehicle should always stop when meeting another on narrow, one-lane roads. Also keep an eye out for cattle and logging trucks on mountain roads. Mishaps can be avoided by driving with care and attention.

- Be sure to carry the "ten essentials" on any wilderness outing to ensure safety and, perhaps, survival:

  1. A topographic map of your travel area and a compass, as well as a working knowledge of their use.

  2. Water and means of purification (a minimum of one gallon per person per day in hot weather).

  3. Sturdy, comfortable footwear and extra layers of clothing.

  4. A signal mirror.

5. Dark glasses and sunscreen.

6. A pocketknife.

7. Waterproof matches and fire starter.

8. A tent, tarp, or some type of emergency shelter.

9. A first-aid kit.

10. Plenty of food.

Most important, always bring a healthy dose of common sense, since the most important factor ensuring an enjoyable outing is safety.

If you'd like to learn more about backcountry hazards, their causes, and how to deal with them, you might want to consider taking courses in first aid and outdoor survival, offered in many communities. At the least, study one or more of the many excellent books on these subjects.

Hiking with Children

With the birth of a child, some new parents might think their hiking and back-packing days are over, at least until Junior is old enough to walk several miles and carry a pack. But when parents forgo hiking trips during a child's formative years, not only are they missing out on some of the most rewarding and memorable experiences to be enjoyed as a family, but the kids will also miss a tremendous learning experience in which they will gain confidence and a growing awareness of the world around them.

Kids can enjoy the backcountry as much as their parents, but they see the world from a different perspective. It is the little things adults barely notice that are so special to children: bugs scampering across the trail, spiderwebs dripping with morning dew, lizards doing push-ups on a trailside boulder, splashing rocks into a lake, watching sticks run the rapids of a mountain stream, exploring animal tracks on sand dunes—these are but a few of the natural wonders kids will enjoy while hiking backcountry trails.

To make the trip fun for the kids, let the young ones set the pace. Until they get older and are able to keep up with their parents, forget about that 30-mile trek to your favorite backcountry campsite. Instead, plan a destination that is only a mile or two from the trailhead. Kids tire quickly and become easily sidetracked, so do not be surprised if you do not make it to your destination. Plan alternative campsites en route to your final camp.

To help children enjoy the hike and learn about what they see, always point out special things along the trail. Help them anticipate what is around the next bend—perhaps a waterfall, or a pond filled with wriggling tadpoles. Make the hike fun, help kids stay interested, and they will keep going.

Careful planning that stresses safety will help make your outing an enjoyable one. Young skin is very sensitive to the sun, so always carry a strong sunscreen and apply it to your kids before and during your hike. A good bug repellent, preferably a natural product, should be a standard part of the first-aid kit. Also, consider a product that helps take the itch and sting out of bug bites. A hat helps keep the sun out of sensitive young eyes. Rain gear is also an important consideration. Kids seem to have less tolerance to cold than adults, so ample clothing is important. If your camp will be next to a lake or large stream, consider bringing a life vest for your child.

Parents with young children must, of course, carry plenty of diapers, and be sure to pack them out when they leave. Some children can get wet at night, so extra sleeping clothes are a must. A waterproof pad between the child and the sleeping bag should keep the bag dry—an important consideration if you stay out more than one night.

Allow children old enough to walk a mile or two to carry their own packs. Some kids will want to bring favorite toys or books along. They can carry these special things themselves, thus learning at an early age the advantages of packing light.

Kids may become bored more easily once you arrive in camp, so a little extra effort may be required to keep them occupied. Imaginative games and special foods they do not see at home can make the camping trip a new and fun experience for kids and parents alike.

Set up a tent at home and consider spending a night or two in it so your child can grow accustomed to your backcountry shelter. Some kids will be frightened by dark nights, so you might bring along a small flashlight to use as a night-light. Kids seem to prefer rectangular sleeping bags that allow freedom of movement. A cap for those cool nights will keep the young ones warm.

Weight-conscious parents of very young children can find an alternative to baby food in jars. There are lightweight and inexpensive dry baby foods available, and all you do is add water.

Children learn from their parents by example. Hiking and camping trips are excellent opportunities to teach young ones to tread lightly and minimize their imprint upon the environment.

Thus the most important considerations to keep in mind when hiking with the kids are careful planning, stressing safety, and making the trip fun and interesting.

There may be extra hassles involved with family hiking trips, but the dividends are immeasurable. Parents will gain a rejuvenated perspective of nature, seen through their child's eyes, that will reward them each time they venture out on the trail.

Many of the hikes in this book are suitable for family day hikes or backpacks, in full or in part. Carefully read each description and prepare for any hazards that may be present.

Hiking With Your Dog

Bringing your furry friend with you is always more fun than leaving him behind. Our canine pals make great trail buddies because they never complain and always make good company. Hiking with your dog can be a rewarding experience, especially if you plan ahead.

Getting your dog in shape. Before you plan outdoor adventures with your dog, make sure he's in shape for the trail. Getting your dog into shape takes the same discipline as getting yourself into shape, but luckily he can get into shape with you. Take him with you on your daily runs or walks. If there is a park near your house, hit a tennis ball or play Frisbee with him.

Swimming is also an excellent way to get your dog into shape. If there is a lake or river near where you live and your dog likes the water, have him retrieve a tennis ball or stick. Gradually build his stamina over a two- to three-month period. A good rule of thumb is to assume that your dog will travel twice as far as you will on the trail. If you plan on doing a 5-mile hike, be sure your dog is in shape for a 10-mile hike.

Training your dog for the trail. Before you go on your first hiking adventure with your dog, be sure he has a firm grasp on the basics of canine etiquette and behavior. Make sure he can sit, lie down, stay, and come. One of the most important commands you can teach your canine pal is to "come" under any situation. It's easy for your friend's nose to lead him astray or possibly get him lost. Another helpful command is "get behind." When you're on a hiking trail that's narrow, you can have your dog follow behind you when other trail users approach. Nothing is more bothersome than an enthusiastic dog that runs back and forth on the trail and disrupts the peace of the trail for others. When you see other trail users approaching you on the trail, give them the right-of-way by quietly stepping off the trail and making your dog lie down and stay until they pass.

Equipment. The most critical pieces of equipment you can invest in for your dog are proper identification and a sturdy leash. Flexi-leads work well for hiking because they give your dog more freedom to explore but still leave you in control. Make sure your dog has identification that includes your name and address and a number for your veterinarian. Other forms of identification for your dog include a tattoo or a microchip. You should consult your veterinarian for more information on these last two options.

The next piece of equipment you'll want to consider is a pack for your dog. By no means should you hold all of your dog's essentials in your pack—let him carry his own gear! Dogs that are in good shape can carry up to 30 or 40 percent of their own weight.

Companies that make good quality packs include RuffWear (888–RUFF–WEAR; www.ruffwear.com) and Wolf Packs (541–482–7669; www.wolfpacks.com). Most packs are fitted by a dog's weight and girth measurement. Companies that make dog packs generally include guidelines to help you pick out the size that's right for your dog. Some characteristics to look for when purchasing a pack for your dog include: a harness that contains two padded girth straps, a padded chest strap, leash attachments, removable saddlebags, internal water bladders, and external gear cords.

You can introduce your dog to the pack by first placing the empty pack on his back and letting him wear it around the yard. Keep an eye on him during this first introduction. He may decide to chew through the straps if you aren't watching him closely. Once he learns to treat the pack as an object of fun and not a foreign enemy, fill the pack evenly on both sides with a few ounces of dog food in resealable plastic bags. Have your dog wear his pack on your daily walks for a period of two to three weeks. Each week add a little more weight to the pack until your dog will accept the maximum amount of weight he can carry.

You can also purchase collapsible water and dog food bowls for your dog. These bowls are lightweight and can easily be stashed into your pack, or your dog's. If you are hiking on rocky terrain or in the snow, you can purchase footwear for your dog that will protect his feet from cuts and bruises. All of these products can be purchased from RuffWear.

The following is a checklist of items to bring when you take your dog hiking:

- Collapsible water bowls
- A comb
- A collar and a leash
- Dog food
- A dog pack
- Flea/tick powder
- Paw protection
- Water
- A first-aid kit that contains eye ointment, tweezers, scissors, stretchy foot wrap, gauze, antibacterial wash, sterile cotton-tipped applicators, antibiotic ointment, and cotton wrap

First aid for your dog. Your dog is just as prone—if not more prone—to getting in trouble on the trail as you are, so be prepared. Here's a rundown of the more likely misfortunes that might befall your little friend.

Bees and wasps. If a bee or wasp stings your dog, remove the stinger with a pair of tweezers and place a mudpack or a cloth dipped in cold water over the affected area.

Heatstroke. Avoid hiking with your dog in really hot weather. Dogs with heatstroke will pant excessively, lie down and refuse to get up, and become lethargic and disoriented. If your dog shows any of these signs on the trail, have him lie down in the shade. If you are near a stream, pour cool water over your dog's entire body to help bring his body temperature back to normal.

Heartworm. Dogs get heartworms from mosquitoes, which carry the disease in the prime mosquito months of July and August. Giving your dog a monthly pill prescribed by your veterinarian easily prevents this condition.

Plant pitfalls. Among the greatest plant hazards for dogs on the trail are foxtails—pointed grass seed heads that bury themselves in your friend's fur, dig in between his toes, and even get in his ear canal. If left unattended, these nasty seeds can work their way under the skin and cause abscesses and other problems. If you have a longhaired dog, consider trimming the hair between his toes and giving him a summer haircut to help prevent foxtails from attaching to his fur. After every hike, always look over your dog for these seeds—especially between his toes and his ears.

Other plant hazards include burrs, thorns, thistles, and poison oak. If you find any burrs or thistles on your dog, remove them as soon as possible before they become an unmanageable mat. Thorns can pierce a dog's foot and cause a great deal of pain. If you see that your dog is lame, stop and check his feet for thorns. Dogs are immune to poison oak, but they can pick up the sticky, oily substance from the plant and transfer it to you.

Protect those paws. Be sure to keep your dog's nails trimmed so he avoids getting soft-tissue or joint injuries. If your dog slows or refuses to go on, check to see that his paws aren't torn or worn. You can protect his paws from trail hazards such as sharp gravel, foxtails, lava scree, and thorns by purchasing dog boots.

Sunburn. If your dog has light skin, he is an easy target for sunburn on his nose and other exposed skin areas. You can apply a nontoxic sunscreen to exposed skin areas that will help protect him from overexposure to the sun.

Ticks and fleas. Ticks can easily give your dog Lyme disease, as well as other diseases. Before you hit the trail, treat your dog with a flea and tick spray or powder. You can also ask your veterinarian about a once-a-month pour-on treatment that repels fleas and ticks.

When you are finally ready to hit the trail with your furry friend, keep in mind that national parks and many wilderness areas do not allow dogs on trails. Your best bet is to hike in national forests, BLM lands, and state parks. Always call ahead to see what the restrictions are.

Appendix C

Hikes Index

Hike 11:   Baker River
Hike 17:   Boulder River
Hike 34:   Lewis River
Hike 36:   Falls Creek Falls

Best Hikes for Geology and Glacier Lovers
Hike 10:   Ptarmigan Ridge
Hike 16:   Cascade Pass
Hike 19:   Gothic Basin
Hike 20:   Ingalls Lake
Hike 22:   Lyman Lakes
Hike 26:   Carbon Glacier
Hike 28:   Comet Falls and Van Trump Park
Hike 31:   Norway Pass
Hike 32:   Tumac Mountain and Twin Sisters Lakes
Hike 39:   Northrup Canyon
Hike 44:   Yakima Canyon Rim (Skyline)
Hike 45:   Ginkgo Petrified Forest

Best Hikes for Wildflower Lovers
Hike 4:   Seven Lakes Basin
Hike 5:   Grand Valley
Hike 8:   Mount Townsend
Hike 13:   Windy Pass/Tamarack Peak
Hike 20:   Ingalls Lake
Hike 22:   Lyman Lakes
Hike 25:   Granite Mountain
Hike 27:   Upper Palisades Lake
Hike 29:   Tatoosh Ridge/Tatoosh Lakes
Hike 30:   Bear Creek Mountain
Hike 32:   Tumac Mountain and Twin Sisters Lakes
Hike 44:   Yakima Canyon Rim (Skyline)
Hike 48:   Oregon Butte